# MILITARY POLICY AND ECONOMIC AID

*A publication of the Mershon
National Security Program of the Ohio State University*

# MILITARY POLICY
# AND
# ECONOMIC AID

*The Korean Case, 1950–1953*

GENE M. LYONS

OHIO STATE UNIVERSITY PRESS
COLUMBUS

*FOR MY WIFE*

# PREFACE

This is a case study of one aspect of American policy during the Korean conflict—the economic aid program. Against the intensity of the controversy over basic strategy, the issue of reconstruction may seem relatively uncomplicated. Nothing would be farther from the truth. Indeed, a study of American policy on Korean reconstruction involves a number of major problems of foreign and military policy: the problem of balancing the relative advantages and disadvantages of multilateral and bilateral economic aid programs; the problem of finding the proper perspective for taking military considerations into account in formulating policy; and the impact of party politics on policy formulation. Above all, perhaps, it becomes clear, in the telling, how narrow military requirements tended to restrict policy alternatives in the absence of positive political objectives to which both military policy and economic aid could be related.

To be of value, a case study of this kind has to probe deeply behind the story told by the public record. For this reason, I was particularly encouraged to undertake this work when Dr. J. Donald Kingsley, first Agent General of the United Nations Korean Reconstruction Agency (UNKRA), agreed to put his personal papers at my disposal. I have quoted freely from these papers with the consent of Dr. Kingsley who also gave me many hours of his time to help bridge the gaps in series of events where documentation was lacking or meaning ambiguous. He also read an early draft of the study and picked me up on a number of points. In all of this, it was clear, however, that what I wrote was my own responsibility. Indeed, Dr. Kingsley and I have not always agreed on the meaning of events or the intentions of people, but I was always aware that my understanding of the issues involved would have been many times poorer without his help and stimulation.

I have also had the wise advice of Professor Leland M. Goodrich of Columbia University, whose own research and writing on American policy on the Korean question made him the most knowledgeable of guides. But more important, perhaps, is the challenge that one gets from Professor Goodrich's own high standard of scholarship and his absolute impatience with mediocrity. I was also fortunate to have been associated with Professor William T. R. Fox during the course of my research. Under an arrangement with the Institute of War and Peace Studies, of which Professor Fox is Director, I prepared a case study on the role of the military in the formulation of Korean reconstruction policy, composed essentially of the material in Chapters I through IV. I have thus had the advantage of having had these sections read and criticized by Professor Fox and his colleagues at the Institute.

In addition, Sir Arthur Rucker, Deputy Agent General of UNKRA from its inception until 1955, was kind enough to read and criticize the four opening chapters; Mr. Robert R. Nathan, who directed the most comprehensive survey of the Korean economy that has been undertaken in recent years, reviewed those sections of the study relating to economic problems; and Professor Leon Gordenker of Princeton University, author of a study of UN commissions in Korea before 1950, not only read most of the study in earlier drafts, but spent a good deal of his time helping me test new ideas. To all three, I am most grateful.

I was also privileged to talk with a number of people who were involved in Korean affairs either as officials of the U.S. government or UNKRA and I am indebted to them for having shared their understanding and experience with me: Colonel Louis Gosorn, Chief of the International Branch, G-4, Department of the Army, in 1950 and 1951 and later Deputy Chief on the J-5 staff, UN Command; Admiral Byron Hanlon who, as J-5, UN Command, was in charge of the military's economic program during most of 1952 and 1953; Mr. Noel Hemmendinger who, as a staff officer in the Division of Far

Eastern Affairs, Department of State, was in charge of the Korean economic program for the Department until the summer of 1951; Professor Philip Jessup who viewed the formulation of our Korean policy during the months following the aggression as a special assistant to the Secretary of State; Mr. David L. Rolbein, Project Coordinator in the Office of the Agent General, UNKRA; Mr. Dean Rusk, Assistant Secretary of State for Far Eastern Affairs during this period until 1952; Mr. William K. Shaughnessy, Special Assistant to the Agent General, UNKRA, from 1951 to 1953; and Mr. C. Tyler Wood, Economic Coordinator, UN Command, and Chief of the Foreign Operations Mission in Korea from the inception of the large-scale bilateral U.S. program in July 1953 until 1956.

Although time and distance prevented me from meeting General William Marquat, the General very kindly forwarded a number of specific questions I had asked, to the Division of Civil Affairs and Military Government (CAMG), Department of the Army, for reply. To General Marquat, who held command of CAMG from the summer of 1952 through 1953, and to the staff of CAMG, I extend my thanks for the time they spent on my questions and for their comments. I should also like to thank Dr. E. Taylor Parks of the Department of State for having arranged a series of meetings for me with officers of the State Department and other government agencies, all of whom had participated in the work on Korean reconstruction and took time to discuss the problems of their work with me.

My research was, for the most part, carried on at Dartmouth College's Baker Library in Hanover, New Hampshire, a rare paradise for scholars. To the library staff and especially to Miss Virginia Close and her associates in the Reference Service, I extend my thanks and my apologies for the unusually large number of requests I made of them. I am also grateful to the editors of *International Organization* for permission to publish material that originally appeared in that journal. I am also indebted to the Mershon Committee on Education in National Security of the Ohio State University for their support in the publication of this book.

Finally, I need, perhaps, tell the reader that I was, myself, associated with UNKRA from 1951 to 1956. For this reason, I feel particularly moved to emphasize that I alone bear full and complete responsibility for what these pages contain.

GENE M. LYONS

August, 1960
Hanover, New Hampshire

# CONTENTS

xi

# CONTENTS xiii

# TABLES

# INTRODUCTION
# THE TWIN FORCES IN AMERICAN POLICY

# THE TWIN FORCES IN AMERICAN POLICY

On June 25, 1950, the American Ambassador to South Korea, John Muccio, urgently informed the Secretary of State that ". . . North Korean forces invaded Republic of Korea territory at several points this morning." He interpreted the attack as "an all-out offensive against the Republic of Korea." [1] Within forty-eight hours President Truman had "ordered United States air and sea forces to give the Korean Government troops cover and support" and by the end of the week had authorized the use of "supporting ground units." [2] With the Soviet delegate absent, the UN Security Council supported the action of the United States by two recommendations: first, "that the Members of the United Nations furnish such assistance to the Republic of Korea as may be necessary to repel the armed attack and to restore international peace and security in the area"; [3] and second, "that such assistance be made available to a unified command under the United States." [4] The approbation of the world organization could not, however, disguise the truth of the situation. American action was as much motivated by a determination to discourage future communist aggression elsewhere as it was by the importance of Korea *qua* Korea to American interests and the defense of the principles of the UN Charter.

The decision of the United States to meet the North Korean aggression by armed support of the Republic of Korea and to assume major military responsibility as a United Nations Unified Command, was quickly followed by a deliberate policy to assist in the reconstruction of the peninsula when hostilities ceased. A Security Council resolution of July 31, 1950, authorized the Unified Command to take charge of the immediate relief problem left in the wake of the fighting. The United States representative, nevertheless, made it clear that "while relief at this moment is . . . an adjunct of the military opera-

3

tions," his government favored early international planning "for the long-run problems of rehabilitation and reconstruction." [5] In the months that followed, plans for the reconstruction of Korea were drawn up under the leadership of the United States. In a resolution passed on October 7, the Assembly established the United Nations Commission for the Unification and Rehabilitation of Korea to represent it in bringing about "a unified, independent and democratic government of all Korea." [6] The Economic and Social Council was, at the same time, asked to draw up a program for Korean relief and reconstruction.

Preliminary investigations already under way were speeded up and by the end of November the Council approved specific recommendations to the Assembly. The work finally reached a climax on December 1, when the Assembly adopted a resolution establishing the United Nations Korean Reconstruction Agency (UNKRA). UNKRA was conceived as a "special authority with broad powers to plan and supervise rehabilitation and relief." [7] In practice, however, the agency's powers could be only as broad as the United States, as initiator, primary source of financial support, and major military power with command responsibility on the UN side in the Korean conflict, wanted them to be.

In sponsoring UNKRA, the United States had acted on the basis of three assumptions. First, the establishment of the agency was predicated on military success and an early cessation of hostilities. Second, military success offered the prospect of creating a unified Korea under international auspices, an aim toward which United States policy had been directed since the liberation of the peninsula from Japanese control in 1945. And third, a unified Korea, striving for independence under the heavy burdens of military destruction, would require large sums of money in economic aid which the United States would be obliged to supply or risk losing Korea after winning the war. Within this general framework, there were distinct advantages in offering aid through the UN, above all, the advantage of following the multilateral policy that had earned the support of all non-communist nations, including the neutralist nations of Asia, for American military action in going to the defense of the Republic of Korea.

Behind all these factors, however, lay the concept of a clear-cut division between active hostilities and political settlement. Subsequent events, triggered by the intervention of Chinese Communist "volunteers" in late October, soon destroyed the illusion that the Korean conflict would follow the pattern of other wars in which the United States had engaged and that a definite line between war and peace could be drawn. The rush of fresh communist forces from Manchuria drove the UN troops from their advanced positions on the Yalu River at the Korean-Chinese border well back of the 38th parallel. As the UN forces began wearily and stubbornly to fight their way toward Seoul during the early months of 1951, the possibility of applying full military force in order to achieve a unified Korea became increasingly dangerous. Any such action risked opening a general war in Asia since the flow of troops and supplies from north of the Yalu River could only be stopped by a direct attack on their sources, an act which might provoke Communist China and possibly the Soviet Union to enter the conflict openly and in force. Moreover, in any general war, there was a grave possibility that the United States would have to use the full range of its strategic power, including atomic weapons, and, by doing so, would assume responsibility for the consequences of opening a nuclear war.

The broad implications of this new phase of the Korean conflict were not immediately and completely clear. The extent to which the Chinese Communists were prepared to commit themselves to battle and the intentions of the Soviet Union were both highly problematical. But beyond these speculative factors, the concept of a limited war had not yet thoroughly entered into the calculations of American strategy. At the same time, support for a multilateral aid program in Korea remained consistent with the broad political objectives of the United States despite the change in the basic assumptions of the original action. The problem was rather a question of timing. On the one hand, UNKRA could be kept inactive until hostilities ceased. The fact that the agency already existed and was supported by other UN members, nevertheless created pressures for its being put to work earlier if there was a reasonable opportunity for its work to be effective.

The identification of what constituted a "reasonable opportunity" for UNKRA to become operative was an issue of serious concern to the military command in the Far East. It presented the possibility of a split authority in a theater of active hostilities since the UN Command had already organized the initial relief operations in Korea along strict military lines. To a certain extent, the possibility of conflict between UNKRA and the military was theoretically mitigated by their complementary objectives. The military mission, following the traditional formula of *preventing disease and unrest* in order to protect the security of the front line troops, was essentially a *relief* mission, emphasizing the provision of consumer goods to meet the immediate needs of the civil population. The mission of UNKRA, on the other hand, was to repair the destroyed economic machinery and bring the country back to the level of agricultural and industrial production it had gained before the outbreak of hostilities. In practice, however, these missions overlapped: first, because the development of the military relief mission carried the *disease and unrest* formula beyond the provision of consumer goods alone; and, second, because the nature of military operations in a limited war began to make it possible to inaugurate a reconstruction program before hostilities had completely ended.

The view of the military was more than a matter of practical approach; it was a matter of doctrine. The experience of the second world war left military leaders with a conviction that civil relief had to be integrated with military supply procedures and with the general economic policy followed in the area. In many ways, this need for an integrated approach only emphasized again a fundamental principle of war: unity of command. Within the broad directive received from headquarters, the military argued that a theater commander had to have complete authority over civil relief and, within the framework of directives from theater headquarters, tactical commanders in the field had to control all phases of the relief work.

Civil relief was, therefore, looked upon as a *command* responsibility that could not be delegated outside the line of military authority.[8]

With the collapse of hopes for early victory, the policy of the military command thus came into conflict with the American commitment to support the inauguration of an UNKRA program. The conflict between these twin forces in American policy dragged on through the long gray period of limited military operations that lasted until a truce was finally signed in July, 1953. During this entire period, there was constant disagreement on how much economic aid was possible under existing military conditions and how tightly the military command had to control economic activities. Questions of civil-military relations were raised but never resolved, except tenuously and temporarily, for lack of a firm political policy on which they could be based. Fundamental to the problem was the difficulty of adapting the military policy of civil relief and the objectives of American economic aid to the situation of limited war. This study is an attempt to analyze the roots of these twin forces in American policy, to isolate and study the principal factors in the formulation of policies to meet the conflict between these forces, and, finally, to judge whether the outcome has been in the interests of the United States.

1. *United States Policy in the Korean Crisis,* Department of State Publication 3922, Far Eastern Series 34 (Washington: Government Printing Office, ʼ950), p. 11.

2. *Ibid.*

3. Security Council Resolution of June 27, 1950.

4. Security Council Resolution of July 7, 1950.

5. UN Security Council, Fifth Year, *Official Records,* 479th meeting (July 31, 1950), pp. 5–6.

6. General Assembly Resolution 376 (V), *The Problem of the Independence of Korea,* October 7, 1950.

7. General Assembly Resolution 410 (V), *Relief and Rehabilitation of Korea,* December 1, 1950.

8. An understanding of this theory as it developed in Army circles out of the experiences of World War II can be had by reviewing articles published in *Military Review* at the Command and General Staff College, Fort Leavenworth. See September 1944 (Vol. 24, No. 6), p. 49; December 1945 (Vol. 25, No. 9), p. 67; June 1946 (Vol. 26, No. 3), p. 25; and April 1948 (Vol. 28, No. 1), p. 29.

CHAPTER I

# THE BACKGROUND OF AMERICAN POLICY IN KOREA

# THE BACKGROUND OF AMERICAN POLICY IN KOREA

The conflict between the twin forces of American policy was continually complicated by the problems of Korean economic and political life. Many of the internal factors that had to be taken into account in formulating a reconstruction policy for Korea after June 25, 1950, had originated in the period of Japanese occupation from 1910 to 1945. Politically, Japanese domination had had the double effect of stimulating fierce Korean patriotism in opposition to foreign rule, while keeping the Korean people at a low level of educational and technical training in order to deprive their patriotism of effective leadership. Economically, Japan so integrated the Korean economy with her own that when liberation came in 1945, the Koreans were left with production facilities that were not made to stand alone and a modern industrial capacity they had no experience in operating.

To the problems of nationalism, a low level of educational and technical training, economic separation from Japan, and inexperience, the circumstances of liberation added the aggravation of political division of a unitary economy. An economic imbalance resulted from the military arrangement of having the Soviet Union accept the surrender of Japanese forces above the 38th Parallel and the United States below that line. The iron, steel, chemicals and power facilities of the north were separated from the agricultural and consumer goods industries of the south. To South Korea, this meant importing fuels, fertilizers and capital equipment while producing few exportable commodities with which to earn foreign exchange.

In the five years from 1945 to 1950 South Korea survived under these hazardous conditions only with considerable aid from the United States. Until 1949, the American military authorities concentrated on two aims: importing foods to sustain

11

a population increasing through the influx of repatriates from Japan and refugees from the north; and stimulating agricultural production by a land reform program designed to eliminate the tenant farmer feature of the Japanese land development schemes.[1] A more ambitious program was planned in 1949 by the Economic Cooperation Administration. Its objectives were to produce or import sufficient consumer goods and raw materials to sustain the people and, at the same time, begin to lay the foundations for a self-supporting economy in South Korea.[2] Although the program was never completed, the South Koreans were, by June, 1950, beginning to create some order out of the economic chaos that had existed in 1945.

During this period, American economic aid was granted within the framework of a policy that had both positive and negative aspects: on the positive side, the United States sought to fulfill the pledge of the Cairo Declaration of 1943 that Korea would become free and independent; negatively, it sought to avert communist domination of South Korea. After mid-1947, the positive objective remained the expressed purpose of the United States as the ultimate goal. But the negative objective of withstanding the spread of communism below the 38th parallel was the major motive behind American policy. From 1945 until the end of 1948, this meant preventing the Soviet Union from extending its occupation throughout the peninsula, and from 1949 it meant preventing the Soviet-dominated regime in North Korea from absorbing the UN-approved Republic of Korea in the south.

During the early period, the deterrent element in South Korea was the armed forces of the American military occupation. Yet, shortly after the turn of 1946, the maintenance of effective troops in that area became an increasing burden to the American military establishment as its reduced postwar force became inadequate for the commitments of the expanding cold war. By early 1947, Secretary of War Patterson began to warn rather persistently that the occupation of South Korea was a risky strain on the Army and urged that the troops be withdrawn as soon as possible.[3] Patterson was supported by military advice that the occupation was dangerously exposing American ground forces to attack on the mainland of Asia, an area General Bradley later prosaically described as "a poor place to fight." [4]

The State Department, however, insisted that, politically, the United States could not withdraw its troops while Soviet troops remained in the north, an opinion shared by the confidential Wedemeyer report on the Far East submitted to the President in September, 1947.[5] The opportunity for gaining the simultaneous withdrawal of all occupation forces began to take shape shortly thereafter when the United States referred the problem of Korean unification from the deadlocked Soviet–United States Joint Commission established under the Moscow Agreement of 1945, to the General Assembly of the United Nations.

The Commission had been entrusted with preparing plans for transferring Korea from occupation status to a four-power (United States, Soviet Union, Britain, and China) trusteeship as a step toward independence. It had never gone as far as determining which Korean groups should be consulted. The United States took the position that all parties and organizations should be heard. The Soviet Union, however, wanted to bar those groups, particularly in South Korea and notably led by Dr. Syngman Rhee, which openly opposed the trusteeship stage. In referring the problem to the United Nations, the United States recommended that elections for a Korean national government be held in the two zones of occupation under the supervision of a United Nations Commission and that the same commission supervise the withdrawal of occupation forces as soon as authority could be transferred. The Soviet Union countered by suggesting almost immediate withdrawal of occupation troops, a proposal rejected by the United States until the broader problems were resolved by the United Nations.[6]

The United States, in this way, made the first move to fill the power vacuum which would be created by the withdrawal of its troops. In using the United Nations as an instrument of policy, it sought the support which comes from acting in accordance with the will of the majority of nations of the world. The General Assembly went ahead to create the machinery for dealing with Korea in only slightly modified form from that proposed by the United States. The Commission established to oversee elections in Korea failed to gain admittance to the northern sector, but proceeded to supervise elections below the 38th parallel. At the 1948 session of the Assembly, the work of the Commission was approved and the Republic of Korea established in the south was recognized by the world body.[7] From the point of view of the effective protection of American interests, however, the action of the United Nations could not replace the United States Army as a deterrent to the communist absorption of the Republic of Korea. To fill the gap, the United States undertook through its ECA program to develop a viable economy in the new state strong enough to support an effective security force trained by an American military advisory group. By the summer of 1949, the State Department considered the support of the United Nations for the Republic to be sufficiently confirmed and the troop training and economic aid programs sufficiently in hand to enable the United States to withdraw the last of its occupation troops.[8]

Although the Soviet Union had announced the withdrawal of its forces in December, 1948, it had created a Democratic People's Republic of Korea in the north with an army of its own. In response to the warning of the UN Commission that there was serious danger of open conflict between the two governments, the General Assembly in 1949 approved a resolution introduced by the United States authorizing the Commission to "observe and report any developments which might lead to or otherwise involve military conflict in Korea." [9] The deterrent to aggression from north of the 38th parallel now became the U.S. supported Republic of Korea and the pledge of United Nations Members to the principles of the Charter. There was, of course, no guarantee that these principles could be invoked effectively. There was, however, a United Nations Commission

# THE BASIS FOR A MULTILATERAL POLICY

## The Machinery for United Nations Action in Korea

President Truman has reported that there was some difference of opinion on the extent of the assistance the United States should offer to the Republic of Korea when it was attacked on June 25, 1950. There was, however, no hesitation on the part of his advisers, civilian and military alike, that the United States had to become involved in the Korean conflict. Questions arose on the timing and need for committing ground troops in Korea, but not on the basic issue.[1] The cold war had reached a point where the risks of backing down in the face of naked aggression were far greater than the risks of open fighting in Korea. This granted, it is but a short distance to American initiative in bringing the matter before the United Nations Security Council and continuing the internationalization of the Korean conflict that had been an essential part of American policy before the outbreak of hostilities.

Ambassador Muccio's first message, reporting the attack, had been received in the State Department at 9:26 on the evening of Saturday, June 24 (Washington time). By telephone, President Truman, from his home in Independence, Missouri, authorized Secretary of State Acheson to bring the issue before the Security Council and declare that an act of aggression had been committed against the Republic of Korea.[2] By the time the President returned to Washington to meet with his top diplomatic and military advisers the next evening, the Council had already met and, by a vote of 9 to 0 with the Soviet Union absent, determined that the North Korean invasion was a "breach of the peace." The Council thereupon called "for the immediate cessation of hostilities," for "the authorities of North Korea to withdraw forthwith their armed forces to the thirty-eighth parallel" and for "all Members to render every assistance to the United Nations in the execution of this resolution and to refrain from giving assistance to the North Korean authorities." [3]

President Truman requested an on-the-spot report from General MacArthur, and the next day a message from the Far East warned that "South Korean units [are] unable to resist determined Northern offensive" and that "a complete collapse is imminent." That evening, June 26, at a second meeting with his advisers, the President authorized the Secretary of Defense to instruct MacArthur "to use air and naval forces to support the Republic of Korea." [4] The following day, he released a statement to the press making his orders public. That same afternoon the Security Council, again with the Soviet Union absent, passed a resolution presented by the United States, recommending "that the Members of the United Nations furnish such assistance to the Republic of Korea as may be necessary to repel the armed attack and to restore international peace and security in the area." [5]

The willingness of the Council to follow the lead taken by the United States was further emphasized when a resolution, introduced by the United Kingdom and France, was passed on July 7 recommending "that all Members providing military forces and other assistance . . . make such forces and other assistance available to a unified command under the United States." Under the provisions of the resolution, the United States was requested "to designate the commander of such forces," which were authorized "to use the United Nations flag in the course of operations against North Korean forces." The United States was also requested "to provide the Security Council with reports, as appropriate, on the course of action taken under the unified command." [6] No provision other than *post factum* reporting was made for United Nations oversight of American direction of the military effort. Thus, for all intents and purposes, the Unified Command was the United States government acting as an executive agent for the United Nations under the broad terms of the Council resolution.

Mention of "other assistance" in addition to military forces in the July 7 resolution, was the first direct reference to aid for the civilian population of Korea. The very first blows of the conflict had already created large numbers of refugees as hundreds of thousands of homeless and hungry people fled before the advancing communist forces. Facing up to this military as well as humanitarian problem, the Security Council on July 31 requested "the Secretary General to transmit all offers of assistance for relief and support to the Unified Command." It also asked "the Unified Command to exercise responsibility for determining the requirements for the relief and support of the civilian population of Korea, and for establishing in the field the procedures for providing such relief and support." As in the case of the direct military operation, no arrangement was made for supervision of the relief work except "to provide the Security Council with reports." [7]

During the discussion on the resolution, the point was made that while relief activities had to be carried out at the same time as military operations, emergency relief was preliminary to a program of reconstruction that would have to be undertaken when hostilities ceased. It was thus immediately at the beginning of the United Nations involvement in the conflict that a distinction was made between relief and reconstruction and the methods of tackling the two problems. Ambassador Warren Austin, the United States delegate, set out the separate approach to each of the programs by suggesting that the specialized agencies "begin to plan ahead for the long-run problem of rehabilitation and reconstruction," after he had emphasized that "relief at this moment is . . . an adjunct of the military operations." [8]

The Unified Command implemented the July 31 resolution by delegating responsibility for the emergency relief program to the United Nations Command, its operating arm in the Far East for military activities. Practically speaking, the program was carried out through the command organization of the United States Army. The Commander-in-Chief of the United Nations Command (CINCUNC), General Douglas MacArthur, assigned primary responsibility for the program to his Assistant Chief of Staff for Supplies and Logistics (G-4) who, in turn, ordered the Eighth United States Army in Korea (EUSAK) to develop a list of basic requirements to meet the needs of the civilian population. The statements of relief requirements were sent through the Army system to United Nations Command Headquarters in Tokyo and then to Washington, D.C., to be filled by the Army's procurement and technical services. There were, however, two new sources of supply made available to the Army to meet the relief requirements: ECA material procured with funds originally appropriated for the economic aid program; and the offers of supplies, equipment and personnel from United Nations Members other than the United States, as well as from specialized agencies and private social welfare and health agencies such as the Red Cross societies.[9] The efforts of all non-U.S. Army agencies were, however, channeled into the Army machinery, those from non-American organizations and governments being processed through a special unit for Korean affairs which was established in the Office of the Secretary-General of the United Nations.[10]

The general organization of the relief operation was thus substantially military in set-up. As a result, a system and staff, already established and prepared to take immediate and unusual action, were placed at the disposal of the United Nations. It is doubtful whether the relief work could have been achieved if this already-existing organization had not been put into action. Conceivably, the procurement and shipping facilities of some of the specialized agencies, especially the International Refugee Organization and the World Health Organization, could have been utilized effectively although they did not have the supply lines in the Far East, nor probably the capacity for the size of the task. What is significant, however, is the fact that only by being able to avail itself of an already established organization like the United States Army, was the United Nations able to implement its relief program in Korea as quickly and, probably, as effectively as it did.

Originally, the relief work had been assigned to a group of American army and civilian personnel in the Public Health and Welfare Section of General MacArthur's Far East Command, assisted by staff from the American Embassy in Seoul and the ECA Korean Mission. The Unified Command's early request for medical and welfare teams to join in the battle against disease and unrest was quickly answered by the specialized agencies of the United Nations and by a number of national Red Cross societies. What had begun as an exclusively American operation soon became a multi-national undertaking as doctors, welfare workers and technicians of twelve different nationalities were posted with the military teams in the Korean provinces. The original unit was, by the end of 1950, raised to the level of a command under the Eighth Army and called the United Nations Civil Assistance Command, Korea (UNCACK). Although UNCACK was part of the over-all military organization, a good portion of its staff was made up of civilians, a number of whom were of nationalities other than American.[11] While using the United States Army as a base for organizing its military and emergency relief operations, the United Nations nevertheless set about establishing organizations on international rather than national foundations to meet the longer-range problems of unification and reconstruction. Its efforts, carried out through the fall of 1950, resulted in the creation of the United Nations Commission for the Unification and Rehabilitation of Korea (UNCURK) and the United Nations Korean Reconstruction Agency (UNKRA).

Two days before the General Assembly started to work, the observation was made that "not on the agenda officially but supplying the background and key to the Assembly will be the struggle between the West and the East for the confidence of the people of all Asia."[12] Very much on the agenda, however, was the problem of Korea, now dramatized as the UN forces, having landed behind the communist lines at Inchon a week earlier, were smashing towards Seoul. The session thus opened with exciting expectations for the future of Korea and, indeed, for all Asia. It was in this atmosphere that Secretary of State Dean Acheson, speaking in the general debate, took the lead in suggesting that the events connected with the establishment of the Republic of Korea, as well as the events of June 25, combined to make the Korean peninsula the place for the United Nations to begin to bring to underdeveloped areas the means and techniques to meet their needs "for food, for land and for human dignity." In Acheson's words, what the United Nations did in Korea could help "set a pattern of coordinated economic and social action in other places where the need is for development rather than for rehabilitation." To this end, the Secretary of State promised that the technicians and resources of his government "now being used to support the United Nations military action" would be made available to a "United Nations recovery force" when the conflict in Korea was over.[13]

The statement of Secretary Acheson did more than just pledge the support of the United States to a program of Korean reconstruction. It gave the program a new dimension by suggesting it would be a pilot project for technical and economic development schemes operated through the United Nations in other areas. In this way, the importance of the Korean program spread beyond the shores of the peninsula. As crucial as was the necessity for restoring the battered homes and workshops of the Korean people, the success of the program was to take on even greater significance and interest if the future development of many of the countries of Southeast Asia particularly, but of the Middle East, Africa and Latin America as well, was to be affected by its progress.

The first act of the Assembly concentrated, however, on the political problem of Korean unification. By October, the United Nations forces had taken Seoul and stood on the 38th parallel. It now became urgent for the United Nations to decide, first, whether to cross the parallel, and second, what machinery to employ to achieve its political objectives once the military objective was gained. These problems were met in a resolution largely drafted by the United States.[14] The Assembly authorized the UN Command to cross the 38th parallel and, at the same time, established the United Nations Commission for the Unification and Rehabilitation of Korea (UNCURK) to "rep-

resent the United Nations in bringing about the establishment of a unified, independent and democratic government of
all Korea." UNCURK was, moreover, to have specified responsibilities in connection with relief and rehabilitation. The nature and extent of these responsibilities were to be determined
when the nature and extent of the program itself were decided.
In order to give the Assembly a basis for working out a program, the Economic and Social Council was requested "to develop plans for relief and rehabilitation on the termination
of hostilities." [15] The Economic and Social Council (ECOSOC)
had actually commenced discussions on relief and rehabilitation in Korea following the Security Council's resolution of
July 31 on the emergency relief program. Although the Security Council resolution had merely requested ECOSOC, together with other United Nations organs and agencies, to assist
in meeting relief requirements as determined by the Unified
Command, the Council had gone a step farther by beginning to
consider the arrangements for long-term economic and social
assistance when hostilities were over.

The work in the ECOSOC was given tremendous impetus by
the results of the conference which President Truman held with
General MacArthur on Wake Island in mid-October. Although
the details of the conference were not available until months
later, it was publicly reported upon the departure of the President from Washington that "the reconstruction of Korea was
. . . to be [the] no. 1 objective in his . . . meeting." It was
also emphasized that while "the United States would assume
a major share of the cost of the proposed reconstruction [the
program] would be carried out under United Nations auspices.
. . . Thus, the United Nations military effort against North
Korea would be translated into a peaceful extension of the
original resolution authorizing armed intervention against
North Korea's aggression." [16] These early reports were confirmed by the statement of the President, himself, on his return from Wake Island. He reported that he and MacArthur
had "devoted a good deal of time to the major problem of

peaceful reconstruction of Korea which the United Nations is facing and to the solution of which we intend to make the best contribution of which the United States is capable." [17] Back in Washington, he then set a staff to work on an appropriations request to meet the American share for the program then being developed by the ECOSOC.[18]

Armed with this high-level pledge of American support, the ECOSOC examined the over-all reconstruction problem in two parts: first, what should be the extent of the United Nations program; and, second, how should the United Nations organize for the implementation of the program? In answering the first question, the Council followed findings of a Temporary Committee which were based on proposals of the Secretary-General and the Unified Command. The Committee called for a program of $250,000,000 to begin on January 1, 1951, and to extend into 1952 if necessary. In its report, the Committee pointed out that this initial program and any further plans for Korean reconstruction were surrounded by a number of uncertainties, including how long hostilities would continue and how much member nations would be willing to provide for such a program. Yet, in the face of these variables, the Council adopted the report of the Committee as a recommendation to the General Assembly without reservations. The Committee's proposals for an initial undertaking of $250,000,000 were subsequently adopted as a program basis after UNKRA had been established.[19]

Proposals submitted by the Secretary-General and the United States delegation on the organization of the reconstruction agency both provided for an executive head with broad operational authority, differing only in that one recommended that the reconstruction chief report through the Secretary-General and the other that he report directly to the General Assembly.[20] By contrast, a draft Australian resolution called for UNCURK to have over-all policy responsibilities for the reconstruction program with an administrator responsible for technical operations, who reported to UNCURK.[21] A joint resolution, developed during a series of private meetings of the United States and Australian delegations, managed to reconcile the differences between these two concepts and provide a basic plan for the establishment of UNKRA.[22]

The United States–Australian proposal set forth three elements of a reconstruction agency: an Agent General as executive head having broad operational responsibility; an Advisory Committee of the General Assembly to which the Agent General reported for approval of program and policy; and UNCURK, which was to advise the Agent General on matters relating to political unification. These elements provided a means of satisfying the essential political interests of potential contributors although they presented the dangers of overlapping responsibilities in practice. The Agent General was theoretically given the freedom of action and decision that he would need in the face of immediate crises which were bound to arise by the very nature and size of the problems in Korea. On the other hand, the nations contributing to the program would have a say in the administration of the agency and, through the Advisory Committee, a check on the authority of the Agent General. Finally, UNCURK was brought into the system in an advisory capacity in order to facilitate the fulfillment of its own responsibilities in the political area. Approved by ECOSOC, the United States–Australian proposals were submitted to the General Assembly which adopted them in a resolution of December 1, 1950, establishing the United Nations Korean Reconstruction Agency (UNKRA).

What UNKRA was, was essentially what the United States wanted it to be. The concept of a multilateral agency for Korean reconstruction fitted the immediate objectives of internationalizing responsibility for Korean affairs, supporting the Republic of Korea, and opposing the communist domination of the peninsula. Moreover, UNCURK, in which the United States, as the major non-Korean contributor to the military effort, could not take an active role, had only a limited part in the rehabilitation work. Major policy responsibility rested

in an Agent General and an Advisory Committee where the
United States could exercise the full weight of its financial
power and political influence.

### Early Implementation of the UNKRA Resolution

Two days before the resolution establishing UNKRA was
voted by the General Assembly, General MacArthur announced
that the United Nations forces in Korea were facing "an entirely new war" against "substantial Communist Chinese
forces." [23] MacArthur's earlier report for the first two weeks
in November already indicated that "Chinese Communist forces
in significant strength have moved across the Yalu River." By
the end of the month, the General described the situation as a
"new war" in place of the "wholesale retreat before unrelenting United Nations pressure" he had proudly reported a month
earlier.[24] What did this do to plans for reconstruction?

At Wake Island, General MacArthur had replied to the
President's request for his views on rehabilitation by warning
that "[rehabilitation] cannot occur until the military operations have ended." Nevertheless, he expressed his belief "that
formal resistance will end throughout North and South Korea
by Thanksgiving" and "that the military should get out the
minute the guns stop shooting and civilians take over." [25] It
was undoubtedly this evaluation of the situation, carried back
from the conference by the President, which provided the
momentum for the intensive work pushed through the ECOSOC
under American guidance during the month of November. During this same month, the Administration was facing not only
increasingly serious reports on the possible effect of Chinese
Communist intervention, but also the first difficulties with Mac-
Arthur over fighting a limited war and keeping it localized.
Following the initial reports that prisoners captured late in
October had been identified as members of Chinese units, Mac-
Arthur, after taking time to ascertain the seriousness and extent of the Chinese intervention, ordered an attack on bridges
over the Yalu River. His orders were at first countermanded,
but later authorized by Washington in modified form on the

basis of the increasing intensity of Chinese infiltration. But Washington refused to go so far as to authorize the bombing of Manchurian bases, which, in the light of the Chinese move, was being requested by MacArthur. The General, moreover, warned that "present restrictions imposed on my area of operation [providing] a complete sanctuary for hostile air immediately upon their crossing the Manchurian–North Korean border, . . . can assume decisive proportions." [26]

Thus, the United States knew that it had a "new war" on its hands well before it proceeded to vote on December 1 for the establishment of a United Nations Korean Reconstruction Agency. The problem of reassessing its commitment to a multilateral aid program in the light of this factor was, however, difficult. The full ramifications of the new situation were not clear while the momentum leading up to the establishment of UNKRA was reaching its climax. A sudden move by the United States to delay the vote on the December 1 resolution or hold up the work of the committee organized to negotiate contributions to the program, would have had severe repercussions on two fronts: Korean morale and Allied cooperation. It remained essential to American policy that both Korean morale and Allied cooperation be kept at a high level no matter what the consequences of the "new war" might be.

As early as November 12, the *New York Times* had reported that many Koreans were already beginning to fear "that Chinese Communist intervention in Korea might prolong hostilities indefinitely and hamper rehabilitation and recovery seriously." The report went on to suggest that "this fact, coupled with the slow realization that rehabilitation and the relief of suffering cannot occur overnight despite promised assistance by the United Nations, has sobered Korean leaders and dimmed the enthusiasm of the man in the street." [27] The relation between Korean morale and the expectation of an aid program was particularly pertinent in the light of the pronouncement of unequivocal support for the Republic of Korea that the President had made at Wake Island.[28] At that time, it was assumed that the fall of the Rhee government would have created an aching void virtually impossible to fill under the conditions of war. The chaotic political consequences would also have undermined the rear echelons and endangered the supporting elements and supply lines of the United Nations forces at the fighting front. The situation was even more obvious once the tide of battle turned. Notwithstanding understandable dissatisfaction on the part of the United States and many of its allies with President Rhee and his colleagues, President Truman seemed determined that the South Korean government had to be maintained in power and the Korean people encouraged to keep up the fight. There would clearly have been severe burdens put on these objectives if any action were taken to abandon or even delay the plans for reconstruction that had been formulated in a more victorious mood.

The problem of continued Allied cooperation in the Korean affair was more complex. From the very beginning, the United States was quite aware that it was going to be difficult to keep the reconstruction program a multilateral concern. The already troublesome history of financing UN economic and social programs was a warning of the difficulties that would be encountered in collecting the high cost of Korean reconstruction. To meet this problem, the United States, at the time Korean relief and reconstruction was before the ECOSOC, proposed that contributions be based on assessments fixed by the General Assembly on those Member States that announced their willingness to assist in financing the program.[29] Thus, while the offer of contribution would be voluntary, the amount would be determined by the Assembly after balancing the requirements of the program against the comparative capacities of contributing nations to meet these requirements. Such a system, it was hoped, would eliminate *token* contributions and would insure an effective multilateral approach. There were also two by-products: internationally, it would isolate the Soviet bloc and embarrass it in the eyes of Asia since all indications were that the Soviets would refuse to contribute to a Korean reconstruction program on such a basis; domestically, it would provide a built-in answer to the frequently voiced congressional complaint that the United States was paying an unduly high share of the costs of maintaining the United Nations and supporting its special programs.

There was, however, immediate and almost unanimous opposition to the American plan. Leading the opposition were states, such as France, that still had post-World War II reconstruction problems of their own, were carrying heavy colonial burdens, and were being pressured into supporting larger military establishments than they felt they could afford. Few states, indeed, wanted to be forced into the position of having to offer public explanation of why they could not contribute as high a percentage of the costs of a Korean reconstruction program as the General Assembly assessed against them. In the light of this opposition, the United States quickly agreed to a substitute resolution to leave the matter of financing the program to the Assembly and have the ECOSOC continue its discussion on the organization and initial program without becoming torn over the controversy over finances.[30]

In the Assembly the problem was turned over to the special Advisory Committee on Administrative and Budgetary Questions on which the United States had strong and influential although not official representation; that is to say, the members of the Committee, while seated as independent experts, were also chosen on the basis of the comparative financial interests of the member states. The Advisory Committee's report recommended that a limited group of states be organized into a Negotiating Committee to take up the matter of contributions with each member state on an individual basis.[31] It would be the function of the committee to convince each government to contribute according to its capacity rather than to have a share set down by the Assembly without the contributor having a part in the determination. This compromise of its original financing scheme was immediately accepted by the United States. The Negotiating Committee could only hope to bring about multilateral support, however, if it was acting from a position of strength. The strongest bargaining position lay in receiving quick and substantial support from the United States which was expected to be the largest contributor and without whose support there would clearly be no program. It was undoubtedly with this in mind that the American representative in the Assembly's Fifth Committee announced, at an early stage, that "the United States Government Executive was ready to ask the United States Congress to authorize a large appropriation for the program of relief and rehabilitation in Korea." He went on to make the assumption that "those States which had already replied so generously to the appeal for emergency supplies would no doubt give a similar answer to the requests of the Negotiating Committee." [32]

This promise of a large American contribution was made some ten days before the creating resolution of December 1 was passed. It was then confirmed less than a week after UNKRA was established when the United States pledged 65 per cent of the initial program to a maximum of $162,500,-000. There was already some consternation among delegates that the "new war" affected the work of the committee and the position that member states might take toward the Korean program. There was an equal determination among the major contributors, particularly the United States, that the basis for financing the program should be firmly established even though the changed military situation might delay its utilization. The United States made its view particularly clear by asserting that so long as the December 1 resolution remained unamended and the purpose of the United Nations unchanged, member states should pledge their contributions on the assumption that the military operation would be successful and the reconstruction program carried out as originally envisaged. By the end of January, 1951, thirteen governments, including the United States, had made firm offers to UNKRA totaling more than $200,000,000 (see Table 1).

The passage of the December 1 resolution and the promises of multilateral financing of the program only created a paper agency. It was still possible for the United States to decide that UNKRA could not become operative because of the change in the military situation. No such decision was made.

TABLE 1 *

STATEMENT OF OFFERS TO THE NEGOTIATING COMMITTEE UNDER THE
GENERAL ASSEMBLY RESOLUTION OF 1 DECEMBER 1950
(AS OF JANUARY 26, 1951)

| | |
|---|---|
| Australia | $ 4,229,000 (maximum) |
| Canada | 7,500,000 (maximum) |
| Egypt | 28,000 |
| Guatemala | "several thousand tons of timber" |
| Indonesia | 100,000 (minimum) |
| Netherlands | 260,000 |
| Norway | 800,000 (minimum) |
| Saudi Arabia | 10,000 |
| Sweden | 1,000,000 |
| Syria | 12,000 |
| United Kingdom | 28,000,000 (maximum) |
| United States | 162,500,000 (maximum) |
| Venezuela | 70,000 |
| Total | $204,509,000 (excluding the Guatemalan offer of timber) |

* Source: UN Doc. A/1769, *Report of the Negotiating Committee on Contributions to Programmes of Relief and Rehabilitation* (26 January 1951), Annex I.

Indeed, by February the United States had concurred in the appointment of an executive head of the agency and the recruitment of a staff, emphasizing again that the change in the military situation did not precipitate a basic change in over-all policy objectives.

A first step toward appointing an agency chief had actually been taken the previous November by Secretary-General Trygve Lie. He suggested that J. Donald Kingsley, then Director-General of the International Refugee Organization (IRO), consider taking on the post of United Nations Agent General for Korean Reconstruction. Lie had had the Korean conflict on his desk almost constantly since June 25 and was known to be anxious to keep enthusiasm and support high for making and keeping the entire operation a United Nations affair. He had, however, been frustrated a number of times in trying to widen the supervisory mechanism over the Unified

Command to provide for greater non-American participation and specifically for participation by the Secretariat.[33] Hopeful that a wider base could be provided for the reconstruction program, he was wise enough in the ways of UN politics to realize that a *sine qua non* of substantial American financial support would be that the Agent General be a United States national. He, therefore, suggested that Kingsley consider taking on the job of Korean reconstruction. Not only was IRO soon to be closed, but from Lie's point of view, Kingsley had the advantage of identity with United Nations operations and also of close ties with the American government. Among several high-ranking posts, he had been a White House aide under President Truman.

Kingsley's first response to the offer of the Korean job was negative. He was then intently interested in maintaining responsibility in the refugee field and was being considered for the new post of UN High Commissioner for Refugees. There was, however, considerable feeling among delegations at the time that since the refugee problem was essentially a European one, the High Commissioner should be European. The post also provided an opportunity to put a non-American into a high United Nations post, a feat often thwarted in the specialized agencies where the United States, under congressional pressure, often had to negotiate for the appointment of an American overseer of heavily United States-financed programs. When the vote for High Commissioner was therefore taken on December 12, Kingsley's supporters were not able to consolidate sufficient votes and the post went to a former member of the Dutch delegation to the Assembly.[34]

Later in December, Lie visited Kingsley in Geneva and again urged him to take on the job as Agent General for Korean reconstruction. Kingsley, now that his plans for continuing the refugee work would not be realized, agreed that Lie might start clearing his nomination through the delegations upon his return to New York. Under the December 1 resolution, the Secretary-General was authorized to appoint the Agent General "after consulting the United Nations Commission for the Unification and Rehabilitation of Korea and the [UNKRA] Advisory Committee." Practically speaking, this meant that Lie had to get the approval of the major contributors, the United States and the British and Commonwealth governments, to Kingsley's appointment. Kingsley had actually been approached earlier by the State Department inquiring as to his interest in the Korean assignment in view of the potential refugee relief problem there. He, also, felt that Lie would not have approached him a second time without having first cleared the move with the major contributors to the program. He, therefore, agreed to the assignment with reasonable assurance that there was strong political support for the UNKRA program.

Kingsley's nomination was cleared by Lie by the end of January and his appointment formally announced on February 7, 1951. It was made clear at the time of his appointment that he was to continue as Director-General of the International Refugee Organization until he could turn the residual problems of that organization over to a liquidator. While this arrangement was dictated by the refugee work that remained and by Kingsley's desire to supervise personally the general closure of operations, it suggests that no one envisaged an all-out crash program immediately upon the appointment of the Agent General. But even with this reservation, the confirmation of Kingsley's appointment served as a clear indication that the American government was going ahead immediately in supporting a multilateral, civilian-managed reconstruction program despite the "new war."

The action taken in agreeing to the activation of UNKRA by the appointment of an Agent General was completely in line with the over-all policy that President Truman was then trying to get across to General MacArthur. The General had continued to request a free hand to extend his counter-offensive to bombing the Manchurian bases and the President sought to explain the "political factors" involved in the government's policy of localizing the conflict. High among the purposes which would be served by "successful resistance in Korea," the

President listed the objective of carrying "out our commitments of honor to the South Koreans and to demonstrate to the world that the friendship of the United States is of inestimable value in time of adversity." In seeking to achieve these purposes, he emphasized that "our courses of action at this time should be such as to consolidate the great majority of the United Nations, . . . [which] is not merely part of the Organization but is also the nations whom we would desperately need to count on as allies in the event the Soviet Union moves against us." [35] While the reconstruction program undoubtedly enjoyed a lower level of concern, its development was conditioned by these same basic factors: keeping the Republic of Korea together and maintaining allied cooperation for the problems of the Korean peninsula.

The intervention of the Chinese Communist "volunteers" into the Korean conflict clearly offered an opportunity to the American government to postpone the actual formation and organization of the reconstruction agency. If the full force and significance of the intervention was not clear on December 1, 1950, when the resolution establishing UNKRA was passed, the fierce fighting and setback suffered by the UN forces in the ensuing weeks made it obvious that the original reconstruction plans were not feasible. It would, therefore, have been completely in order not to appoint an Agent General until the military situation had settled down and future events could be more clearly anticipated. Nothing like this was done. Indeed, the American government seems to have insisted that no step be taken that would even imply the possibility of defeat of the UN forces or disappointment for the Republic of Korea. The decision to go ahead and set up UNKRA cannot be deemed to have been carefully determined after deliberate assessment of the new situation. It seems rather the result of the momentum started up the previous September and an accompanying indisposition to upset the applecart of a multilateral spirit in Korea. What can be thus said with greatest certainty is only that the United States could not take advantage of the opportunity that was offered to stop the momentum leading up to the activation of UNKRA without endangering the bases of its long-range objectives in the Korean conflict.

1. Harry S Truman, *Memoirs,* II (Garden City, N.Y.: Doubleday and Co., Inc., 1956), 334–35.

2. *Ibid.,* p. 332.

3. Security Council resolution of June 25, 1950.

4. Truman, *Memoirs,* II, 336–37.

5. Security Council resolution of June 27, 1950.

6. Security Council resolution of July 7, 1950.

7. Security Council resolution of July 31, 1950.

8. UN Security Council, Fifth Year, *Official Records,* 479th meeting (July 31, 1950), pp. 5–6.

9. United Nations Command, *Civilian Relief and Economic Aid—Korea: 7 July 1950–30 September 1951* (Tokyo: United Nations Command Headquarters, 1952), pp. 1–4.

10. UN Doc. E/1851/Rev. 1, *Report of the Secretary-General on Assistance for Civil Population of Korea,* Economic and Social Council, Eleventh Session (resumed), (October 11, 1950). Very shortly after the appointment of the Agent General of UNKRA, these duties were transferred to his office.

11. United Nations Command, *Civilian Relief and Economic Aid—Korea,* pp. 9–12.

12. Article by A. M. Rosenthal, *New York Times,* September 17, 1950, Sect. IV, p. E.7.

13. UN General Assembly, Fifth Session, Plenary Meetings, Vol. I, *Official Records,* 279th meeting (September 20, 1950), pp. 26–27.

14. Leland M. Goodrich, *Korea: A Study of U.S. Policy in the United Nations* (New York: Council on Foreign Relations, 1956), p. 129 n.

15. General Assembly Resolution 376 (V), *The Problem of the Independence of Korea,* October 7, 1950.

16. *New York Times,* October 12, 1950, p. 1.

17. *Ibid,* October 15, 1950, text on page 5.

18. *Ibid,* October 19, 1950, p. 1.

19. UN Doc. E/1864, *Report by the Temporary Committee on Provisional Programme for Relief and Rehabilitation Needs of Korea,* Economic and Social Council, Eleventh Session (resumed), (November 1, 1950).

20. UN Doc. E/1851/Add. 1, *Suggested Organization for Korean Relief and Rehabilitation Programme of the United Nations,* submitted by the Secretary-General, Economic and Social Council, Eleventh Session (resumed), (October 9, 1950) ; and UN Doc. E/1858, *Plans for Relief and Rehabilitation of Korea,* draft resolution submitted by the United States, Economic and Social Council, Eleventh Session (resumed), (October 17, 1950).

21. UN Doc. E/1852, *Assistance to Civil Population of Korea,* draft resolutions submitted by Australia, Economic and Social Council, Eleventh Session (resumed), (October 9, 1950). See especially Draft Resolution II, *Rehabilitation Functions of Commission and other Machinery.*

22. UN Doc. E/1858/Rev. 1, *Plans for Relief and Rehabilitation of Korea,* joint draft resolution submitted by the United States and Australia, Economic and Social Council, Eleventh Session (resumed), (October 26, 1950).

23. Special communiqué of November 28, 1950, *New York Times,* November 29, 1950.

24. *Reports of the UN Command Operations* (Eighth Report: for the Period October 16–31, 1950; and Ninth Report: for the Period November 1–15, 1950), reprinted in the Department of State *Bulletin,* XXIV, No. 601 (January 8, 1951), 43–50.

25. *Substance of Statements Made at the Wake Island Conference* on October 15, 1950, compiled by General Bradley, from notes kept by the Conferees from Washington. Prepared for the use of the Committee on Armed Services and the Committee on Foreign Relations, U.S. Senate, 82nd Congress 1st Session (Washington: Government Printing Office, 1951), p. 1, (Hereinafter referred to as *Wake Island Conference Notes.*)

26. Truman, *Memoirs,* II, 374–77.

27. *New York Times,* November 12, 1950.

28. *Wake Island Conference Notes,* p. 8.

29. UN Doc. E/114, draft resolution submitted by the United States of America; for discussion see Economic and Social Council, Eleventh Session (resumed), *Official Records,* 431st through 433rd meetings (November 6 and 7, 1950), pp. 439–54.

30. UN Doc. E/L. 125, draft resolution submitted by the United States of America; for discussions see *ibid.*

31. UN Doc. A/1526, report of the Advisory Committee on Administrative and Budgetary Questions; for discussion see General Assembly, Fifth Session, Fifth Committee, *Official Records,* 268th Meeting (November 21, 1950), pp. 195–202.

32. UN General Assembly, Fifth Session, Fifth Committee, *Official Records,* 268th Meeting (November 21, 1950), p. 200.

33. Trygve Lie, *In the Cause of Peace* (New York: Macmillan Co., 1954), pp. 333–34, 336.

34. UN General Assembly, Fifth Session, Plenary Meetings, Vol. I, *Official Records,* 325th Meeting (December 14, 1950), p. 674.

35. See General Marshall's testimony, *Military Situation in the Far East,* Part I, p. 503.

# CHAPTER III

# THE SEARCH FOR A *MODUS VIVENDI*

## *The First UNKRA/UNC Contact*

## *First Proposal for an UNKRA/Unified Command Agreement*

## *Independent Status for UNKRA*

# THE SEARCH FOR A *MODUS VIVENDI*

## *The First UNKRA/UNC Contact*

The immediate impact of the fighting on the South Korean economy is virtually impossible to measure. Reliable statistics are noticeably lacking. There is, however, some measure of magnitude in the estimate that production immediately fell to one-third the rate attained in 1949–50, a period when the people enjoyed little more than the bare necessities of life and this with the support of almost $80,000,000 in ECA aid.[1] Physical assets such as homes, factories, farm and industrial equipment, estimated at a minimum value of $1.5 billion, were destroyed. Additional loss was incurred through a lack of repair and maintenance facilities, through disuse, and through the almost complete disruption of the distribution system. What facilities were left intact, moreover, had to be converted from the production of basic commodities of livelihood to military defense; also, imported foods and raw materials had to yield valuable port and reception space to the influx of military aid. Finally, the generation of young men and women whose energies and skills had only begun to be trained to lead their country to recovery had to be thrown into battle.

The destruction and military conversion of resources and manpower were crippling to the South Korean economy not yet recovered from the effects of economic separation from Japan and North Korea. Between June, 1950, and March, 1951, the retail price index rose from 430.4 to 1506.8 as a mal (20 liters) of rice jumped in price from 5,380 won to 18,000 won. The amount of paper money in circulation rose fivefold over the same short period, while the amount of goods and services for civilian consumption dropped to dangerously low levels. In addition, and of most immediate importance, almost four million refugees from North Korea and the provinces near the 38th parallel swarmed among the twenty-one million peo-

41

ple in the Republic of Korea already struggling to live on inadequate food and housing.[2]

This was the situation that the recently appointed Agent General of UNKRA wanted to see at firsthand as he arrived in Tokyo on February 15, 1951. The purpose of his trip was to hold discussions with the military authorities of the United Nations Command on the part the agency could play under existing military conditions. The United Nations troops were now engaged in hard fighting to regain Seoul after having been thrown back as a result of the intervention of the Chinese Communists. Once more they were pushing toward the 38th parallel and waiting for a decision whether or not to cross the line again. Several times the Joint Chiefs of Staff had requested political guidance from the State Department on how far north MacArthur should be allowed to move his troops. The Department, however, preferred to delay forming any such specific political objectives until there was a clearer picture of the situation military operations might bring about.[3]

In this rather fluid state of affairs, Kingsley had been briefed by the Unified Command in Washington before leaving. Details were left for Tokyo. It was obvious, however, that there was considerable concern over the difficulties Washington was having with General MacArthur. There was no way to be sure what the General's reaction would be to the presence of a civilian-directed agency in a theater under his command. But, as if anticipating difficulties, members of the State Department working on multilateral programs advised against accepting any perfunctory dismissal by the military of UNKRA's immediate initiation of some program, albeit modest in the light of the continuing hostilities. At the decision-making level, however, there seemed no real anxiety to come to grips with MacArthur on this particular issue, at least at this particular time.

Kingsley was accompanied to the Far East by members of his own staff, including a high-ranking retired U.S. Army officer who knew many of MacArthur's staff personally. His task was to explain that UNKRA, although international and civilian in direction, would have a good understanding of the problems of the military in a theater of active operations. In Washington, the party was joined by two representatives of the Unified Command, one representing the Department of State and the other, an Army officer, representing the Department of Defense. Their presence seems to have indicated confirmation that support of UNKRA was a basic tenet of American policy. Nevertheless they carried no positive instructions to the field except to facilitate Kingsley's trip and participate in the general review of the situation. The military representative, moreover, made it quite clear that it was premature to begin to think about an active UNKRA program.

Arriving in Tokyo, Kingsley had an immediate interview with MacArthur before going on to Korea. MacArthur was quite moving as he spoke about the enormity of the refugee problem and the utter chaos and want into which the peninsula had been thrown. He admitted that the acute civilian distress was a major danger to his military operations and he feared the growing demoralization of the Korean people might prove as formidable an obstacle as the enemy troops. Describing these problems, MacArthur encouraged Kingsley by welcoming any help he could get to keep the Korean people alive and keep their hopes from disappearing altogether. But he cautioned that he had a war to fight and couldn't have anyone getting in his way. If Kingsley followed that rule and could find ways to get something done, then MacArthur promised every bit of help he could give. Armed with this promise, Kingsley flew to Korea with the chief of the United Nations Command's Korea Economic Aid Section to meet with staff of the Eighth Army's field units in order to try to work out some basis for UNKRA operations.

As a promise, MacArthur's general statement of policy might have meant partial success to Kingsley, but as an order what could it mean to subordinate staff officers? What was involved was the responsibility of deciding that one UNKRA project did not get in the way of MacArthur's conduct of military operations, but that another did. A general instruction in a fluid situation is more difficult to execute the farther down it gets in any bureaucracy; in an army, the difficulty is multiplied tenfold. A military commander, at any level, is personally responsible for the achievement of his mission and cannot excuse his failure by accusing his commanding officer of being vague. Few officers, it must be assumed, could resist saying "no" rather than take the chance of approving a civil affairs project for implementation on the basis of their own judgment that it would not affect military operations. Civil and military affairs were so interwoven that few could discern where one left off and the other began. Also, the farther down the line a decision on the feasibility of a reconstruction project was sent, the more it would suffer from the tensions between military and civilian personnel in the field. The fact is that there were frequently outbursts of conflict between civilians and the military and this, together with the nature of the military hierarchy, augured ill for an easy transfer of the MacArthur promise into practice.

The civilian relief teams, as has already been noted, included both United Nations civilians, many of them non-Americans, and U.S. Army officers, all integrated into the command structure of the Eighth Army. During their processing, the United Nations civilians were required to sign an agreement to work under the command of the military authorities. This was done at the request of the Unified Command to insure that there would be no rude surprises when a civilian was put under military command and to minimize problems which might arise should the civilian come armed with instructions from his parent organization which were not entirely consistent with standard army operating procedures. While using United Nations civilians throughout its relief operation, the Eighth Army made sure that control remained in military hands. The central Civil Affairs Section of EUSAK (later set up as a separate command with the title of United Nations Civil Assistance Command in Korea, UNCACK), while composed of military and civilian personnel, was controlled by the military element. Moreover, this section was the ultimate source of authority over provincial teams where civilian influence might be greater, although each team was under the command of a military officer of the rank of colonel or lieutenant-colonel. A good many of the UN civilians were veterans of the UNRRA experience in World War II and still remembered, frequently with disfavor, the strict military control under which the field teams in Europe had had to operate. Working through the army again in Korea often proved frustrating although the problems were not unlike those found in many other headquarters/field relationships. One civilian, for example, complained that "the military machinery was ponderous and the czars of the Civil Affairs Section of EUSAK were as ignorant of local conditions as they were anxious to be of help." He went on to say that while "they invited comments and recommendations from the United Nations experts and wherever feasible the recommendations were acted upon . . . often by the time any action was taken, the emergency had either ceased to exist or some improvisation had taken place." [4]

There was clearly a good deal of misunderstanding on the part of sponsoring organizations of exactly how tightly the U.S. Army controlled the relief work. The United Nations specialized agencies were apt to think that requests for technical personnel meant that they were going to staff the program in their particular fields rather than just fill the gaps in the Army organization. There was also the natural desire of the agencies and the Red Cross Societies that their assistance be properly recognized by the Koreans and, through appropriate publicity, by the rest of the world. Two cases may serve to illustrate the problems that arose in the field. The first involved the World Health Organization, which, after the first call for medical assistance, quickly recruited a number of teams for Korea, including doctors and sanitary engineers. In organizing their contingent, they designated one doctor to act as senior medical adviser and to report to WHO Headquarters on the work as it progressed. Arriving in Korea, this senior medical appointee, a conscientious and competent British doctor, informed the Army of his designation by WHO as Director of Medical Services. The Army was undoubtedly somewhat taken aback and proceeded to tell the doctor exactly what place he held in the scheme of things, i.e., subordinate to the military medical authorities. Notwithstanding the rather obvious warning, he took the liberty of holding a press interview during which he publicly announced that he had been appointed Director of Medical Services and, the inference was, intended to carry out those duties. Quite understandably the military considered this an act of deliberate insubordination contrary to the agreement all United Nations civilians signed before arriving in Korea and quickly asked that the senior doctor be recalled.[5] The case was a perfect example for those in the military who were warning that loyalty was indivisible under conditions of active operations and that the Army had to have complete and unquestioned control of all civilian relief activities until hostilities were definitely over.

Another case, that of the Red Cross insignia, came up for discussion at a higher echelon and also did little to help civilian/military relationships in the field. Early in February, a number of welfare teams organized by the British, Canadian, and Danish Red Cross Societies arrived in Tokyo ready to be assigned to Korea. While being briefed at UNC Headquarters, they were told that they would be required to wear U.S. Army-type uniforms without any special insignia. The members of the teams immediately requested permission to wear the Red Cross emblem which their societies required. Permission was refused and the teams, in turn, refused to proceed to Korea.[6] A spokesman for the United Nations Command explained that "all civilian welfare groups in Korea must operate under United Nations Command, pooling their supplies and personnel and not acting as independent organizations." He went on to say that welfare personnel had to wear prescribed uniforms with the United Nations shoulder patch, but it may show the identity of their parent organization. The disagreement with the Red Cross Societies, he explained, did not therefore concern insignia, but the larger question of independent or unified operation of the civil relief operations. What really troubled the military was that "representatives of the League of Red Cross Societies in this theater have stated that they may not, as a matter of principle, become members of the United Nations Command, nor may the League of Red Cross Societies donate supplies to the command pool, but that they must operate as a separate Red Cross organization and that Red Cross–donated supplies must be distributed separately under their supervision." [7]

The establishment of separate supply channels by the Red Cross was, of course, intolerable from the point of view of the military under the conditions of heavy fighting then going on in the Seoul sector. The insignia ban, however, was literally heard around the world. The League of Red Cross Societies took the matter up with the Secretary-General of the United Nations, the British Embassy in Washington approached the State Department, and the British government in London was asked to explain in the House of Commons what action it was taking to reverse an order that was unacceptable to the British Red Cross Society. Ten days later, the ban on wearing Red Cross insignia was lifted by MacArthur's Headquarters, undoubtedly on instructions from the Unified Command in Washington. [8] Red Cross supplies, however, continued to be distributed through military channels. The Medical Director case and the Red Cross insignia ban are two examples of the tensions in Tokyo and in the field between the civilians who sought to maintain the identity and prestige of their sponsoring organizations and the military authorities who refused to tolerate any sign of divided loyalty or separate supply channels in a war situation.

Immediate responsibility for the military Korean Aid program had been assigned to Colonel W. H. Hensey, Jr., in October, 1950, with the mission to provide "civilian relief in Korea to prevent disease and unrest and to further military objectives." [9] Specific responsibility for civilian relief had been formalized by a Presidential directive of September 29, 1950, which had clarified the roles of the Army and the ECA in Korea, the first to take over emergency relief and the second, long-term rehabilitation work pending the establishment of permanent United Nations machinery. The Army, in fact, needed no specific directive to set about the organization of civilian relief. In defending its request for appropriations to meet its relief responsibility, the Army witness pointed out that "to carry on successful [military] operations . . . the indigenous population, friendly or unfriendly, must be sustained to the point that unrest, disease, starvation, and so forth, will not jeopardize the success of the military operation." [10] Thus, while not in fact creating Col. Hensey's mission, the Presidential directive supported it. Moreover, it later proved a basis for the Army to expand its activities beyond emergency relief by "assuming" ECA responsibilities under the directive when "due to the intensity of the military operations, the Economic Cooperation Administration found it increasingly difficult to operate and gradually phased out." [11]

Given the military concept of civilian relief, the civil-military tensions in the field, and the conditions of MacArthur's promise, the position taken by Col. Hensey in his meeting with Kingsley in Taegu late in February was not surprising. He made it quite clear that within the broad framework of General MacArthur's policy statement in Tokyo, he simply could not see any possibility of UNKRA's operating substantial independent projects in Korea while the military situation remained critical and troop requirements were already overtaxing the available supply and transport facilities. He was emphatic in stating that the actual military situation required unity of authority in the theater of operations and that any United Nations activities would, as had non-military relief assistance, have to be integrated into the Army's program. At the time, Kingsley made no positive comment on this view of the situation. He was, however, forced to respond to the difficulties it posed when he encountered a completely opposite opinion in his subsequent meeting with the United Nations Commission for the Unification and Rehabilitation of Korea (UNCURK).

By February, it was becoming clear that UNCURK's primary purpose to "represent the United Nations in bringing about the establishment of a unified, independent and democratic government of all Korea" could not be achieved by peaceful means and few, like President Rhee, were advocating its accomplishment by force of arms. Indeed, by early June, Secretary of State Acheson was willing to admit publicly that "the intervention of the Chinese Communists . . . made it militarily difficult, if not impossible, to achieve the political objective of the United Nations . . . of unifying Korea under free and democratic institutions." [12] Its primary mission frustrated, UNCURK turned to its secondary purpose, to "exercise . . . responsibilities in connection with relief and rehabilitation in Korea." In the debates in the ECOSOC in November, the Australian and Chilean delegations had exerted particular efforts to gain a policy-making role for UNCURK in the field of relief and rehabilitation. Defeated in the main by pressure from the United States, they were forced to satisfy themselves with a somewhat perfunctory advisory role restricted to the general political considerations which might affect the reconstruction program.[13] UNCURK was, however, according to the establishing resolution of October 7, 1950, "the principal representative of the United Nations in Korea" and, in this capacity, had begun, under the stimulus of its Australian and Chilean members, to take a more active role in relief and reconstruction matters than its advisory duties probably warranted. As early as December 5, 1950, several days after UNKRA had been established by the General Assembly, the Commission set up a special sub-committee on economic questions which proceeded to consider such problems as policy recommendations to the Agent General, food production and land reform in the Republic of Korea, and economic and financial conditions.[14]

Meeting with UNCURK after seeing Col. Hensey, Kingsley explained that General MacArthur had been firm in insisting that no reconstruction project interfere with the conduct of military operations. Specifically, this made it impossible to establish any supply routes outside existing military facilities which were already being heavily taxed and were handling as many civilian supplies as they could under the emergency relief program. This, he explained, made any substantial project impossible and made him seriously doubt the practicality of establishing an operational organization in Korea without very much to do. He told the Commission that he was, however, considering what possibilities there might be to provide technical assistance to the Republic of Korea which would not require the transportation, warehousing and distribution of supplies and equipment, but would be of considerable help to the government during these days of crisis and provide the economic groundwork for the future reconstruction program. The Commission was not entirely satisfied and expressed the view that some operations should be begun by the Agent General as soon as possible. Specifically, in addition to technical assistance, they suggested planning operations and building up a staff, conducting surveys to determine needs, importing relief goods and other supplies where military arrangements permitted and actually beginning rehabilitation work in areas where there were no military operations. The Commission also felt free to advise Kingsley that he should immediately establish his Headquarters in Korea and begin developing more of a nucleus than the United Nations civilian element of UNCACK for taking over full responsibility for relief and reconstruction when the military situation permitted.[15]

Leaving Korea after his meeting with UNCURK, Kingsley was convinced in his mind that the advice of the Commission was impractical. The Commission itself had agreed that the military authorities had to play a major part in all relief work while the future remained indefinite. Granting this, Kingsley was not prepared, as UNCURK was suggesting, to try to loosen the rigid line Colonel Hensey had taken in explaining exactly how tight army control had to be. From his own experience, he knew and appreciated that, outside of immediate and complete peace (which was not in view), only a specific directive from higher authority would succeed in changing the United Nations Command's position. Without the support of such a directive from Washington, he felt that his position, if he set himself up in Korea, would be weakened by constant disputes that were bound to arise on one side or the other as he sat between UNCURK and the United Nations Command. He was also aware of the pressures generated by the Koreans who would be constantly asking why the UNKRA program could not start producing results.[16]

Stopping in Tokyo on his way home, Kingsley had a final talk with MacArthur's staff and quite frankly agreed that under the actual military situation and the operating conditions, the United Nations Command would have to have over-all authority as it indeed had over-all responsibility in Korea. At this stage, he made no effort to contend that, within this structure, UNKRA could undertake certain independent projects. There was, however, agreement on all sides that emergency relief was not enough even in this fluid state of affairs. The wheels of the South Korean government had slowed down to a dangerously slow pace; the economy was constantly being strained under the pressure of skyrocketing inflation and inept handling. Soon even military success might have little meaning for the Korean people. The military pointed out that ECA had not been able to operate under the Presidential directive of September 29, 1950, and no longer had the staff in Korea to cope with the task of bringing the South Korean governmental and economic structure through the bedlam of the war. It was possible that UNKRA should now undertake this work. If so, the United Nations Command insisted that the Agent General recognize the ultimate authority and responsibility of the military and work on a technical assistance level under military supervision, just as the specialized agencies and Red Cross were working under military oversight in the relief field.

### First Proposal for an UNKRA/Unified Command Agreement

During February and March, the split between the Unified Command and General MacArthur was growing ever deeper. Among the decisive incidents was the refusal by the Joint Chiefs of Staff to allow the bombing of the North Korean city of Racin, a port of reception for Soviet-originated supplies and equipment just 17 or 18 miles from the Russian border. The refusal of the Joint Chiefs had been based on the political objections of the State Department not to risk hitting Soviet territory and opening the "big war." [17] Incidents, like the Racin bombing, opened up the whole question of the weight to be given to political considerations in limiting military recommendations and the relationship between a theater commander and the central authority in Washington. Although it is difficult to identify direct contact, the thinking in Washington and Tokyo on these issues must have affected the status of UNKRA. An independent role for the agency depended on these same questions: how valid and forceful were the political factors favoring its activation; and, to what extent was the central authority willing to overrule the theater commander?

As Chairman of the Joint Chiefs of Staff, General Bradley saw the problem in terms of shifting balances. He later testified that "When the Joint Chiefs of Staff express their opinion on a subject, it is from the military point of view, and is given with a full realization that considerations other than military may be overriding in making the final decision." [18] And again, he later elaborated in saying that "the end results of a war are a combination of military and political considerations and you use the military to obtain your political objectives." [19] Accepting Bradley's position as that which prevailed at the time, we can say that the objectives of economic reconstruction had to be balanced with the military objectives of the United States. The fact that the military objectives were actually in the process of change was therefore of some consequence in terms of determining the status of UNKRA.

It is, of course, difficult to pin down exactly when, after the setback of November and December, 1950, the United States decided it was not willing to risk open war with Red China and possibly the Soviet Union to create a situation which would permit the early unification of Korea. By March, 1951, however, the government in Washington seems to have been coming around to the position of consolidating the Republic

of Korea behind the 38th parallel and leaving the matter
of unification where it was before June 25, 1950: an ideal to
be achieved through peaceful negotiation but with little chance
of success within the near future. This seems clear in the reluctance of the State Department to respond to the request
of the Joint Chiefs for "political guidance" during February
and March, particularly with regard to crossing the 38th parallel again. Within the framework of the limited objective of
pushing the aggressors back, little success could be claimed
even here if the Republic of Korea was to be crushed by the
burden of defending itself. Clearly, reconstruction had to start.
Were there, nevertheless, political considerations that were sufficiently compelling to override, within the Bradley formula,
the traditional and logical military stand of the United Nations Command that authority and responsibility could not be
divided in a theater of active hostilities? In the case of the
bombing of Racin, political considerations had prevailed under the pressures of avoiding the "big war." Were there any
pressures that even approached this level in the case of providing some sort of independent status for UNKRA in Korea?

Political pressures in this direction began to manifest themselves when the March 11 issue of the *New York Times* announced what were reportedly the UNKRA Agent General's
plans following his return from the Far East. High among
these was the news that "a special staff for coordinating all
civilian relief and reconstruction activities in Korea will start
functioning by April 1 in Tokyo." It was, however, also noted
that "this staff, while appointed by Mr. Kingsley, will be integrated completely with General of the Army Douglas Mac-
Arthur's headquarters and will in fact form the Civil Assistance staff of that headquarters." Special mention was made
that "Mr. Kingsley . . . put complete integration of all civilian supply and assistance work with the United Nations military establishment first among his immediate objectives," and
he was quoted as saying that "we are not going to try to run
separate programs, separate lines or separate anything because there would be no sense in it." [20]

The news of these plans immediately aroused a storm of protests from several directions. Secretary-General Trygve Lie cabled Kingsley that the idea of UNKRA's planning and advisory staff being under Army command was contrary to the concept of Member Governments during the ECOSOC and Assembly debates. If Lie seems to have neglected considering the vastly changed military picture since these debates, he went on to emphasize that subordination to military command would complicate fund-raising for UNKRA. He asked that Kingsley clear any proposals with the Advisory Committee and UNCURK before releasing them to the press.[21] Lie's fears on fund-raising were promptly justified. Delegations representing major contributors after the United States quickly informed his office that it was extremely unlikely that their governments would be willing to support a United Nations reconstruction program that was under the command of what was really the United States Army.[22] What was generally left unsaid was that their governments lacked trust in the American field command under MacArthur, especially since the question of limiting the Korean conflict was again a burning issue.

Replying to Lie, Kingsley did not deny or even attempt to modify the substance of what had been reported. He rather pointed out that he had thus far agreed with MacArthur only in principle on the broad lines of a "practical operating arrangement for an interim period." "Agreement in principle" did not, of course, necessarily mean that there was still room for an independent UNKRA program on a limited basis. Kingsley did not, however, go further to suggest any alternative at that time to complete integration. Indeed, he took the opportunity to remind Lie that while he appreciated the support of the Secretary-General's office, he had been, and would continue, contacting governments and explaining his position directly.[23] What Kingsley was, in fact, telling Lie was that he had to run his own show.

Kingsley seems to have been concerned particularly with the necessity of dealing directly with the United States. In the establishment of the Unified Command, care had had to be taken that no supervisory functions be left in UN bodies where the Soviet Union—which opposed the UN action—could wield influence. But beyond this, the United States went so far as to reject any supervision of the military operations even by a committee composed entirely of non-Communist states.[24] The coordination that was carried out with those governments that contributed armed forces to the United Nations Command, moreover, took place through diplomatic channels in Washington and not at the seat of the United Nations. The establishment of UNKRA as a special body, separate from the Secretariat of the specialized agencies, was thus consistent with what seems to have been a deliberate policy of the United States to minimize the possibility of influence either by the Soviet Union as a UN member or by Soviet nationals in the Secretariat over United Nations operations in Korea at every level. While it is true that the UNKRA program was a nonmilitary undertaking, the agency, nevertheless, would have to operate in the theater of military operations and to post personnel in areas of acute military concern. These activities would, in turn, pose a security problem to American military commanders in the field. Given these relationships, it seemed expedient for Kingsley to deal directly with the United States government on all issues. The protests of the Secretary-General could, therefore, be met somewhat sharply, without even trying to answer them completely.

The protests from other contributors against operating UNKRA under complete army command were, nevertheless, quite clearly something else. What they represented was the possible loss of support needed to maintain a multilateral effort in Korea. As such, they provided political considerations to balance against the military recommendation for undivided authority. It must be admitted that these considerations hardly seem formidable when compared with the intensity of allied opposition to a military recommendation such as "hot pursuit" of communist planes over the Manchurian border.[25] This is, perhaps, because there is little to compare after looking at the immediate stakes involved. Yet, in terms of long-range objectives, it remained important to hold together the failing economy and morale of the Korean people and maintain allied cooperation in the reconstruction program. It was, therefore, of some importance that an opportunity to force the issue of UNKRA's status in Korea came soon after these protests were made. The occasion arose when, toward the end of March, the State Department asked UNKRA to send out an economic advisory team, presumably independent of military supervision, to organize an attack on the almost-uncontrollable inflation rampant throughout South Korea. The Agent General refused, explaining that any attempt by UNKRA to begin activities before completing operational arrangements, particularly with the Unified Command, would be both politically and administratively unwise.[26] Kingsley clearly seemed to suggest that the United States government had to decide what instructions it was going to send its military representatives in the field and how far it was going to support UNKRA operations in Korea under the present conditions, before the agency began to undertake any projects.

By the end of March, however, the explosion between President Truman and General MacArthur was about to take place. It was probably the least propitious moment for Washington to counter the recommendations of the theater commander on a reconstruction program that could not, under the best of circumstances, be fully implemented for some time to come. The State Department, therefore, acting for the Unified Command, responded to Kingsley in terms that were designed to meet the position of the United Nations Command. Basic to the proposal was an assertion that responsibility in Korea could not be divided until peace and security were established. It was therefore suggested that UNKRA operate under military supervision in the fields of technical assistance and long-range planning while continuing to supply medical and welfare staff for the civilian relief program.[27] Some hope for an active operation was held out in the promise that UNKRA would be given freedom of action in areas which did not affect the military mission of the Commander-in-Chief of the United Nations

Command (CINCUNC). In fact, this was nothing more than MacArthur's earlier pledge now formalized and confirmed by Washington. Nothing, however, was said to suggest that it would be interpreted any more broadly than Col. Hensey had done in his Taegu meeting with Kingsley in February.

Kingsley's immediate action was to inform Washington that the proposals were not acceptable. While he was prepared to accept the priority of the military position, he maintained that the activities of technical assistance and planning staff would not affect the mission of CINCUNC and, therefore, should be given complete freedom of action, including freedom from military supervision. He made considerable point of the necessity of relating authority and responsibility: where the United Nations Command had responsibility in the field of civilian relief, let them have full authority; where it was logical for UNKRA to assume responsibility, for economic and financial advisory services and planning its own future program, let UNKRA have full authority. He promised and even encouraged effective coordination between UNKRA and the United Nations Command, but declared that he was "most reluctant to assume responsibility without commensurate authority and while such may be necessary within limits, I am anxious to narrow those limits as much as possible." [28]

Kingsley's demands for the separate (but coordinated) status were in large part motivated by the discussions he had had with representatives of Great Britain and several of the Commonwealth governments. These followed protests against the prospect that their contributions might be used for projects that would not be entirely controlled by UNKRA. The governments made it clear that if circumstances did not allow UNKRA to gain independence within a definite sphere of action, limited though it may be, they preferred that the agency delay commencing operations rather than place them under military supervision. Delay, however (as not only Kingsley but also a number of State Department officials realized), if too long, might very well mean quiet death, given the problem of collecting contributions, the increased difficulties when the ardor of the UN approach to the Korean affair had waned, and the ever-cooling support of other governments for the Rhee regime. The possibility thus existed that UNKRA might never become operative if it did not get into the field quickly. Kingsley, therefore, took the initiative in seeking an immediate modification of the military stand for "undivided authority and responsibility." For the State Department, his action was forcing a choice of opposing the policy of the military authorities or abandoning the plans for a multilateral approach to the problem of Korean reconstruction.

By early April, the basis of the split on the role of UNKRA in the "new war" situation was thus clearly defined. The United Nations Command held that authority could not be divided in a theater of active hostilities. Thus, if it was determined that UNKRA had to begin activities before peace and security had been established, then these activities had to be restricted to a sphere that did not hamper effective military operations, and the limits of these activities had to be left to the determination of the Commander-in-Chief of the UN Command. The Agent General of UNKRA was prepared to recognize the realities of the situation and the priority of military needs. He nevertheless maintained that a substantial area existed where UNKRA could provide technical assistance and long-range planning services without affecting the military mission of the UN Command and that activities within this area did not require military supervision. To a great extent, his position was a response to the insistence of other major contributing governments that their contributions were not to be used unless UNKRA was in a position to undertake independent activities. If nothing was done to respond to these views, it was possible that the agency would be put into a permanent status of inactivity. Here were the first consequences of having allowed the original momentum for the establishment of a Korean reconstruction agency to have continued unarrested despite the basic complication brought on by the entrance of Chinese Communists into the conflict.

## Independent Status for *UNKRA*

The position of the military authorities in the UNKRA issue had very firm roots in the experience of the Second World War. Early in the war, General Marshall, then Army Chief-of-Staff, had warned that "orderly civil administration must be maintained in support of military operations in liberated and occupied areas." It was the strong view of Secretary of War Stimson, supported by Secretary of State Hull, that this responsibility for maintenance of civil administration was initially a military one. Although President Roosevelt was prone to be suspicious of the military's assuming any civilian duties, he was eventually brought around by Stimson's persistent and telling arguments to agree that "the War Department must assume the responsibility for civilian relief in all liberated areas during the first six months after their liberation." [29] Thus, early in 1942, the War Department began preparing for its civil affairs responsibilities by training specialists in public service, particularly at the School of Military Government in Charlottesville, Virginia.

Prior to D-Day, General Eisenhower's Headquarters anticipated the civil problems that would be encountered by the Allied Armies. It issued an elaborate handbook providing guidance to insure "that conditions exist among the civil populations which will not interfere with operation against the enemy, but will promote these operations." Eisenhower himself, however, cautioned Civil Affairs Officers just before D-Day that "you are not politicians or anything else but soldiers." [30] The instructions from Supreme Headquarters were later interpreted at the level of the 12th Army Group as orders "to control the civilian population during combat, to organize trustworthy police assistance in keeping military roads clear of refugees so that troops and supplies could move uninterruptedly, to provide emergency care for refugees and displaced persons, and generally to aid in re-establishing friendly local governments in our rear capable of restoring law, order and essential civilian services." The scope of these duties in liberated countries was, as the G-5 section of the 12th Army Group later reported, all-encompassing because "a military operation in a heavily populated country disturbs every organized civilian activity." [31]

Like the Korean problem later, the Army's civil affairs mission had to be related to the establishment of an international agency, the United Nations Relief and Rehabilitation Administration. UNRRA was founded to administer emergency relief and assist in initial rehabilitation efforts in countries liberated by the Allied Armies. Not unlike the experience of UNKRA, the UNRRA Council had had to recognize that the agency, established in the midst of the war, could not commence operations until some months after liberation. Indeed, the first resolution of the Council provided that "in the case of a liberated area in which a government or recognized national authority does not yet exercise administrative authority, the administration [UNRRA] will operate from such a time and for such a purpose as may be agreed upon between the military command and the administration and subject to such control as the military command may find necessary." The primacy of military responsibility for civilian relief in liberated areas was thereupon recognized by UNRRA in accepting the concept of what the military called a "military relief period." In definition, the Combined Chiefs of Staff of the Allied Powers had established that "(the military relief period) was to last 6 months during which the Director-General (of UNRRA) would be kept informed, within the limits of military security, regarding the military programs." They also stipulated that "the period could last less or more than 6 months but the determination would be a military one with UNRRA being given as much notice as practicable of when it could be expected to take over." [32] For all practical purposes such a policy put the situation completely in the hands of the military authorities.

The relation of UNRRA to the Army's civil affairs mission was particularly important in the displaced persons operation.

Here the military authorities decided to bring UNRRA into
the European Theater before the end of hostilities. A request
that UNRRA furnish 200 teams to staff centers in Germany
was followed up by an instruction from Supreme Headquarters
to all field commands that "UNRRA personnel should replace military personnel to the maximum extent and as soon
as possible in the handling of displaced persons and refugees
subject to the requirements of the military situation."
UNRRA personnel recruited in accordance with this request,
however, became subject to the command and control of the
appropriate military authorities in the area in which they were
posted.[33] Their status was accordingly established in the field
by the G-5 section of the 12th Army Group under the admonition that "UNRRA personnel will operate under military control and all reports by such personnel to UNRRA will be
submitted through military channels." [34] There could hardly
be a more complete parallel between this situation and the
UNKRA situation in 1951.

The position taken by the UN Command in 1951 was thus
based on historical experience. This is not surprising. From a
military perspective, experience is a surer guide than innovation. The insistence that UNKRA be given even limited independent status was an innovation that could only be supported
if the basis of proven historical experience could be challenged.
This was not easy to do even though, with the dismissal of General MacArthur, the United States now publicly limited its
military objective to pushing the aggressors back beyond the
38th parallel. The challenge, theoretically at any rate, lay in
the essential differences between a limited war of political objectives and a war in which the primary objective was the over-
riding military one of forcing the unconditional surrender of
the enemy. Practically speaking, however, a good deal depended on the conjuncture of events and personalities since the
complexities of limited war had not yet entered into the lexicon
of American planning.

Responding to Kingsley's position on their first proposals,
the State Department now pursued the argument, in negoti-

ations with the Pentagon, that authorities in the field had to
accommodate their civil affairs mission to the political consideration of keeping responsibility for Korean relief and reconstruction internationalized. The Army, in turn, counter-
attacked with almost absolute defense of a commander's need
to have complete operational authority within the limits of
broad policy guidance. General MacArthur's fall from glory
notwithstanding, the Army's position remained fixed despite
the insistence by the State Department that the undivided
authority of a theater commander had to be regarded not as
dogma but as policy which could be modified given particularly
important political considerations. To this, the Pentagon responded by suggesting, by inference, that if the UN Command
in Tokyo would take the initiative to agree to limited autonomy for UNKRA in the field, there would be less resistance
by the military authorities in Washington. This, in turn, was
made clear to the UNKRA Agent General. The problem
thus became one of having UNKRA make arrangements directly with the UN Command in Tokyo in order to provide a
situation in which the State and Defense Departments could
come to an agreement on the status of the agency in the field.
In mid-April, therefore, Kingsley sent his deputy, Sir Arthur
Rucker, to the Far East with instructions to negotiate a *modus
operandi* with the UN Command.

In Tokyo, Rucker encountered the beginnings of an expanding concept of the military mission of preventing "disease,
starvation, and unrest." As of April, 1951, the civil affairs
program of the UN Command technically operated under the
authority of two directives: first, the Security Council resolution of July 31, 1950, which requested the United States government, as the Unified Command, to take over the relief operation; and, second, the Presidential directive of September
29 of 1950 which had made the military responsible for whatever short-term rehabilitation could be undertaken. Despite
the provision in the Presidential directive that this was an interim arrangement pending the formation of a UN agency for

relief and reconstruction, no further instructions had been sent to the field when UNKRA was established. With the increasing inability of ECA to mobilize its efforts in the midst of active hostilities, the UN Command assumed, by fiat, the essential functions that had been the responsibility of ECA under the Presidential directive. This assumption of short-term economic responsibilities was, furthermore, covered under the umbrella of authority that the UN Command had for all activities in the theater of military operations. Referring specifically to the Security Council resolution of 31 July 1950, and the Presidential directive of September 29, the Command now began to draw up a program to provide not only supplies and equipment to prevent disease, starvation and unrest, but also equipment and raw materials for the initial rehabilitation of Korean agriculture and industry. At the same time, Colonel Hensey's Korea Aid Division drafted a comprehensive economic aid agreement for submission to the Republic of Korea, to replace the now lapsed accord under which ECA aid had been granted to the Republic of Korea prior to the outbreak of hostilities.[35]

Against the obstacle of an ever enlargening program being assumed by the military authorities, Sir Arthur Rucker enjoyed support from two quarters in his negotiations. The first, operating at the Washington level, was being watched carefully by the Agent General, engaged in private negotiations in conjunction with the talks in the Far East. During the budget review of the Department of Army estimates for appropriation for the fiscal year 1952, a number of questions were directed at the inclusion of an amount of $50,000,000 for raw materials and commodities under the military relief program in Korea. The questions seemed to have been provoked by the assumptions, first, that the Army had sufficient funds to meet its over-all obligations in Korea in its budget request without this particular $50,000,000, and, second, that this particular request, if granted, would have authorized the Army to move into an area of operations beyond the normal civil relief mission. The Army, indeed, interpreted the questions as being an attempt to restrict them to a relief operation that they claimed would not be adequate to maintain stability within the country "if conditions continue as they are now." [36]

Army representatives admitted that "it is felt that the military should be concerned only with the direct relief, immediate relief, which results from military operations." They nevertheless insisted that "it had earlier been determined that, upon [the] cessation [of ECA operations in Korea], the Department of Defense would assume responsibility for the supply of sustaining type of imports to augment Korean resources and productive capacity since it had been firmly established that such augmentation is far less expensive than the furnishing of only finished-type relief items." The almost over-logical observation was made that "to the extent that crops can be increased by fertilizer, raw materials processed into cloth, the fishing catch aided by rehabilitation of the fishing fleet, or industrial plants repaired, the requirements for finished consumer items . . . are reduced." [37] The Army's position seemed to make good sense. It was, however, an admission that port and handling facilities were now available for receiving rehabilitation equipment and materials even if it was argued that these facilities had to be controlled by the military authorities in the event there was need to convert quickly to meet the needs of a new flare-up in the fighting.

Rucker also found support in his negotiations with the UN Command from the American Embassy in Seoul. The Embassy staff looked upon the plans of the military authorities to support the South Korean economy as too closely resembling the military government methods of the period immediately following World War II. Having been accredited to the Republic of Korea at the time of its founding and recognition by the United States, Ambassador Muccio would have undoubtedly found it difficult to accept any plan which would impair the overt independence of the government the United States had been so expensively supporting since its inception.[38] The Embassy, also, must have been interested, in line with State Department policy, in maintaining a multilateral approach to the Korean conflict. It is to be remembered that UNCURK had expressed displeasure when Kingsley had agreed in February to subordinate his staff and program to the military command. The members of the Commission might have difficulty in communicating their views directly to the military authorities in Tokyo, but they could easily operate at the diplomatic level and make the American Embassy aware of their deep concern that a UN-originated and directed program be set in motion as soon as possible. Indeed, thoughts such as these were reinforced by Andrew Cordier, executive assistant to the UN Secretary-General, on a visit to the Far East at this very time. Cordier made it clear to General Ridgway and his Chief-of-Staff, General Hickey, that other UN members would not be willing to support the UNKRA program if it was subordinate to the United States military authorities.

During the latter part of April, Rucker, therefore, carried on negotiations with General Hickey in an attempt to work out a *modus operandi*. The General, whatever may have been his private reservations, was undoubtedly aware of the possible budget restrictions on the military relief program. Moreover, he was apparently by now convinced that it was the policy of his government to keep the Korean affair internationalized and that the price of keeping other UN members interested in the relief and reconstruction program was to provide limited autonomy for UNKRA for immediate activities in Korea. Also, there seems to have been no specific objection voiced by the Army in Washington to an independent UNKRA in Korea if the theater commander could accommodate his responsibilities to its presence. It was obvious, however, that the Army did not want to *order* the theater commander to accept UNKRA.

The results of the Rucker/Hickey discussions actually became the basis for the formal agreement which UNKRA signed with the Unified Command in Washington in July. It was not easy sailing. The military authorities made it clear that there were risks in permitting an independent civilian-directed

agency to become established in Korea. It not only weakened
military control in the Korean peninsula, but it also weakened
the position of the UN Commander in bringing the sometimes
difficult Korean allies into line. If General Hickey was prepared to come to some agreement with UNKRA, it was clear
that it was under the pressure of political considerations. Thus,
the UN Command was ready to accept an independent
UNKRA in Korea, provided that certain specific controls
were established. Primarily, the military insisted that while
UNKRA might conduct independent activities on an advisory or planning level, the agency should not be assigned
operational responsibilities which would require the establishment of separate supply channels. Any operational personnel which UNKRA had in Korea was to be integrated into
military units. They would later provide the continuity necessary when UNKRA assumed full control and authority
for the rehabilitation operation. Any specific operating projects which UNKRA might wish to implement would be considered supplemental to the military program and would require
specific agreement and authority by the military command.
Only in the case of technical advisers provided to the South
Korean government, would UNKRA staff report directly to
the Agent General. Even here, however, there was tacit agreement that the work of these experts would be coordinated with
military personnel functioning in the same field. The military
authorities in Tokyo were thus brought around to agreeing
that an independent UNKRA staff be established in Korea.
Their basic consternation nevertheless remained. It was re-
vealed when, on relaying the basis of their agreement back to
Washington, they emphasized that "CINCUNC regrets the
necessity for any division of any responsibility at this stage
but is prepared to accept the above solution provided safeguards are rigidly enforced." [39]

The Department of State immediately recommended that
the Unified Command approve the procedures for establishing an independent UNKRA staff in Korea that had been

worked out in Tokyo. The Department of the Army, however, was in no hurry to agree. The delay in the Army seems to have stemmed from concern that while the field command had agreed to permit independent UNKRA staff to function in Korea it had only done so with reluctance. Indeed, the Army in Washington might well have interpreted the reservations of the UN Command as an indirect rejection of UNKRA demands. Kingsley attempted to find out why the Unified Command delayed in formally agreeing to the procedures already worked out in Tokyo. The only explanation he received was that the Army was continuing to consider the safeguards, in terms of military responsibilities, which the UN Command considered must be tied to any concession toward an independent UNKRA. Delay in the Pentagon only tended to emphasize the split between the military and the State Department.

Late in May, the Agent General informed his Advisory Committee that discussions had taken place in Tokyo on how to set up an independent UNKRA staff in Korea for long-range planning and technical assistance without interfering with military operations. He told the Committee that procedures had been worked out and that it remained only for the Unified Command to confirm them if the agency was to operate in Korea at all. The Committee thereupon approved the broad principles behind these procedures by a unanimous vote, including that of the American delegate. The United States was, therefore, put in the ambivalent position of having approved an independent status for UNKRA in Korea as a member of the agency's Advisory Committee but not yet as the Unified Command. Armed with the approval of the Committee, Kingsley then informed the Secretary of State early in June that the delay in implementing the agreement which had been worked out in Tokyo almost five weeks earlier was creating an impossible situation for the UNKRA staff already receiving requests for assistance from the Republic of Korea. He therefore warned that unless there was immediate action taken to implement the agreement he would have to inform all governments that it had been impossible to attain the agreement of the Unified Command for a limited program for UNKRA at the present time.[40]

Agreement, however, was still over a month away. Considerable concern now seemed to have been exercised both at the policy level of the Joint Chiefs of Staff and the working levels of the Department of the Army about the problems involved, in principle and in operations, by a division of responsibility in a theater of military operations. Aware of these concerns, the Agent General instructed his Washington representative to assure the Unified Command that while it was necessary for UNKRA to have the maximum freedom possible in order to satisfy the demands of other UN member governments, he would pledge that all UNKRA activities would be reasonably coordinated with the military authorities in Korea. He made it clear, however, that whatever was set down in writing had to provide for complete autonomy for UNKRA in the limited areas of long-range planning and technical assistance. Anything less, he warned, would alienate the support of other UN members, particularly the British and Commonwealth governments.[41]

The procedures worked out in Tokyo had made it certain that UNKRA would not establish separate supply channels, but would only implement operational projects with the prior agreement of the UN Command. Any supplies which UNKRA was going to import into Korea would, therefore, be known to the Command long before their arrival and could be brought in under agreed shipping arrangements and at an agreed time so as not to interfere with military requirements. Here the Command retained full authority. The issue of divided responsibility, therefore, was, from an operational point of view, now related to the advisory functions which UNKRA would undertake under the proposed agreement. While prepared to allow UNKRA to place specialists with the government of the Republic of Korea, the military sought to restrict their activities to technical advice concerning the operations of the ministries. These experts would thus be prohibited from offering advice on policy which would affect the economic aid mission of the UN Command. In any cases where policy nevertheless seemed to be involved, the military wanted assurance that they would be advised beforehand, that no advice would be given which might lead to the Koreans' undertaking or requesting economic recovery projects not part of the military program, and that any projects which were implemented as a result of technical advice from UNKRA specialists would be undertaken under military aegis.

A strict interpretation of what the military authorities considered proper safeguards against the dangers of divided responsibility, thus would have restricted UNKRA, as an independent agency, to advising the South Korean government on the problems of bureaucratic management. In any other projects, the UNKRA specialists would, for all intents and purposes, be working under the military command. Such an arrangement would have frustrated the *paper* autonomy of UNKRA: first, because the South Korean government was not going to be content, at a time when their house was falling down under the stresses and strains of an all-out war effort, with advice on how to make their bureaucracy more efficient; and, second, because it was sure to be almost impossible to determine where *technical* advice ended and *policy* began. Thus only as broad an interpretation of what was policy as to frustrate all independent action by UNKRA, could possibly satisfy the military demand of undivided responsibility.

At the level of the Joint Chiefs of Staff, the concern over divided responsibility was undoubtedly more a matter of principle than of the details of who was going to be responsible for what in Korea. The geographical circumstances of the Republic of Korea—about the size of New Jersey and surrounded on three sides by water and on the other by an enemy force— made it necessary to consider the whole area the battleground.[42] To have granted UNKRA independent authority over any activities within this limited and potentially dangerous area might have been considered to have made a mockery, from the military point of view, of any attempt to keep the theater commander responsible for the maintenance of supplies to his troops and readiness to repel any new attack from the north.

The position of the Joint Chiefs was, however, based on military considerations and, under General Bradley's formula, "given with a full realization that considerations other than military may be overriding in making the final decision." [43] This meant that if the State Department insisted that there were "over-riding considerations," it had to assume responsibility should the divided authority for economic assistance result in instability in the rear echelons. The State Department was, however, forced to support autonomy for UNKRA in Korea in order to keep other governments involved and interested in the reconstruction program and to follow up its own action in approving the Toyko-discussed proposals as a member of the UNKRA Advisory Committee. But beyond these points, the Department also seems to have been motivated by considerable anxiety lest complete capitulation to military demands be interpreted as a precedent for the military authorities to assume control of economic aid programs in all areas where the military assumed operational responsibility. [44] With these alternatives, the Department chose to accept responsibility for supporting UNKRA, but simultaneously chose to minimize the risks that might be involved.

The last weeks of June and first week of July saw a flurry of drafting and redrafting to try to reconcile the various interests involved. Essentially, the problem was how to get UNKRA into the economic aid picture in Korea as an independent agency without jeopardizing the ultimate authority of the UN Commander for *military* operations. By July 11, sufficient agreement had been worked out at sufficiently high levels in the Departments of State and Defense for specific proposals to be submitted to Kingsley on behalf of the Unified Command. [45] The proposals were essentially based on the procedures agreed by Sir Arthur Rucker and General Hickey in Tokyo about two months earlier. It was, first of all, clearly stated that "the responsibility of the United Nations Command for the operation of the United Nations Command programs of relief and short-term economic aid will continue until such time as the military operations will permit the transfer of this responsibility to UNKRA." Nevertheless, "with a view to making the transfer as smooth as possible, it is desired to introduce UNKRA into the entire operation as it progresses." Here military responsibility for economic aid beyond the normal relief mission was recognized and acknowledged, as was the political necessity to get UNKRA established in the field immediately despite the continuing hostilities.

The period of military responsibility for relief and short-term economic aid was conveniently called "phase (1)" and the period after transfer of responsibility to UNKRA "phase (2)." During "phase (1)" it was suggested that "UNKRA will have responsibility for long-range planning and high level technical assistance to the Korean Government and for any program of economic aid additional to the United Nations Command program which the military situation may permit UNKRA to implement." In order to undertake its responsibilities, "UNKRA personnel operating in Korea would consist of two groups": first, a group of technical advisers and program experts "who will operate as a group under the direction of the Agent-General and be responsible to him"; and, second, personnel engaged in "relief and short-range rehabilitation and reconstruction" who "may be integrated in staffs or units of the United Nations Command" and whose duties "will be as prescribed by the United Nations Command."

The first group of experts offered UNKRA an independent toehold in the economic aid picture in Korea and thus sought to satisfy the political considerations of the State Department. The argument of the Department of the Army and the Joint Chiefs of Staff that divided authority in a war theater was a danger to military operations was, however, satisfied by the further stipulation that "such plans or recommendations as may be made [by UNKRA experts] will be coordinated with the United Nations Command for determination as to whether or not they affect the mission of the United Nations Command"

and those "plans or recommendations which affect its mission will be implemented only with the concurrence of the United Nations Command." In addition, the proposals wound up with a final admonition that "These arrangements are considered workable only if the procedures . . . for ensuring close coordination and avoiding any action by UNKRA which would conflict with the military necessities are carefully observed." To emphasize this point, "the final authority and control of the Commander-in-Chief, United Nations Command, on the ground during hostilities are not intended to be affected by these arrangements."

Whatever recognition the proposals offered to the political considerations favoring autonomy for UNKRA in Korea, there was no doubt that, in the final analysis, the United Nations Command retained complete control. The one free element was the group of technical and program experts who, before they came to a point of making "plans or recommendations" that might "affect the mission of the United Nations Command," were in no way responsible to the United Nations Commander. This was some concession, though modest. Those in the State Department who had fought for this recognition, slight though it may have been, nevertheless, considered that it was a considerable victory for their position. Moreover, in accepting the proposals several days later, Kingsley announced that they comprised "a significant new stage in the development of United Nations action in Korea" and that "[the] adoption of the two-phase approach to rehabilitation is the solution to the problem that has plagued every civilian agency trying to work in the area of military operations in recent years—namely, how to handle the transition from military to civilian control of supply operations." [46]

Almost simultaneously, truce negotiations were opened at Kaesong on July 10, 1951. These followed Jacob Malik's suggestion that, as a first step toward a settlement of the armed conflict in Korea, discussions should be started between the belligerents for a cease-fire and an armistice providing for a mutual withdrawal of forces from the 38th parallel. More than on the limited freedom of its technical experts, the future of UNKRA depended on the prospects of peace in the Korean peninsula. There must have been some encouragement in the coincidence of the achievement of limited autonomy and the Malik proposals.

1. *A Preliminary Report on the Economic Reconstruction of Korea,* a report prepared by Robert R. Nathan Associates for the United Nations Korean Reconstruction Agency, 1953, pp. 1–6, I–9 (Mimeographed). (Hereinafter referred to as *Preliminary Nathan Report.*)

2. *Ibid.,* p. I–8.

3. General Bradley's testimony, *Military Situation in the Far East,* Part II, pp. 920–22.

4. Edgar Kennedy, *Mission to Korea* (London: Verschoyle, 1952), p. 108. See also pp. 115–19.

5. An incomplete version of this incident is found in Kennedy, *op. cit.,* p. 57.

6. *New York Times,* February 17, 1951, p. 3.

7. *Ibid,* February 18, 1951, p. 3.

8. *London Times,* February 27, 1951, p. 7; also *London Times,* March 1, 1951, p. 5. See also *New York Times,* February 28, 1951, p. 3.

9. *New York Times,* October 16, 1950, p. 3.

10. Testimony of General Reeder, Deputy Assistant Chief of Staff, G–4. Hearings before a Subcommittee of the Committee on Appropriations, House of Representatives, 82nd Congress, 1st Session, *Department of Defense Appropriations for 1952* (Washington: Government Printing Office, 1951), p. 1056.

11. Testimony of General Reeder, Hearings before a Subcommittee of the Committee on Appropriations, House of Representatives, 82nd Congress, 2nd Session, *Urgent Deficiency Appropriations for 1952* (Washington: Government Printing Office, 1952), p. 100.

12. Bradley, *op. cit.,* Part III, p. 1735.

13. See above, pp. 26–27.

14. UN General Assembly, Sixth Session, *Official Records,* Supplement 12 (A/1881), *Report of the United Nations Commission for the Unification and Rehabilitation of Korea,* pp. 4–5. (Hereinafter referred to as *UNCURK Report to the 6th Session.*)

15. *Ibid.,* pp. 37–38.

16. While in Korea, Kingsley and his party had seen President Syngman Rhee who had shown them plans he already had for the rebuilding of Seoul. Rhee had also indicated some disappointment when Kingsley told him that little money had as yet been collected and that, once collected, funds would be expended by the Agency and not by the Republic of Korea.

17. Bradley, *op. cit.,* General MacArthur's version, Part I, pp. 17–19; General Bradley's version, Part II, pp. 750 and 1063–64.

18. *Ibid.,* Part II, p. 729.

19. *Ibid.,* Part II, p. 899.

20. *New York Times,* March 11, 1951, p. 5.

21. Cable from Secretary-General Lie to Agent General Kingsley dated

March 12, 1951 (Kingsley papers). Almost two weeks later, UNCURK raised the same question when the *New York Times,* March 11 edition, finally reached Korea.

22. Cable from Secretary-General Lie to Agent General Kingsley dated March 13, 1951 (Kingsley papers).

23. Cable from Agent General Kingsley to Secretary-General Lie dated March 14, 1951 (Kingsley papers).

24. Leland Goodrich, *Korea,* p. 119.

25. Testimony of Secretary Acheson, *Military Situation in the Far East,* Part III, pp. 1879–80.

26. Cable from Agent General Kingsley to the Department of State dated March 27, 1951 (Kingsley papers).

27. These proposals were contained in a letter from Assistant Secretary of State Hickerson to Agent General Kingsley dated March 29, 1951 (Kingsley papers).

28. Letter from Agent General Kingsley to Assistant Secretary of State John D. Hickerson dated April 16, 1951 (Kingsley papers).

29. Henry L. Stimson and McGeorge Bundy, *On Active Service in Peace and War* (New York: Harper & Bros., 1947), pp. 553–54.

30. Forrest C. Pogue, *The United States Army in World War II: The European Theater of Operations; the Supreme Command* (Washington: Office of the Chief of Military History, Department of the Army, 1954), pp. 76–84.

31. *Report of Operations (Final After Action Report),* 12th Army Group, Vol. VII, G-5 Section (Germany: 1945), pp. 6–9.

32. United Nations Relief and Rehabilitation Administration, *Report of the Director General to the Second Session of the Council,* Council II, Document I (Washington: 1944), pp. 10–11, 18.

33. United Nations Relief and Rehabilitation Administration, *Report of the Director General to the Council for the Period 1 January 1945 to 31 March 1945* (Washington: 1945), pp. 19–20.

34. G-5 Operational Instruction No. 13, *Control and Care of Displaced Persons and Refugees in Germany,* dated 17 April 1945, reprinted in *Report of Operations (Final After Action Report),* 12th Army Group, Vol. VII, G-5 Section (Germany: 1945), see appendixes.

35. See Footnotes 10 and 11. The Second Report of the Command on Civil Assistance and Economic Aid in Korea (for the period 1 Oct. 1951–30 June 1952—Headquarters, United Nations Command, Tokyo, 1952) clearly showed this expanding mood in stating "When the previous report [for the period 7 July 1950–30 Sept. 1951] was prepared, the emphasis was primarily on emergency civilian relief and direct military necessities. Improvement in the world-wide political situation in the past year has permitted changes in the approach to the relief and economic aid program. The establishment of relative stability and the restoration of order among the population resulted in a change from the emergency provision of subsistence, clothing, shelter, and medical supplies to a well-organized and smoothly operating program. *Meanwhile, the prevention of unrest took on new aspects having connotations of long-range planning for the stabilization of finances, the development of a self-sustaining economy, and the improvement of social services essential to the future welfare of Korea"* (italics added), p. iv. See also p. 28.

36. Testimony of Colonel Louis Gosorn, Chief, International Branch, G-4, Department of the Army. Hearings before a subcommittee of the Committee

on Appropriations, House of Representatives, 82nd Congress, 1st Session, *Department of Defense Appropriations for 1952* (Washington: Government Printing Office, 1951), p. 1054.

37. Testimony of General Reeder, Committee on Appropriations, U.S. Senate, 82nd Congress, 1st Session, *Department of Defense Appropriations for 1952* (Washington: Government Printing Office, 1951), p. 1220. See also Colonel Louis Gosorn, "The Army and Foreign Civilian Supply," *Military Review,* XXXII, No. 2 (May, 1952), 27–42. As Chief of the International Branch, G-4, Colonel Gosorn's views undoubtedly influenced the Army's program.

38. The prime objection of the government of the Republic of Korea to the military-drafted aid agreement was that certain of the provisions impaired the sovereignty of the Republic of Korea.

39. Paraphrase of message of May 4, 1951, from CINCUNC, Tokyo to Department of the Army, Washington (Kingsley papers).

40. Cable from Agent General Kingsley to Secretary of State dated June 6, 1951 (Kingsley papers).

41. Record of telephone conversation, Agent General Kingsley and Acting Chief, UNKRA Washington Office, on June 9, 1951 (Kingsley papers).

42. All of South Korea, including the Civil Assistance Command, was still under the command of the Eighth Army. Not until the summer of 1952, over a year later, did the Army consider the situation sufficiently stable to create a Communications Zone and confine the area of responsibility of the Eighth Army to the northern sectors close to the battle lines, at the same time transferring direct supervision over civil affairs and economic aid from Eighth Army to UN Command Headquarters, Tokyo.

43. See above, p. 52.

44. The situation in Washington was known to the Agent General through reports from the UNKRA office there. The above is based on Personal Report No. 3, dated June 17, 1951, as well as on interviews. (These reports are in the Kingsley papers.)

45. Letter from John D. Hickerson, Assistant Secretary of State to Agent General of UNKRA, dated July 11, 1951.

46. *New York Times,* July 19, 1951, p. 3.

CHAPTER IV

# A MARRIAGE OF CONVENIENCE

*Implementation of the July Agreement*
*Inflation in South Korea*
*The Memorandum of Understanding*
*The End of the First Year*

# A MARRIAGE OF CONVENIENCE

## Implementation of the July Agreement

The early weeks of discussions on a cease-fire were not particularly heartening. Disagreement quickly arose over whether the 38th parallel or the actual line of battle, extending in several places across the parallel where the UN forces had advanced in order to consolidate and strengthen their positions, should be accepted as the truce line. While this argument remained unsettled, the negotiations were suspended from August 5 to 10 and from August 23 to October 25 because of alleged violations of the neutral area in which the talks were being conducted. From the very beginning, the United States made it quite clear that while it had definitely rejected the policy of unifying the peninsula by force, it was equally determined to maintain a position of strength in Korea. Thus, when the communist side suggested that all foreign troops withdraw immediately, Secretary of State Acheson issued a statement that said: ". . . The United Nations forces are in Korea . . . to repel aggression and to restore international peace and security in the area." It went on to emphasize that "if there is an effective armistice, a United Nations force must remain in Korea until a genuine peace has been firmly established and the Korean people have assurances that they can work out their future free from fear of aggression." [1]

There are several explanations of what was behind the Malik proposals for cease-fire negotiations in the first place. At the very minimum it seems clear that the Soviet Union, no less than the United States, had decided that it was not going to risk opening up the big war over the Korean issue. Nevertheless, there was not sufficient evidence that the Soviet Union had either given up its design to unite the peninsula under a communist regime or was prepared to let the northern sector be absorbed in a non-communist union of all of Korea. The most that could

79

be safely assumed was that the Soviet Union was prepared to accept a divided Korea. This did not exclude exerting pressure over a long period of time to a point where the United States might break down and provide an opportunity for North Korean and Chinese Communist armies to conquer the southern provinces, preferably without involving foreign troops. A more optimistic view, of course, would be that the Soviet Union was prepared to accept a peaceful settlement of the Korean question provided that its interests, short of a communist government for a united peninsula, could be protected. This, however, assumed that the interests of the Soviet Union could be guaranteed, from the viewpoint of the Soviets, without a communist government in Korea.

At any rate, American policy seems clear. The United States agreed to negotiate a cease-fire arrangement, but rejected the proposal for the withdrawal of foreign troops and determined that U.S. troops would remain in Korea until a genuine peace was achieved. In point of fact, the United States thus accepted the existence of a divided Korea until such time as it was certain that a peaceful unification of the peninsula could be gained. This certainty depended on the proven good will not only of the Soviet Union but of Communist China as well. Since the United States could not be optimistic about the intentions of either, it seems reasonable to conclude that American policy now assumed the condition of a divided Korea for some time to come, at least until there was a sharp change for the better in the course of the cold war. If it can also be assumed that, after consolidating their positions to the maximum, the UN forces could contain North Korean and Chinese forces behind the present battle line, then it is equally reasonable to conclude that, from the point of view of military security, it may have been feasible to start on the beginning of a program of reconstruction.

It was within this context and the general calm that set over the battleground from the time negotiations started, that the establishment of UNKRA in Korea as a semi-autonomous agency under the terms of the July agreement, occurred at an

opportune moment. The agreement itself, however, was no assurance that the agency would be able to function successfully.
Ultimate authority continued to rest with the United Nations
Commander and to a large extent the success of the agreement
depended on what instructions were sent to him from Washington with regard to the implementation of its provisions. Unfortunately, no specific instructions seem to have been sent until
late in September, although the final paragraph of the Unified
Command proposals asked the Agent General to advise the
Command "as soon as possible [if these proposals are accepta-
ble] so that the understanding may be officially communicated
to the Commander-in-Chief of the United Nations Command
and put into operation promptly." Primarily, delay seems to
have been caused by the difficulty in getting all departments to
agree on an over-all directive on Korean relief and reconstruction to replace the Presidential directive of September 29,
1950. The latter remained the latest word despite the withdrawal of ECA from Korea and the acknowledgment in the
July agreement with UNKRA that the military authorities
now held responsibility for short-range economic aid, as well
as for emergency relief. Among the questions which the Army
considered still unresolved was how economic assistance to
Korea was to be financed, although this may only have been
a practical consequence of the controversy over how far the
military commanders should have authority over economic affairs in areas of military concern.[2]

The Army's request for funds for its relief program was, as
noted earlier, restricted to $50 million for consumer supplies.
At the same time, the Department of State was asking Congress
to authorize $112.5 million in new appropriations for UNKRA
and the transfer of $50 million of unexpended balances from the
old ECA program for Korea. These two amounts made up the
total U.S. pledge of $162.5 millions against the projected pro-
gram of $250 million. The inclusion of these requests in the
authorization bill had been one reason why the Army's request
for an additional $50 million for ECA-type supplies had been
questioned during the budget review of estimates.[3] Although

the July agreement had acknowledged that the military mission now extended to short-term economic aid and that UNKRA operations would only be supplemental to the UN Command program until hostilities ceased, the budget process had undoubtedly gone too far for the bills to be changed and the basic Army bill still included only $50 million for emergency relief. Under the emergency of military operations, the Army, however, had the advantage of being able to transfer funds from other categories to meet its rehabilitation program and account for the total expended at a later date.[4] The military were, therefore, in a position to carry out an expanded program despite budget restrictions.

In requesting that the full amount of the United States pledge to UNKRA be authorized at this early stage, the State Department sought to achieve something of the same financial flexibility that the Army enjoyed, in order to be in a position to act quickly should an opportunity arise. When Congress showed concern that the request for the full United States contribution was premature, Assistant Secretary of State (for Far Eastern Affairs) Dean Rusk explained to the Senate Committee on Foreign Relations that "the continuation of military operations would leave the primary responsibility [for Korean relief and rehabilitation] in the hands of our military forces." He nevertheless emphasized that it was important "to clear the way for a broad, United Nations program of rehabilitation in order that the necessary machinery can be put in readiness to step in quickly at the time that the military operations themselves actually stop." [5] Beyond this practical aspect Rusk told the committee that if the Koreans "do not see forthcoming preparations for a substantial and effective reconstruction program, they cannot help but be greatly discouraged as they face these very difficult days that are ahead in any event." At the same time, "It would be of great benefit to us in seeking contributions from other members of the United Nations if we would be certain about the scale of contributions which we would be in a position to make." [6]

Rusk was supported by the Assistant Secretary of State for

UN Affairs, John Hickerson, who went so far as to tell the Committee that "this legislation is requested on the assumption that the situation in Korea is going to be stabilized within this fiscal year sufficiently for the rehabilitation task to be undertaken." Lest he be caught too far out on a limb, however, he added that, "if that expectation does not come true, funds will not be turned over to the UNKRA in any major amount and will not be spent." In response to questioning, Mr. Hickerson went even farther in assuring the Committee that due caution would be taken. He emphasized that "the money [for UNKRA] will not be spent unless and until the United Nations Command, that is General Ridgway, as authorized by the Joint Chiefs of Staff, says that the time has come when the United Nations Rehabilitation Agency can take over this task." [7] Indeed caution had, in many ways, been the order of the day when the same bill had been considered by the House Committee on Foreign Affairs several days earlier. Congressman Vorys had particularly indicated anxiety, undoubtedly shared by many of his colleagues, that what constituted a cessation of hostilities could not be decided by the UN. He emphasized the need for "guarantees that hostilities are not going to start again." The State Department spokesman for the bill quickly agreed that "we would have to have some sort of guaranty, or at least a good chance that hostilities would not start again," or "there would be no point in taking in supplies just to have them endangered again by the enemy." [8]

The State Department did not get the financial flexibility it requested, but neglected to defend. The House Committee cut the request for new funds down to 10 per cent ($11,250,000) and the Senate Committee by almost one-half.[9] Later, in October, a joint conference set the authorization at $45 million in new funds and $50 million of unexpended ECA funds, but the new funds were never appropriated.[10] Congressional skepticism on whether UNKRA could become sufficiently operative until peace was assured, augured ill for anything less than a strictly military decision on when this might be. In response, the State Department offered no alternative. Indeed, departmental spokesmen agreed that the military had to say when UNKRA could engage even in a limited operation and that until that time, American-contributed funds would be used sparingly so as not to be dissipated for projects which might be destroyed with a new outbreak of fighting.

The State Department does not seem to have related the reconstruction program to the circumstances of a limited war that was developing into a long drawn-out stalemate. Nor did the Department do very much to convince Congress, so soon after the trying sessions on the MacArthur dismissal, that there were strong political considerations for initiating major UNKRA projects immediately even over military protests. Indeed, by the end of August, the State Department seems to have been sufficiently set back by its experience with Congress to consider seriously asking that even less than the authorized amount be appropriated. These tactics seem to have been rationalized on the theory that Congress would appreciate a realistic approach to the problem. It might consequently act quickly and positively in cooperation with the Department should a sudden turn in the truce negotiations offer a sufficiently bright prospect for peace that UNKRA operations could expand.[11] The consequence of such tactics, however politically realistic, nevertheless fall at the other end of the bureaucratic spectrum from financial flexibility.

This cautious approach, as events were to show, left UNKRA somewhat isolated. The agency's staff had already started to draw up a number of specific projects that would require a broad interpretation of the July agreement in order that they be implemented. It was clear that the only way to gain the confidence and support of the Koreans, so necessary to the operation of the full program after a truce, was to begin to put a number of concrete projects into operation immediately. The Koreans were skeptical of planners and long-range programs and quick to lose respect for foreigners who produced no results.[12] Any substantial project, however, required the importation of supplies and equipment which, in turn, required that the military authorities grant permission for UNKRA to utilize the limited supply channels into Korea. To meet both sets of issues meant developing a program that did not over-burden supply facilities or, through the expenditures of local currency, add appreciably to the ever-rising inflationary pressures. UNKRA thus began to develop individual projects which, while directed toward a particularly acute economic need, would require only the minimum use of military supply channels and the minimum expenditure of local currency. Among these were the importation of draught animals, the development of breeding and agricultural experiment stations, the establishment of vocational training and medical rehabilitation centers and the improvement of education facilities. Included also were plans for dredging the harbor of Kunsan on the west coast in order to provide eventually separate port facilities for civilian relief and rehabilitation supplies.[13] These projects were conceived of as examples only, as promises of what UNKRA could do. At the same time, plans were also made to initiate preliminary projects of more comprehensive long-range programs in the fields of housing, public health, industrial rehabilitation and education. These would be continuing efforts to be more fully and actively implemented when UNKRA took over complete responsibility for the rehabilitation program.

The July agreement had not spelled out definite channels for clearing UNKRA projects under the provision that "UNKRA will have responsibility . . . for any program of economic aid additional to the United Nations Command program which the military situation may permit UNKRA to implement." The military authorities may never have seriously expected that this particular provision would be implemented. In the final analysis their control of the available ports and transportation provided a check that no project was undertaken without their approval. Sir Arthur Rucker, working on the actual development of the projects, sought to rely on rather informal meetings with the commanding general of the UN Civil Assistance Command in Korea (UNCACK) to meet the provisions of the agreement referring to the coordination of operational activities.

Ultimately, what UNKRA hoped to achieve was agreement for the agency to undertake rehabilitation work in specific areas of the economy without having to request the approval of the military for each individual project. In the meanwhile, they sought to put a few tangible signs of their efforts in the field to justify their presence in Korea to the Koreans.

The activities of the UNKRA staff in Korea could not very well be kept secret from the military authorities. UNKRA experts working on plans for the projects had to contact either their counterparts in UNCACK or the Korean ministry concerned to get new data or check on their facts. When they wanted to travel outside Pusan, where they were billeted, they had to request military travel orders and indicate the purpose of the trip. The increasing UNKRA activity, moreover, was running up against increasing activity by the military themselves. They were then busily drawing up a new table of organization for the Civil Assistance Command to staff it to assume its new responsibilities in the field of short-range economic aid.[14] This simultaneous organizational expansion, the details of each largely unknown to the other, but each smacking of competitive "empire-building" to the other, inevitably wove a net of mutual suspicions in the field.

In Washington, the Army seemed to be taking an attitude toward UNKRA that was as unenthusiastic as that of the field command was suspicious. The announcement that UNKRA was planning to import draught cattle into Korea caused the G-4 staff to ask how UNKRA ever thought it was going to bring the cattle into the country. Having been forced to accept an independent UNKRA in Korea for "political reasons," the Army was undoubtedly unprepared to allow any impairment of the safeguard it had insisted upon in agreeing to the July proposals: recognition by all parties concerned of the necessity for "avoiding any action by UNKRA which would conflict with the military necessities." When, therefore, instructions were finally sent from Washington to Tokyo in September, 1951, over three months after the July agreement had been signed, they not only de-emphasized the independent status of

UNKRA but gave the theater commander almost complete discretion over the conditions under which UNKRA could be introduced into the Korean economic assistance program.[15]

In what was essentially a unilateral interpretation of what constituted "the military necessities," the Army, in effect, preserved the indivisibility of a theater commander's armor of authority that some members of the State Department thought they had pierced. The instructions to the UN Command acknowledged that under the July Agreement UNKRA possessed "limited non-operational responsibilities" to furnish technical advisers to the South Korean government. It was nonetheless stipulated that these responsibilities would be assumed only "in coordination with" the theater commander who continued "to exercise the broad responsibilities of the Unified Command for relief and support of the civilian population of Korea" under the "31 July 1950 resolution of UN Security Council." With regard to allowing UNKRA to implement "any program of economic aid additional to the United Nations Command program," the instructions authorized the theater commander "to the extent you deem appropriate . . . [to] seek the active cooperation and assistance of UNKRA in carrying out [relief and economic aid] activities."

This rigid and narrow interpretation of the July Agreement left little hope for the freedom of action the Agent General and his Deputy hoped to cultivate. It offered less hope that UNKRA would be given wide areas of responsibility in which the agency could begin to operate long-range programs without having to clear individual projects with the military authorities. For under this interpretation, UNKRA technical experts would, in the name of coordination, be under the virtual supervision of the military authorities. At the same time the agency would presumably have to wait to be asked to assist the military authorities in operating their own programs, thus, in this area as well, subordinating UNKRA to direct military supervision. The logic of the military's position was undoubtedly founded on the same factors that had made them resist an independent UNKRA for Korea in the first place: the question of principle involved in sole responsibility of a theater commander for all operations; the realities of the limited supply channels; the precarious security problem where bands of Communist guerrillas were operating in South Korea and creating grave risks for non-Korean civilians stationed in isolated villages without adequate means of protection; and the common jealousies of competing organizations. Nevertheless, the success with which the military were able to apply the logic of their position rested in no small measure on the weakness with which the State Department defended its interests.

## Inflation in South Korea

As the truce talks continued and a stalemate in military operations developed to make an economic aid program more feasible in South Korea, the economic condition of the country began to have as great an influence on responsibility for the program as the war itself. By the fall of 1951, Korea was moving toward a state of such high inflation that the Republic was in danger of complete collapse and any reconstruction program, the Army's or UNKRA's, was in danger of failure before it even started.[16]

Early in 1951, the UN Command had revived the Korean-American Joint Economic Stabilization Committee. This had been set up at the suggestion of the Economic Cooperation Administration before the war as a watchdog committee to make recommendations on halting inflation and stabilizing the economy. Under the stress of heavy fighting during the first six months of 1951, the Committee was hardly effective as a counter-inflationary force. The retail price index for commodities (1947 at 100) which had risen from 257.2 in December, 1949, to 825.5 in December, 1950, now soared to 2,889 by August, 1951.[17] The Committee became, instead, a forum where charges could be directed against the military representatives by the government of Syngman Rhee. Rhee's main stand was that the inflation could be directly attributed to the advances of local currency (won) his government had been making to the UN Forces to meet their maintenance costs in Korea.

He broadly argued for two essential steps before his government could take effective stabilization measures: the repayment in dollars for the local currency advances at the rate of exchange fixed by his government; and the importation of aid goods by the United Nations to drain off excess currency already on the market.

Even though there was considerable justice in Rhee's position, the military authorities refused to acknowledge that the won advances to the UN forces were the sole, or even the most important, cause for the hyper-inflation. They also rejected the basis on which the Rhee government claimed repayment and insisted that counter-inflationary measures to restrict credit and non-essential government spending could and should be taken by the government immediately without waiting for settlement of the advances. What was behind the military stand was a refusal to see several tens of millions of dollars put into the hands of the South Korean government without prior agreement on how the government was to spend its foreign currency or how the rate of exchange was to be calculated. Suspicion of the Rhee government was undoubtedly justified. It was not, however, reason for failure to acknowledge the facts: that the local currency advances were a major inflationary factor and that the Koreans had already made considerable efforts since March to restrict non-military spending. Indeed, the Koreans were very conscious of their own efforts and were surely disturbed that these were not recognized. Finance Minister Paik Too Chin later told a reporter: "You thought back there last March [1951] I couldn't do it, didn't you? Well, we have! And with enough left over after the first six months of curtailed costs to total about 28,000,000,000 won cash surplus. We've strictly followed one rule—spend out of revenue; and if no revenue, then don't spend." [18]

The full effect of the local advances to the UN forces comes through statistically. By the end of June, 1951, the amount of currency in circulation had increased since June, 1950, by 397.8 billion won, of which 198.2 billion won represented advances to the UN forces.[19] These advances had been made under an agreement signed with the Republic of Korea by the American Ambassador shortly after hostilities commenced. On the one hand, the Korean government had agreed to furnish the Commander-in-Chief of the UN Command with local currency and credits "in such amounts, of such types and at such times and places as he may request, for expenditures arising out of operations and activities in Korea." On the other, it was agreed that "settlement of any claims arising from the provision and use of currency and credits under the Agreement . . . shall take place directly between the Government of the Forces concerned and the Government of the Republic of Korea." It was, however, stipulated that "such negotiations shall be deferred to a time or times mutually satisfactory to the respective governments and the Government of the Republic of Korea." [20]

Under the terms of the Agreement, it was perfectly possible for the military authorities to claim that there was no legal obligation that required payment to the Korean government for the won advanced to the UN forces. Taken against the tremendous amounts being spent by the United States, particularly, in coming to the defense of South Korea, the won advances could (somewhat unrealistically) be considered part of the contribution of the Koreans themselves toward the war effort. There was, however, little illusion that the Republic of Korea, even at best, could finance the local maintenance of a large modern mechanized army. The real purpose of the military was to whittle the claim down to reasonable costs that the United States was willing to pay. This meant deducting from the Korean claim the costs of services which the United States Army supplied to the South Korean forces and calculating the resulting obligation at the free market rate of 6,000 won to the dollar rather than the government-pegged rate of 1,800 won to the dollar. It also meant gaining some assurance that the dollars paid over to the Republic of Korea would be used wisely and efficiently in counterattacking the inflationary pressures.

The South Korean government, however, rejected both the attempt to decrease its total claim and the demand to control its foreign exchange. It met the attempt to decrease the claim by arguing that the UN Command had the duty and obligation of seeing that these forces under its control, Korean or others, had the equipment and services they needed to engage in combat. The controversy over the rate of exchange was spiced by Syngman Rhee's simple but uncanny logic that if you wanted a low rate of exchange, you arbitrarily set it low and then brought in sufficient goods and foreign exchange to support it.[21] There were, however, other and more fundamental reasons why he rejected the free market rate for dollars. For one thing, a low exchange rate meant more dollars for the won advanced to the UN forces; for another, when applied to the transfer of won to a counterpart fund in payment for imported aid goods, it meant paying less than the value on the open market for the supplies than if a higher rate were applied. To have accepted the high rate of 6,000 won to the dollar, also, would have admitted culpability on the part of his government for bringing on economic instability. This, in turn, would have weakened the argument that the advances to the UN forces were behind the financial precariousness of the country.

Beyond his relations with the American military, Rhee was also aware of the repercussions of the problem on internal Korean politics. First, the possession of foreign exchange and aid goods at considerably less than their marketable value left a wide margin of profit, which could be passed on to favored private traders who might otherwise be tempted to form a nucleus of middle class opposition to the Rhee regime. And second, the increased dollars which a low exchange rate would have handed over to the Rhee government on any settlement on won advances to the UN forces, represented an indirect form of economic aid over which Rhee would have sole control. This foreign exchange could have then been used by the South Korean government to pursue its practice of importing grains and other goods for distribution to government employees and other favored groups, thus artificially protecting them from the worst effects of the inflation and preserving another powerful segment of political support.[22]

In refusing to meet the full Korean claim for repayment of

the won at the Rhee rate of exchange, the military authorities thus fell into the complex web of South Korean politics. Moreover, in insisting that repayment had to wait
upon an economic aid agreement that provided for military
control over the utilization of foreign exchange, they gave
Rhee a weapon of considerable political power, defense of Korea's sovereign rights. The repeated dedication of Rhee to the
political unity and independence of Korea stimulated his resistance to outside control over the limited means he had to
trade in world markets. While the UN Command approached
the problem with the logic of reasonableness and cost accounting, he was happily placed in the position of seeking to meet
the vital needs of his country and the essential protection of its
national sovereignty. There was bound to be conflict. The trag-
edy of the conflict was that it meant a delay of over a year before any substantial aid program could be undertaken, either
by the UN Command or by UNKRA.

In such a situation, UNKRA became little more than a complicating factor as far as the military authorities were concerned. UNKRA had local currency expenses which had to be
financed by loans from the Bank of Korea since the agency was,
as yet, in no position to import commodities for sale in order
to cover administrative and maintenance costs. More seriously,
however, was the complication that arose when, under the terms
of the July Agreement, UNKRA supplied economic advisers
to the South Korean government. Any serious economic advice
for recovery had to emphasize the need to repay the won advances and import aid goods without delay whatever the equi-
ties of the position taken by the military negotiators. Not that
UNKRA was alone, for it seems certain that the U.S. Embassy
had also been urging a more lenient attitude on the part of the
military authorities to avoid a major collapse of the government in power during the precarious months of war. This seems
evident from events that occurred in Washington late in the
summer of 1951. In August, the South Korean Ambassador
boldly presented the State Department with a bill for $100,-
000,000, and made a point of publicly announcing that "John

Muccio, United States Ambassador in Korea, recommended the payment be made and that the State Department also favored it." [23] Noticeably, he said nothing about the United Nations Command.

Despite the efforts of the State Department to keep the negotiations quiet, the Ambassador's announcement brought a flood of congressional and public inquiries, most of which asked how the United States could possibly be in debt to a country to which it was contributing millions of dollars in military and relief supplies, let alone the best part of its fighting force. From the point of view of domestic politics, the task of the State Department in encouraging payment was clearly an unpopular assignment. Something of the dichotomy in United States policy was evident in the information the Department was forced to give reporters once the Korean claim was known. It was stated that "[without accepting] the $100,000,000 figure nor the Korean claim that [the United States] had an obligation to make payment, . . . serious consideration is being given to the fact that South Korea's economy has been unbalanced by the war. The basis for present studies is a belief that it probably would be well to make some payment to South Korea in view of this country's over-all interest there." Almost anticipating a possible charge of financial irresponsibility the Department made sure to point out that "if it should come down to a matter of presenting bills, the United States bill for equipment and services would more than offset any claim the Koreans properly could make. However, authorities said they thought the problem should be approached on both sides on the basis of the real interests of the two countries and not as a financial transaction." [24]

The State Department failed to get the military, let alone the Koreans, to agree to a basis for the settlement of the full account. The best that could be achieved was agreement that an interim payment of slightly more than $12,000,000 be made immediately and that the settlement of other Korean claims and such questions as the rate of exchange and control of foreign exchange be left to future negotiations in the field.[25] While clearly nothing more than a stop-gap move, this partial settlement had the advantage of propping up the South Korean economy without either the Koreans or the military losing face. The Korean Ambassador, on the one hand, could report that he had received $12,000,000 without conceding his government's right to set a low rate of exchange or to reject outside control over foreign resources. The Department of the Army, on the other, could inform the field command that they could proceed with the negotiation of an economic aid agreement with the concurrence of the Department of State. Thus, once more, the State Department could be said to have recognized the practical necessity, so often reiterated by the military, that the theater commander have ultimate authority in all matters, including economic affairs, so long as an active state of hostilities prevailed.[26]

The increasingly strong position the military authorities began to take in matters of economic policy could not help but fan the flames of suspicion between the military and UNKRA civilian experts. Granted professed vows of cooperation on either side and the possibility that given good will and a frank exchange of ideas, the two agencies could work together, it was perhaps inevitable that the Koreans, with Oriental virtuosity, began to play off one group against the other and seek the support of UNKRA in trying to force the military authorities to meet their demands. It was also most unfortunate that one of the chief economic experts seconded to the South Korean Ministry of Finance, assumed the role of *éminence grise* behind the Minister. He undoubtedly provoked the suspicion that he was the source of many Korean attacks and counterattacks during the frustrating negotiations on the proposed economic aid agreement during October. Indeed, a later report described this man as one who "seemed to regard himself as an employee of the ROK office to which he was attached and invariably referred to his advisee as 'my Minister.' "[27]

Despite the stop-gap payment of $12,000,000 and the recognized authority enjoyed by the military authorities, the negotiations on the proposed economic aid agreement were soon

deadlocked and the possibility of initiating a coordinated reconstruction program grew more and more remote as the military continued to insist on the prior conclusion of an aid agreement. In this chaotic situation the bitter dissension between
the South Koreans and the UN Command prevented the inauguration of any reconstruction work in which UNKRA
might participate and turned UNKRA technical advice to the
Koreans into a source of deep suspicion. The July Agreement,
in so far as it was implemented, was a complete failure. Its inactivity in programming brought UNKRA the displeasure of
the Koreans; its activity in technical assistance brought the
distrust of the UN Command. Faced with what he considered
to be an impossible position between the frying pan of Korean
scorn and the fire of military wrath, the Agent General therefore decided to propose a modification of the July Agreement.
His aim was a more advantageous position from which to
influence the economic policy of the government of the Republic of Korea and the economic aid programming of the UN
Command.

## The Memorandum of Understanding

Operating under the July Agreement had raised difficulties
not only in UNKRA's relations with the government of the
Republic of Korea and the UN Command, but also with its own
Advisory Committee. Caught in the never-never land of neither
war nor peace, the Committee found it virtually impossible to
offer general policy guidance within which the Agent General
could operate. The Committee was undoubtedly somewhat
shaken by the realization that UNKRA could not be abandoned
even though the agency had, it turned out, been formed prematurely. It therefore sought to steer a course between hopeful determination to fulfill its assignment and realistic caution
to protect contributions until they could provide an identifiable
impact on the Korean economy. In this situation where the best
UNKRA could hope for was to carry out a few isolated projects while waiting for peace, the only guidance the Committee
could offer would have to apply to the individual projects.

Such an arrangement had the members scrutinizing the details of the projects until the Committee would come to direct the program rather than oversee the operation running under the executive management of the Agent General.

Seeking a way out of dickering over details on the one hand with the UN Command and on the other with the Advisory Committee, Agent General Kingsley, by the end of September, decided it was time to attempt to achieve a more integrated approach than prevailed. What he had in mind was an amalgamation of the UNKRA and UNCACK staffs in Korea under the military authorities and the implementation of an integrated program of reconstruction in which UNKRA would be a full partner in the planning, funding, and operation of projects. As a full partner, Kingsley hoped to stimulate the immediate importation of commodities to start building up a supply of goods in line with the supply of money already on the Korean market. In return for immediate action, the Koreans would be required to pursue more stringent credit and spending policies than they had in the past. With UNKRA participating on a large scale, despite the fact that the whole program would be "technically" under military supervision, the Advisory Committee could not possibly get into all the details of the operations, but would have to be content with setting general policy and leaving the operations to the Agent General.

Kingsley adopted the strategy of clearing the new procedures in principle in Washington and then fully developing them in the field as a working interpretation of the July Agreement. He therefore broached the idea to the State Department sometime around the first of November. The reaction in the Department was split. On the one hand, there was disappointment that Kingsley was giving up what had, at the time, been considered by some to be a victory in achieving recognition of civilian responsibility for economic policy. Beneath this disappointment there undoubtedly lay a resentment that UNKRA had not capitalized on this victory by vigorously inaugurating independent projects under the terms of the July Agreement. This argument had little support, however, when taken against the limitations on the operations of the agency: first, as a result of the Army's message of September 28 that practically authorized the military in Tokyo to administer the agreement as they wished; and, second, as a result of the concurrence of the State Department in the assumption of responsibility by the UN Command for a program of economic stabilization.

There was, on the other hand, a certain resignation in the Department that they had few weapons in any battle with the military authorities on the issue of authority and responsibility in a theater of military operations. Even in the relatively minor matter of gaining military concurrence for the few projects UNKRA wanted to implement immediately, there seemed little heart to get into an argument with the Army on whether UNKRA supplies should take priority over military supplies which the Army could undoubtedly prove were necessary to the successful pursuit of military operations. When all views were expressed, it was, therefore, accepted that any agreement with the Army on the status of UNKRA would have to leave ultimate authority in the hands of the UN Commander as had the July Agreement. It was also now clear that the UN Commander would interpret UNKRA's role in the narrowest sense possible, that the Pentagon would support the theater commander, and that Congress would support the military position should any request be made for funds to implement an expanded UNKRA program against military advice. These factors did not, of course, minimize the problems of maintaining a multilateral pattern for the Korean program. Here it was decided that a major effort had to be made to convince other major contributors that because the largest share of the military expense was being carried by the United States, it was necessary to concede to the judgment of the American military commanders until an armistice had been achieved. Finally, there were the fears of the Republic of Korea, real or otherwise, that military government-type procedures would be established to infringe on their newly found, but threatened, national independence. Here it had to be assumed that the needs of South Korea were so great that it had to accept the program the United States offered, no matter what form it took.[28]

Taken on balance, therefore, Kingsley's proposals made sense to the Department. To the extent that UNKRA staffed important posts in the military civil assistance organization, the day-to-day operations with Korean officials would be civilian-oriented, as would policy recommendations sent up through the command structure. A single organization in the field would also offer a more direct channel for the implementation of an integrated reconstruction program utilizing the combined resources of the UN Command and the Republic of Korea, as well as UNKRA. Hopefully, UNKRA participation in an integrated program would be maximum and would provide UNKRA with experience and staff to take over the complete program at a definite point after a cease-fire. Thus, ideally, a reconstruction program could be started during the gray period of truce negotiations with considerable international cooperation to maintain South Korean confidence in UN and United States promises but without sacrificing the military requirement for unrestricted authority as long as a state of hostilities existed.

About ten days after preliminary discussions in Washington, the Agent General formally presented his proposals to the Department of State as the most practical basis on which he felt the work of the Agency could now proceed.[29] Specifically, the proposals called for "Phase 2," the period when UNKRA would assume full responsibility for the reconstruction program, to begin 180 days following the cessation of hostilities. In the meanwhile, the United Nations Command would have sole responsibility for the operation of all projects of relief and economic aid, including technical advice to the Republic of Korea, with all UNKRA experts being seconded to the military Civil Assistance Command. UNKRA would, however, undertake reconstruction projects to be cleared through UN Command/UNKRA Joint Committees. These would also provide a mechanism whereby UNKRA planning teams would be afforded full information in the military reconstruction program so that all efforts would be geared to the same pattern and UNKRA would be in an operating position once "Phase 2" began.

Compared to the July Agreement, the negotiations leading up to the signing of a memorandum of understanding embodying the substance of Kingsley's proposals were a relatively tame and simple affair. Perhaps one explanation is that objections to UNKRA's self-denial of autonomy in Korea could hardly hope to gather effective support given Kingsley's stand, the entrenched position of the military, and the demonstrated frustrations of trying to work outside the military structure. The principles having been privately accepted, the proposed text was circulated for bureaucratic clearances. The State Department had an opportunity to reconsider if it was really giving up very much and the military an opportunity to assure themselves that the proposals were no trojan horse. On November 24, Kingsley, in confidence and impatience, announced the essence of his proposals to the press before they had been sent to the Pentagon for transmittal to the field. In releasing the information, it was emphasized that "the merging of most of Mr. Kingsley's field staff with the military organization . . . is in no sense abandonment of the principle of civilian responsibility for reconstruction." On the contrary, the Agent General felt that the new "kind of close working relationship with the military, which in this field means almost exclusively the United States Army, is worth more than a nominally independent status that, in fact, would mean exclusion of his staff from participation in the practical work they will need to know when the responsibility is shifted to civilian shoulders." [30]

The early release of the new arrangement may have possibly hastened the grinding of bureaucratic wheels. Shortly afterwards the State Department sent the proposals to the Pentagon with a recommendation that the military interpret UNKRA's role in a coordinated program as broadly and liberally as the military situation permitted.[31] The Pentagon, in turn, authorized the UN Command to negotiate and conclude an agreement with UNKRA along the lines of the proposals which Sir Arthur Rucker had actually already discussed in Tokyo. It is difficult to know, however, whether or not the State Department's auxiliary recommendation was seriously passed on. For in discussions with Rucker, the military sought to provide that "Phase 2" would commence with the establishment of "peace and security" rather than simply with the cessation of hostilities. Such a suggestion, seeking to preserve the primacy of the military position as long as possible, gave little hope for much flexibility while hostilities still ran on. Nevertheless, by December 21, minor points of disagreement had been ironed out and Rucker signed the Memorandum of Understanding with the Command.

The Memorandum ended the independent status which UNKRA had had (if not enjoyed) in Korea since the July Agreement. The UN Command was given "sole responsibility for the operation of all projects of relief and economic aid in Korea." The only UNKRA staff not under direct military supervision would be members of the UNKRA "Planning Liaison Team" whose "primary duty" would be "to prepare, and keep up-to-date, plans for UNKRA operations to begin at the commencement of Phase 2." A mechanism for UNKRA participation in Phase 1 operations was provided in "Joint Committees . . . in Tokyo and Korea," with the committee in Korea responsible "for the preparation of plans" and the committee in Tokyo responsible for approving projects "UNKRA will undertake . . . additional to the UNC program." It was specifically stated that the "technical assistance and advice" UNKRA was to furnish to the government of the Republic of Korea, under the July Agreement, would be "furnished through the UNC; and technical experts required for this work will accordingly be members of the staff of the [military] Civil Assistance Command." In addition to the technical experts, UNKRA also would employ and loan other civilian operational staff for service with the Civil Assistance Command "to such extent as may be mutually agreed." It was made clear that "such personnel shall be considered members of the United Nations Command," however. Finally, Phase 2 would commence "180 days following the cessation of hostilities in Korea, as determined by the UC [Unified Command]."

## The End of the First Year

It would be incorrect to conclude that the Memorandum of Understanding was nothing more than a reversion to the agreement the Agent General had made with General MacArthur during his first trip to the Far East in February. Then, there had been no UNKRA staff to loan to the military; by the end of the year, a sizable force was already in Korea, plans were in operation to amalgamate all specialized agency and Red Cross personnel into UNKRA, and recruitment machinery was being organized to fill additional posts. Thus, it was possible to provide a much broader and more compact international base for the relief and rehabilitation work in the field than would have otherwise been possible. Organized by one single agency, the international civilian segment of UNCACK presented promise to the South Koreans that the resolutions of the United Nations were not hollow gestures. Through the Joint Committees, also, UNKRA would be involved in the program planning operations with the military authorities and with the Koreans themselves, a position of advantage and prestige that most assuredly would have been denied in February.

The assumption of full operations by UNKRA, however, continued to be tied to the cessation of hostilities with little thought having as yet been given to the need to re-evaluate this timing in the light of the decision to limit military objectives and the recognition that Korea would undoubtedly remain divided. A limited war gave the enemy as much say over when hostilities would cease as those who decided to withhold the means of forcing the enemy to surrender. This seems to have been recognized most clearly by the South Koreans. Even at this early date, they began to warn that the Communist truce negotiators were deliberately throwing blocks in the path of the talks (by now transferred from Kaesong to Panmunjom) in the expectation that the South Korean economy would crumble, the Rhee government fall, and the communist absorption of the whole peninsula involve only a mopping-up campaign. This admonition was as much an attempt to stimulate more and quicker economic aid as it was a show of dissatisfaction with the decision to negotiate with the communists at all.

The recognition that Korea would continue to be divided no matter what the results of the truce talks might be, was, by necessity, recognition that a continuing military danger would exist in which the United States would be involved either through the commitment of its own forces or through support of a South Korean defense establishment; any other conclusion would deny the correctness of the action of June 25, 1950. Indeed, as early as March, 1951, the Department of the Army had already carried out a preliminary study to determine what size the South Korean Army had to be to protect its position once the military position had stabilized and all foreign troops were withdrawn from the peninsula.[32] With the "cessation of hostilities" indefinitely postponed and the certainty of military danger in the peninsula even when hostilities formally ceased, the basis for a civilian-directed international aid agency operating in Korea badly needed reassessment. In October, 1950, the formula had been to allow the military to carry on relief work while putting a quick end to enemy resistance and simultaneously to organize an international aid agency to pick up the relief task and begin a more extensive reconstruction program. By November, the formula was unworkable and over a year later no comprehensive alternative had been worked out except to expand the military civil relief mission in order to fill the vacuum that was being created. Nevertheless, by then, the need for a reconstruction program had grown more immediate and the military situation became sufficiently stable to make a program feasible. But the military did not consider it to be so stable as to warrant giving a civilian-directed agency even limited freedom of action in the area of operations.

There were, unquestionably, misgivings over this expansion of the military relief mission. These were evident in the questioning of the inclusion of ECA-type aid items in the Army's

Korean relief program and the insistence on an independent status for UNKRA in Korea. The Army's message of September 28 to the UN Command also had recognized this consternation. Here, the Army had explained quite frankly that a draft of a comprehensive directive on civil affairs to replace the Presidential Directive of September 29, 1950, had cleared the Department of Defense. It would have been forwarded to the President for approval but for objections by the State Department to granting the military blanket authority over the South Korean economy. This being so, there is perhaps a lesson to be learned in the way the Department of the Army nevertheless proceeded to issue interim instructions to the field command which accomplished the very same purpose, albeit on an "interim basis." [33]

The new situation following the intervention of the Chinese Communists and the decision to limit military objectives, created two problems: what should be the role of the military in civil affairs in Korea during the long gray period of truce negotiations, and what should be the role of the United Nations in relief and reconstruction now that political division and military danger were sure to continue? The policy-makers may have faced up to these questions but they did little to answer them. It was perhaps too early in limited war experience for anything more than the pragmatic attempt to keep UNKRA in the picture in order to maintain international interest in the program. The foundations of UNKRA's future, however, were already very shaky. The opportunity to strengthen them might not have been lost, however, if political support had been exerted from Washington through the joint committee system at an early stage of its operation.

1. Department of State *Bulletin*, XXV, No. 631 (July 30, 1951), 188.

2. Department of Army message to Commander-in-Chief, United Nations Command, DA 82719, dated 28 September 1951, subject: *Interim Civil Affairs Directive for South Korea* (Reprinted in *United States Agreements with the Republic of Korea*, collection of documents published by the Korean Civil Assistance Command, December, 1954), p. 27. Hereinafter referred to as *DA Message of September 29, 1951;* the collection of documents will be referred to as *KCAC Documents.*

3. Testimony of Colonel Gosorn, Hearings before a subcommittee of the Committee on Appropriations, House of Representatives, 82nd Congress, 1st

Session, *Department of Defense Appropriations for 1952* (Washington: Government Printing Office, 1951), p. 1059.

4. The Army had, by March 31, 1952 (the end of the third quarter of fiscal year 1952), already expended $98.7 million from "general military funds" in addition to the $50 million appropriated for the UN Command's relief mission. See testimony of General Honnen, Chief, Budget Division, Department of the Army, Hearings before a subcommittee of the Committee on Appropriations, House of Representatives, 82nd Congress, 2nd Session, *Urgent Deficiency Appropriations for 1952* (Washington: Government Printing Office, 1952), p. 77.

5. Hearings before the Committee on Foreign Relations and the Committee on Armed Services, United States Senate, 82nd Congress, 1st Session, *Mutual Security Act of 1951* (Washington: Government Printing Office, 1951), p. 535.

6. *Ibid.*

7. *Ibid.*, pp. 670–73; also 683.

8. Testimony of William O. Hall, Office of International Administration and Conferences, Department of State, Hearings before the Committee on Foreign Affairs, House of Representatives, 82nd Congress, 1st Session, *The Mutual Security Program* (Washington: Government Printing Office, 1951), p. 1031.

9. Report of the Committee on Foreign Affairs, *Mutual Security Act of 1951*, House Report No. 872, 82nd Congress, 1st Session (Washington: Government Printing Office, 1951), p. 29. Also, Report of the Committee on Foreign Relations and the Committee on Armed Services, *The Mutual Security Act of 1951*, Senate Report No. 703, 82nd Congress, 1st Session (Washington: Government Printing Office, 1951), p. 31.

10. Conference Report on the Mutual Security Act of 1951, House Report No. 1090, 82nd Congress, 1st Session (Washington: Government Printing Office, 1951), pp. 5, 18.

11. The Agent General was informed of this thinking in a report from staff in the UNKRA office in Washington dated August 31, 1951 (Kingsley papers).

12. Something of the Korean attitude on "planners" can be learned from a remark of Paik Too Chin several years later. Paik, then prime minister, and finance minister in 1951, was asked if the plans ECA had made had helped in post-war rehabilitation work. He replied, "No, no. Circumstances change and at that time in accordance with the recommendations of the ECA we hired Day and Zimmerman Co. for surveying purposes, and they made a big book for the reference of reconstruction. We read it, but that doesn't feed us."— Hearings before a subcommittee of the Committee on Government Operations, House of Representatives, 83rd Congress, 2nd Session, *Relief and Rehabilitation in Korea* (Washington: Government Printing Office, 1954), p. 10.

13. Mr. Kingsley announced some of these plans on arriving in New York for a meeting of the Advisory Committee. *New York Times,* August 9, 1951, p. 2.

14. Writer's personal observations on trip to Korea, September–November, 1951.

15. DA Message of September 29, 1951, *KCAC Documents,* p. 27.

16. In its report of September 30, 1951, the UN Command understated the problem (undoubtedly because of the "public" distribution of the report), thus: "The unusual expenses of the present war have inevitably speeded up the inflation until it is now in a serious state."—*United Nations Command, Civilian Relief and Economic Aid—Korea,* 7 July 1950–30 September 1951 (Headquarters, UN Command, 1952), p. 38.

17. For the prewar work of the Economic Stabilization Committee, see A. Bloomfield and J. Jensen, *Banking Reform in South Korea* (Federal Reserve Bank of New York: March 1951), p. 22. For rise in price index, see *UN Command Report, 7 July 1950–30 September 1951,* p. 38.

18. *New York Times,* January 3, 1952. Minister Paik's pleasure was somewhat confirmed by the report of the Agent General on the inflationary situation during the second year of the conflict from June 30, 1951, to June 30, 1952: " . . . The Government . . . had managed by drastic retrenchment of an emergency nature coupled with heavy taxation to attain a surplus of revenues over expenditures and to reduce its overdraft (with the Bank of Korea) below the level of June, 1951." Unfortunately, a loose credit policy had offset the decrease in government expenditures and maintained the inflation at a high point. UN General Assembly, 7th Session, *Official Records,* Supplement No. 19 (A/2222), Report of the Agent General of the United Nations Korean Reconstruction Agency, p. 10.

19. *Ibid.* The total increase in currency for the period July 1, 1951, through June 30, 1952, was 699.8 billion won, of which 388.3 billion won resulted from advances to UN forces.

20. Agreement between the Government of the United States of America, and the Government of the Republic of Korea regarding Expenditures by Forces under Command of the Commanding General, Armed Forces of the Member States of the United Nations, *KCAC Documents,* pp. 13–14.

21. The rate of exchange controversy endured for years. An excellent statement of Rhee's position is found in an editorial in *The Korean Republic,* an English language newspaper printed in Seoul as a propaganda organ of the government (December 20, 1954): " . . . Aid administrators have sought to maintain that black market prices are 'realistic,' and should be accepted automatically as a yardstick for pricing goods into the Korean market. This is a very strange philosophy, considering that black market prices are sky-high because of the acute shortage of aid goods and of U.S. dollars."

22. Some of the political purposes for which President Rhee used the aid program were recognized by at least one member of the special Economic Mission sent to Korea in the spring of 1952; see Clarence Heer, *Report on Relationship of Proposed UNKRA Program to Counter-Inflationary Objectives of the Agreement on Economic Coordination* (Chapel Hill, North Carolina, 1952), pp. 4–5. For an economic criticism of the way the South Korean government sought to protect favored groups from the worst effects of the inflation, see *Preliminary Nathan Report,* pp. III–13 and X–10.

23. *New York Times,* August 17, 1951, p. 2.

24. *Ibid.,* August 18, 1951, p. 6.

25. *Ibid.,* October 11, 1951, p. 3.

26. In a letter from the State Department to the Acting Chief of the UNKRA office in New York dated October 9, 1951, it was stated: "The Department agrees that under the present circumstances it would be desirable that a CINCUNC-ROK agreement be negotiated as soon as possible and that [UNCACK] assume responsibility for the stability of the Korean economy until such time as UNKRA can become operational."

27. See Heer, *Report on Relationship of Proposed UNKRA Program to Counter-Inflationary Objectives of the Agreement on Economic Coordination,* p. 15.

28. Many of the problems on the status of UNKRA summarized above were reviewed in a staff study prepared for the Agent General on November 1, 1951 (Kingsley papers).

29. Letter from Agent General Kingsley to James E. Webb, Acting Secretary of State, dated November 10, 1951 (Kingsley papers).

30. *New York Times,* November 24, 1951, p. 2.

31. The Agent General was informed of this in a cable from the State Department dated November 23, 1951 (Kingsley papers).

32. Captain Robert K. Sawyer, *United States Military Advisory Group to the Republic of Korea, a Monograph* (Washington: Office of Military History; Department of the Army, 1955), Part III, pp. 269–71. The Army assumption was, however, presumably, nullified by the determination voiced almost four months later by Secretary of State Acheson that the UN forces would stay in Korea until a genuine peace was achieved.

33. See DA Message of September 28, 1951, *KCAC Documents,* p. 27.

CHAPTER V

# THE FAILURE OF AMERICAN POLICY

*The Joint Committees in Action*
*The Meyer Mission*
*Coordination in Washington*

# THE FAILURE OF AMERICAN POLICY

## *The Joint Committees in Action*

The Memorandum of Understanding was an attempt to provide the best of all possible worlds. But the attempt failed. At best, the joint committee system was a bureaucratic technique; it was not a policy. The fact of the matter is that the system proved cumbersome and no integrated relief and reconstruction program, which was a policy, came out of the committees. Indeed, during the first six months of 1952, the military program was never specifically discussed at any committee meeting and those UNKRA proposals that came up for review were treated as isolated projects without being related to an over-all integrated program. Two reasons for the failure of the joint committee system to get a coordinated program into operation stand out in retrospect: the lack of a positive reconstruction policy by the United States to act as a guide for committee action and the failure of the system to provide for the direct participation of the government of the Republic of Korea.

The joint committee system was rounded out by the conclusion of a Supplemental Memorandum of Understanding between the Unified Command and UNKRA in March. The Supplemental Memorandum set up a joint committee in Washington to act as the apex of the system by reviewing proposals sent up through the Tokyo Committee and, most importantly, "major policy questions relating to mutual responsibilities for civil assistance operations in Korea." [1] Here, in theory, was a mechanism for the coordination of United States government policy through the participation of both the Department of State and the Department of Defense, and for the coordination of American policy with UN activity through the participation of the Agent General.

Unfortunately, the Washington Committee never got off the ground. It was hoped that the State and Defense Departments would be represented at the Assistant Secretary level while UNKRA would be represented by the Agent General so that decisions of a policy nature could be made with minimum referrals and delay. The State Department did, in fact, designate the Assistant Secretary for UN Affairs, Mr. Hickerson, as its representative but he never attended any of the meetings of the committee after a preliminary session on general procedures. The Defense Department never did designate its member, but was represented by the chief of the recently reconstituted Civil Affairs and Military Government Division, who had only recently been appointed and knew nothing of the problems involved. As Agent General, Mr. Kingsley left the work of the committee to the chief of his Washington office, acting as Deputy Representative, so long as the other members did not send high level representation. Left to subordinate officers, the Washington Committee held only two meetings between the time the Supplemental Memorandum was signed and the end of June. The first meeting dealt principally with organizational matters of the committee itself. The major subject discussed at the second meeting was the question of granting UNKRA responsibility for the rehabilitation of education in South Korea. No conclusions were reached except that it was agreed that the Department of Defense would seek the views of the field in this matter. The focus remained in the Far East, and particularly in Tokyo.

Joint committee meetings had been convened in both Tokyo and Pusan almost as soon as the Memorandum of Understanding had been signed and were generally held on a monthly basis after that. Briefly, procedures were developed whereby an UNKRA project would, first, be presented to the Korea Committee where, if all agreed that it was operationally appropriate and feasible, it was "approved in principle." The project was then submitted to the Tokyo Committee for review to determine whether it was consistent with the over-all military program and, if found to be in line, for "approval in principle" at this higher echelon. Approved in Tokyo, the project would then be developed in detail by the staff in Korea. Full information on the organization, procurement and operation was then submitted to the Korea Committee for transmittal, through Eighth Army channels, to the Commander-in-Chief of the UN Command for final approval.

Needless to say, these procedures were most frustrating and by the constant concentration on details, the committees were almost always lost in the morass of specifics with no general framework within which to work. A number of UNKRA projects were approved by the committees during the first months of operation under the system. These were, however, mainly projects that UNKRA staff had been working on since the previous summer in consultation with the military and which could be presented in detail without too much trouble. They included plans for the importation of hatching eggs and mobile public health clinics, the establishment of a merchant marine academy and the construction of a laboratory for mineral analysis. Admirable as these projects were, they were not part of a total recovery program but only single efforts mainly stimulated by the enthusiasm of a Korean minister or an UNKRA specialist.

The difficulty in getting an integrated program organized did not stem primarily from any difficulty in UNKRA/military coordination in the field (although difficulties did exist) but rather from the continued difficulty of the military in gaining agreement with the South Korean government on counterinflationary measures. In the interim, there was literally no firm policy in Washington on the reconstruction program except the weakly voiced hope that the United Nations Command would interpret the terms of the Memorandum of Understanding liberally to enable UNKRA to act as an effective partner in the work in Korea. Without an integrated program, however, there was no basis for a partnership except on an *ad hoc* arrangement. In an attempt to achieve partnership functionally, therefore, UNKRA continued to pursue the policy of seeking broad authority in delegated areas of interest with a particularly strong effort being made to gain authority in the field of education.

At the first meeting of the Tokyo Committee early in January, the UNKRA representatives admitted that the agency was not yet in a position to undertake any large-scale rebuilding in connection with educational rehabilitation. He nevertheless ventured to suggest that while the military might handle construction needs, there were decided advantages to education's being the responsibility of a United Nations civilian agency, especially questions relating to the printing and distribution of textbooks, teacher training and school curricula. The military members merely expressed doubt that educational rehabilitation could as yet be completely detached from military supervision, but agreed that UNKRA might be allowed to carry on particular projects in the field after further discussion in the Committee.[2] When the question was again raised in the February meeting, the UN Command announced that, in its own program, it was undertaking to restore educational facilities to a point where normal schooling could be carried on. It invited UNKRA to work out specific projects in the Korea Joint Committee in support of these efforts.[3]

During the next three months, the Korea Committee discussed and eventually approved UNKRA projects for the purchase of textbooks and laboratory equipment, presumably to be used in the classrooms to be constructed under the military program. While these individual projects worked their way painstakingly through the joint committee system, however, Agent General Kingsley attacked the problem more broadly during discussions in Korea in early May with General Van Fleet, the commander of the Eighth Army. Kingsley underscored his belief that "the time has come when it is not only feasible but desirable that UNKRA be charged with responsibility for assisting the Korean Government in the reconstruction of education, with the exception of school buildings and furniture." He went on to suggest that "education is, by its very nature, a long-term proposition and questions of teacher training, curriculum, fundamental education, vocational and professional training, and the like, are matters which can most readily be approached through civilian assistance." Kingsley expressed the thought that "this is the general view of the educational profession, without whose whole-hearted assistance and support educational reconstruction would be difficult to achieve." [4]

The problems of educational rehabilitation could, it was felt, be attacked at the outset on a long-range basis as well from the short-term need to rebuild facilities and refurnish equipment and materials. The problems of Korean education, moreover, were complicated by the need to reorient the method and content of education from the techniques of the Japanese regime, to reform the Korean written language in order to make the learning process easier, to train administrative and teaching staffs, to stimulate research and scholarly investigation, to develop a system of adequate financial support for education and to try to break down the highly centralized, bureaucratic control of education. [5]

Kingsley's proposals on education, originally taken up at a meeting with General Van Fleet and President Rhee, were part of a fifteen to twenty million dollar program he sought to get approved *in toto* at a high level without having to nurse each project through joint committees. Despite this attempt to short-circuit the committee system, his proposals came back to the Tokyo Committee for discussion at its May and June meetings. At the May meeting, the military representatives repeated that they could not relinquish their responsibilities for education as Kingsley had suggested, but that they hoped to clarify the picture by presenting a full policy statement on education to the June meeting. [6] The statement presented several weeks later only re-emphasized the military position by asserting that assistance "in the rehabilitation of the South Korean school system" could not be delegated by the United Nations Command because it was "required by the directive to the UNC to prevent unrest among the civil population to further accomplishment of the Military Mission." [7]

Something of the power wielded by Tokyo in the field of civil assistance is emphasized by this unilateral assertion of responsibility and authority. For almost a year the State Department had repeatedly expressed the view that education was an ideal field for UNKRA. The Department also expressed concern that the military should not begin to get involved in questions of educational policy. The military authorities in Washington had, at first, been wary of such a move for fear of UNKRA establishing its own supply channels to meet the physical needs of Korea's schools. However, by May, 1952, when the question was raised in the Washington Joint Committee, the Army representative seemed to be willing to agree to UNKRA's assuming responsibility for education subject to the precaution of ascertaining the views of the theater commander. With this background, which must have been communicated to the field, and with General Van Fleet's agreement to Kingsley's proposals, the UN Command was still able to issue a statement reaffirming its responsibility for education under the authority of its civil affairs mandate.

Despite the theory that the joint committees would provide a mechanism for civilian influence over the reconstruction program, the military authorities comprised the dominant party in the system. The State Department was only represented in the Washington Committee which must be judged as having been completely ineffective. In both the Korea and Tokyo committees, UNKRA was continually on the defensive since the agency had to present individual projects for military review without any more support than could be developed through informal contacts in the field and the State Department's desire that UNKRA's role under the Memorandum of Understanding be interpreted as broadly as the military situation would allow. Yet it seems fair to say that so long as no more positive policy was sent forward from Washington, the military command in Tokyo was justified in not taking the risk of releasing any of its authority to UNKRA. By this time, General Mark Clark had assumed command in Tokyo and felt strongly that "in order to prosecute the war effectively, it was necessary to make certain that unrest, disease and starvation were eliminated or at least minimized in South Korea . . . and this meant . . . I had to have the authority to make decisions which would funnel relief and reconstruction aid money into

projects that would be beneficial to the war effort at the same
time that they helped the Korean economy." The General thus
concluded that "I . . . couldn't afford to let a group of UN
economists decide to rehabilitate textile factories, for instance,
with money we sorely needed to dredge a harbor or a channel to
make way for our supply ships." [8]

The episode of the joint committee system demonstrates
rather clearly that the military will not, indeed, cannot be expected to modify their policy of relating everything in a theater of operations to the objective of maintaining the security of
their forces. Who can say that they were too cautious? Is it
the proper role of the military to take the risk of *not* seeing
everything from the viewpoint of military objectives? If political considerations are ever to be considered valid in modifying
normal military operations, then clearly it is incumbent
upon the political departments of the government to specify
the framework within which the military are to operate. The
State Department never assumed any such responsibility in
outlining a firm policy for Korean reconstruction. Why should
the Department of Defense have done more?

The search for reasons why the United States had no policy
for Korean reconstruction except to wait for an armistice that
was ever more elusive and already gave little promise of satisfaction even if achieved, leads, as so often, back to the problems
of the South Korean economy and the relations of the United
States with the Rhee government. The military's policy statement on education issued in early June was further strengthened by the tasks they were now charged with under the terms
of an economic agreement signed with the Republic of Korea
by a Presidential Mission that had been sent from Washington
in April. And some explanation, if not excuse, for the do-noth-
ing attitude of the State Department might lie in the uncertainty that existed until the agreement was signed.

## The Meyer Mission

The negotiations between the UN Command and the South
Korean government on an economic aid agreement had been

broken off in November, 1951, over Korean protests that they could not accept the Command's control over their foreign exchange. If they had accepted such control under the pre-war ECA agreement, they contended that the struggle since June, 1950, had stirred up such strong nationalist sentiment that it would be disastrous for the government to accept any veto over its independence of action. Between November and February positions hardened.[9] The South Korean government compromised to the extent of agreeing that it would work out, jointly with the military command, plans for the utilization of dollars received in payment for won advances to the UN forces. They were adamant, however, that while they were prepared to offer periodic information on how they used other foreign exchange, they would not consent to outside control beyond this point. The military authorities, on their side, continued to contend that the government had to begin to gets its economic house in order. This meant that until there was an agreement on joint control of all foreign exchange resources, there could be no extensive aid program nor further repayments for local currency advanced to the UN forces. By January, the government was, however, stubbornly maintaining that only the won advances remained as an obstacle to its own counterinflationary program and threatening to cut off future won advances unless steps were taken to repay previous drawings.

In this struggle, the American Embassy seems to have been cast in the role of mediator. The Embassy sought to convince the government that an agreement with the military authorities would pave the way for a coordinated economic program which would, in turn, act to stabilize the South Korean economy and provide an opportunity for reasonable settlement of the won advances in the process. If the government was not completely convinced by the logic of the Embassy's reasoning, it seemed to respond to this more conciliatory tone and agreed to new negotiations in February. But these talks, like those before, were wrecked on the same rocks of contention: the refusal of the Republic of Korea to accept military control over its foreign exchange or to allow the rate of exchange for won to drop to open market values.

The difficulties encountered in negotiating with the South Korean government soon found their way to Washington, and after the February talks collapsed, the UN Command asked that a special mission be sent to the Far East to take over the negotiations. Two requirements seem to have been considered important in forming the mission: first, that it be granted full authority to sign an agreement while in Korea; and, second, that the various departments interested be represented. The mission was, thus, designated by the President to insure its prestige and powers and was composed of nominees from the State, Defense and Treasury departments, as well as the Mutual Security Administration. If anything, however, military representation was the strongest. Four Army officers, a civilian economist with the Division of Civil Affairs and Military Government, and an outside economist appointed by the Secretary of Defense, comprised six of the eight-man team under Dr. Clarence Meyer, former head of ECA in Korea.[10] While designated by the President, the authority of the mission was deemed to derive from the resolutions of the Security Council of July 7 and July 31, 1950, which had set up the Unified Command under the United States and asked the Command to assume responsibility for civilian relief.[11] The United States was, thus, acting under the authority it had received from the UN in negotiating with the Republic of Korea, although there seems to be no evidence either that other nations involved in the Korean conflict were consulted in the work of the mission or that UNKRA was consulted (although the agency was informed of the purpose of the mission a few days before it left for the Far East).

The Meyer Mission arrived in Pusan early in April and spent the first few weeks going over the same arguments and coming to the same point of deadlock with the Koreans as had the military negotiators before them. The mission does not seem to have been tied to any definite proposals but to have had fairly broad discretion in settling the problems of the won advances and an aid agreement. This very flexibility seems to have given the head of the mission the opportunity to break out of the deadlock in private talks with the South Korean Finance Minister, Paik Too Chin: first, by agreeing to an organizational setup to oversee an aid program which would enhance the government's prestige and act to compensate for any restrictions on its unilateral control over its foreign exchange; and, second, by settling on a stop-gap solution of the local currency question which avoided the issue of the rate of exchange.

By the end of May, details had been worked out and Dr. Meyer signed an Economic Coordination Agreement with the government which provided for the creation of a Combined Economic Board as the focal point of a program designed to achieve economic stability.[12] The Board was to consist of two members, one representing the Republic of Korea, and the other, the United Nations Command. It was stipulated that the Board was to be a "coordinating and advisory" rather than an "operating body" to "consider all economic aspects of the Unified Command programs for assistance to the Republic of Korea and all pertinent aspects of the economy and programs of the Republic of Korea, in order that each of the Board's recommendations may be a part of a consistent over-all program designed to provide maximum support to the military effort of the Republic of Korea and develop a stable Korean economy." In considering proposed economic projects, the Board was also to insure that expenses in both won and foreign currency were kept to a minimum and that funds and material provided for the economic assistance of Korea were not diverted to other purposes. According to the letter of the Agreement, the Board became the control point over the economy of South Korea. But if this gave the military authorities a say over the Koreans' use of their foreign exchange, it also gave the Koreans a say over the military's aid program, a concession for which Syngman Rhee had long been fighting.

Under the agreement, the United States undertook to assist the Republic of Korea in providing the basic necessities to "prevent epidemics, disease, and unrest," after both parties had ascertained aid requirements in consultation. The agreement, thus, geared U.S. assistance to the basic military mission and reaffirmed the primacy of the United Nations Command in the relief and rehabilitation program, even to the extension of the Command's authority over economic affairs. The agreement did, however, recognize that changes would be required "as responsibilities of the Unified Command are assumed by the UN Korean Reconstruction Agency." It noted that, under the Memorandum of Understanding, UNKRA was to assume responsibility for all UN relief and rehabilitation in Korea 180 days after termination of hostilities unless "military operations do not so permit at that time."

The question of local currency advances to UN forces was settled by an exchange of notes accompanying the basic agreement. For won supplied by the South Korean government for the first five months of 1952, the United States agreed to pay at an exchange rate of 6,000 won to the dollar. There was, however, no settlement on outstanding amounts supplied prior to January, 1952, nor agreement on the rate of exchange to be used for the repayment of advances after June. In order to avoid the inflationary consequences of won advances in case of delay in agreeing to a rate, the United States agreed to pay $4,000,000 a month to the South Korean government with these monthly payments later being taken into consideration when a rate of exchange was agreed upon and the exact amount of reimbursement calculated.[13]

The establishment of the Combined Economic Board filled the need for a central point not only in settling economic problems and policy, but also in tying the government of the Republic of Korea down to written decisions in order to minimize the possibility that the Koreans could ignore their responsibilities. The frustrating experience of negotiating with the Rhee government seems to have deepened the distrust with which South Korean intentions were regarded. Thus, a suggestion from the State Department that UNKRA be granted a seat on the Combined Economic Board was vetoed by the military authorities.

They viewed such a move as weakening their own position (by dividing authority and providing a basis for their being overruled) in keeping the South Korean government in line while armed forces were still committed in the peninsula.

At least one member of the Meyer Mission felt strongly that the mere presence of UNKRA in Korea, even in a subordinate position outside the Combined Economic Board, was a distinct danger to the pursuit of a counterinflationary program by the Board.[14] If these views were in the minority among members of the mission, they nevertheless dealt with the realities of the situation and seem to have reflected the opinion of the military authorities, particularly in Tokyo. This school of thought was based on the undoubtedly correct assumption that the representative of the Republic of Korea on the Board would encourage inflationary measures, such as a liberal credit policy, under the pressure of domestic politics. It was thus evident that the UN Command member would have to use every power at his disposal, particularly the power to stop or limit further aid from all sources, to force the counterinflationary program through. The very presence of UNKRA with any kind of independent program was immediately a handicap to these efforts and, thus, a potential danger to the counterinflationary program.[15] Such objections to UNKRA were basically no different from the military fears of divided authority that had led to an abandonment of UNKRA's independent status and the frustrations of the joint committee system.

Substantively, the objections to an UNKRA program were rooted in the methods to be used to attack the hyper-inflation in South Korea. Stated rather simply, the Agreement emphasized the need to import the maximum amount of consumer goods for sale to drain excess currency off the market and, through the Combined Economic Board, to restrict investment until reasonable stability had been achieved. By very definition, the UNKRA program of "reconstruction" called for immediate investment projects which would create purchasing power without concurrently creating finished goods to counteract the inflationary pressures thus produced. Whether it was necessary, or even appropriate in the case of South Korea, to follow a rigid policy of restricting investment while attacking inflation was a question that was disputed several months later. For the moment, the rigid anti-investment policy accepted by the Meyer Mission and the military authorities was simultaneously anti-UNKRA whether deliberately or simply as a by-product of applying traditional economic theory to a tradition-shattering situation.

The Combined Economic Board actually began to operate early in July under Finance Minister Paik Too Chin and the Deputy Commander for Civil Affairs, Eighth Army, Major-General Thomas W. Herren. Almost immediately, General Herren informed UNKRA that the agency was expected to work within the framework of the recently signed Economic Coordination Agreement:

In order to enable me to discharge my responsibilities as Representative of CINCUNC, it is essential that all commands, echelons, and agencies engaged in furnishing relief and economic aid to the Republic of Korea:

    a. Operate within the framework of the Economic Agreement.
    b. Follow policies enunciated by CINCUNC.
    c. Coordinate and integrate all their activities into one over-all program.

It is my opinion that the Resolution of the Security Council of July 31, 1950, and the Memorandum of Understanding between the UNC and UNKRA of 21 December 1951, place upon the United Nations Command (CINCUNC) responsibility for the aid and relief program, and the procedures for providing relief and support to the Republic of Korea.

.   .   .   .   .   .   .   .   .   .   .   .

My first objective is to minimize won drawings and maximize the receipt of won from the sale of aid goods. The Republic of Korea is being encouraged to utilize foreign currency in such a way as to produce the maximum won returns from it. These measures, however, will not stop inflation unless administration expenses are reduced to the lowest possible level, avoiding wage increases from present scales except through payments in kind, adopting and adhering to uniform wage scales, and avoiding major construction projects which directly or indirectly require the use of indigenous labor. Goods imported for sale must be of such a nature that they can be readily utilized without the expenditure of additional won. For instance, the importation of building material for sale is not considered sound, in that the end use of such material requires the use of additional won for indigenous labor engaged in construction. The Bank of Korea is being enjoined to restrict loans to short periods and to make loans only to businessmen for import purposes.[16]

The immediate objectives of the military command, as explained by General Herren, of limiting new currency drawings to the absolute minimum and stimulating the importation of finished consumer goods for sale, were potentially crippling to UNKRA in Korea at this particular moment. The agency had continued to finance its local administrative expenses through won advances from the Bank of Korea. If the first objective were pursued without discretion, it was clearly possible for the UNC member of the Combined Economic Board to refuse to agree to any further loans to UNKRA, thus making it impossible for the agency to operate in Korea until it was in a position to import consumer goods for sale in order to earn won. Even if this stage were reached, however, and permission granted to UNKRA to use the port, warehouse and transportation facilities that would be needed for such an operation, the total effect might still be considered inflationary since the won then earned would be put back into the market in form of wages and payments for contractual work rather than kept out of circulation altogether.

As had to be expected, the objective of importing finished goods which could be immediately sold without the further expenditure of won (except, presumably, to cover minimum distribution costs) ruled out almost every UNKRA project which had been approved "in principle" by the joint committees in the last six months. Each project, no matter what its status under joint committee procedures (which had not, as yet, been superseded), now had to stand the ultimate test of review by the Combined Economic Board and particularly the military member to determine whether it conformed to the counterinflationary policy of the Board. Wherever a project called for the importation of building materials (and almost every UNKRA project did), it was automatically disqualified under the rigid formula followed by General Herren since the consequent construction costs, no matter how minimal, would produce new purchasing power.

If the full effect of the new economic organization momentarily threatened the future of the UN agency, it could well be rationalized as an unfortunate by-product of the need to resist compromise in pursuing the policy laid down by the Meyer Mission. Conceivably, the South Korean government might seize upon preferential treatment to UNKRA as justification for pursuing the loose credit program that was as serious an inflationary threat as the won advances despite Syngman Rhee's refusal to recognize this weakness.[17] Yet the ultimate conclusion of the economic policy being pursued by the U.S. government agencies in Korea was certainly running counter to American policy in continuing to support UNKRA. There was, nevertheless, a role for UNKRA to play since the counterinflationary program also called for a coordinated recovery program in which UNKRA could participate. Within such a program, the inflationary impact of any single project would not be a matter of critical concern since its effect would only be temporary provided that the total program was balanced. But the fact of the matter was that in July, 1952, there was no coordinated ROK/UNC/UNKRA program. The joint committees had not been able to develop any such program because of the piecemeal approach taken by the committees and the absence of Korean representation. The Combined Economic Board was not equipped to develop a program since it was "a coordinating and advisory body" and "not . . . an operating body" and did not have UNKRA representation. Finally, there was no basic economic blueprint upon which to develop a program, no indication of the intended role of South Korea in Far Eastern economic planning or in American political and military policy.

## Coordination in Washington

While the military authorities were elevated to a position of ultimate power in economic affairs through the arrangement established under the Meyer Agreement, their means to wield power were being drastically cut in Washington. For one thing, there were renewed efforts to restrict the Army to a narrow interpretation of the "disease and unrest" formula. But, more important perhaps, the Army's new request for funds to meet its civil relief commitments in Korea was now based on "responsibility for civilian aid in Korea . . . [being] transferred to the United Nations Korean Reconstruction Agency" after December 31, 1952.[18] There seems little explanation how the United Nations Command could successfully resist UNKRA participation on the Combined Economic Board when the budget process, at any rate, was simultaneously operating in Washington on the basis of responsibility for the relief and reconstruction work being transferred to the UN agency under the terms of the Memorandum of Understanding by the end of the calendar year!

There was a very clear relationship between the Army budget for aid to Korea and the appropriations covering the U.S. contribution to UNKRA for the fiscal year 1953. Included in the funds intended for UNKRA was an amount of $66 million to be made available from funds or supplies under the Army program still in the military pipeline at the time of transfer.[19] Great stress was placed by both civilian and military witnesses before congressional committees on the necessity for keeping a steady stream of aid goods flowing into Korea during the transition period. In its budget estimates for the previous fiscal year, the State Department had substantially justified its request for funds for UNKRA on political grounds: the need to demonstrate to the Korean people, to other UN members involved in the conflict, and to uncommitted peoples of Asia that the Administration, supported by the Congress, was determined to begin the reconstruction of Korea despite the temporary setback brought on by the entrance of Communist Chinese into the war. But for fiscal year 1953 the emphasis was more on the practical rather than political reasons for appropriating funds for UNKRA, as if, despite what was happening in the Far East, American support for a UN reconstruction program and the full inauguration of the program itself were both assured.

The State Department representative before the House Appropriations Committee did not, it is true, explicitly say (as had military witnesses) that UNKRA was going to take over responsibility for the program under the terms of the Memorandum of Understanding. He did, however, request appropriations for UNKRA on the basis of there being "no way to avoid the disaster of a gap, a great empty space occurring in [the supply] pipelines, unless appropriation has taken place and funds are available for disbursement to UNKRA very quickly when the responsibility for that pipeline is transferred from the military to UNKRA." [20] The military had been much more precise in assuming a transfer of responsibility on a specific date. When asked what would happen if the committee failed to approve funds for Korean relief under the UN Command program for the period from July 1 through December 31, the Army witness answered: ". . . If you did, then General Ridgway, or General Clark, now, would have a fit, because the plan is that UNKRA will take over this activity six months after the end of hostilities, which take-over is now predicted as December 31. They are a welfare organization without, perhaps, the well-knit operation that the Army has, and if they do not find a pipeline in existence when they take over they will probably fall down on the job . . . ." [21]

Although the truce negotiations were strung high on the prisoner repatriation issue, there seemed little doubt that the UN military position was secure.[22] A rehabilitation program was feasible, even though the Meyer Mission had emphasized that rebuilding had to wait until greater economic stability had been achieved through a counterinflationary program. Plans were thus made, in the budget process, for the Army to continue its relief program for the first six months of fiscal 1953 with UNKRA assuming responsibility early in 1953 and picking up the funds and supplies in the military pipeline to start its own program. While this planning seems quite logical, there is no evidence that either the field or higher echelons were brought into the picture very closely.

On the very day (June 17) that the State Department was up before the House Committee on Appropriations requesting that the Army be authorized to make $66 million in supplies and/or funds available as part of the United States contribution to UNKRA, the Army Chief of Staff, General Collins, was testifying before the Senate Committee on Appropriations on the bill which included military funds from which the $66 million would be taken. The General ran into considerable trouble with Senators Knowland and Ferguson who were most dissatisfied with the high proportion of the burden for the Korean conflict that the United States was taking on in comparison with other UN members. Senator Knowland, particularly, wanted assurances that the United States would at least control any funds it turned over to a UN agency for Korean relief and protect them from being used where the Soviet Union could interfere.[23] Quickly, General Collins assured the Senator: " . . . We deliberately . . . kept [the relief program] in the hands of the military to be sure that there would be no interference with the actual military campaign." And "that is the reason why we still frankly had to carry the load on this thing." The General then went so far as to say that "[I] will put it in the record right now *subject to correction*, moneys appropriated here, if appropriated, will be expended wholly under American supervision. That is, no international organization will be involved in the expenditure of these funds." [24] The General was not corrected, as he should have been, and the committee went ahead to recommend "the appropriation of . . . funds [for the relief of civilians in Korea] only on the understanding clearly expressed at the hearing on behalf of the Department of the Army that these funds are to be expended only by the Army and that no representatives of the United Nations Korean Reconstruction Agency will have any function or responsibility therewith." [25]

On the very next day, Senator Dworshak noted this particular point in the Committee's report. On the Senate floor he asked for "clarification because the Mutual Security Act stipulates that certain amounts, in one instance, $67,000,000 shall be made available by the Department of the Army for expenditure by the Korean Relief Agency." [26] The Senator then insisted that "it is the responsibility of the Senate to determine whether we are expending millions of dollars for Korean relief under the Mutual Security Program, whether we are turning over $175,000,000 to the Department of the Army for civilian relief in Korea, or just what we are doing." [27]

Senator Knowland immediately took it on himself to explain that the language of the Mutual Security Act authorizing the Army to make transfers to UNKRA "relates to a condition after peace has been established in Korea. Such a condition has not been brought about." He also reminded the Senate that another reservation in the appropriations bill required the Army to submit a complete report "on the manner in which all sums appropriated or to be appropriated have been or will be expended" and, accordingly, "none of the funds [can] be turned over without both making a report and coming before the committee and making full justification, regardless of the language in the [Mutual Security Act]." [28]

In what must be considered an unfortunate impulse to bow to shortsighted congressional pressure, General Collins thus invited the Senate to participate in the administration of the Memorandum of Understanding with UNKRA. Senator Knowland's remarks might well have been left a matter of record. But there were risks in employing such tactics since the questions involved in turning over responsibility to UNKRA in the event of a truce would include several of importance, in principle, to the Senator; among these were, especially, a determination of the degree of peace actually achieved in a truce that gave no assurance of a unified Korea and an evaluation of the degree of participation in manpower and resources of other nations in the Korean conflict. The Senator would not have let these matters rest lightly if there is any lesson to be learned from the storms that rose over similar questions during the hearings on the MacArthur dismissal.

As things turned out, the Knowland reservations were never

tested since, by the time a truce was gained, the whole problem
of Korean reconstruction had taken new shape. For the moment this congressional episode serves only to illustrate the contradictions that arose in not relating Korean relief and reconstruction to the total picture of American policy in the Far
East. If there was any basis for transferring authority to
UNKRA, it had to lie in some firm expectation either that a
truce was on its way or else that the military situation was sufficiently secure to transfer almost complete authority to a UN
civilian agency. Yet either assumption should have been of sufficient importance to be of concern to the Army Chief of Staff
and prominent in his mind when testifying before a congressional committee. Indeed, it should also have been of sufficient
importance to have some effect on the agreement which the
Meyer Mission had signed with the government of the Republic of Korea. Yet General Collins' remarks on June 17 and the
Meyer agreement signed on May 24 did not take into account
either of these possibilities, but appear clearly predicated on
the continuing responsibility of the military command for relief and rehabilitation. Yet if this was, indeed, still the policy
of the American government, what was the basis for cutting off
Army funds by December 31, 1952?

The vagaries of the Korean truce and the requirements of
United States government procedures undoubtedly made planning difficult. Both the State Department and the Army had to
be ready for a change-over if the terms of the Memorandum of
Understanding had any meaning. It might very well come in
the middle of the fiscal year and the Executive Branch had to
be ready. There were several possibilities of how the situation
could be handled. Total funds for a year's operation could be
requested by the Department of the Army. This was objectionable since it would put funds in military hands for an ex-
pansive interpretation of the "disease and unrest" formula and
might lead to a dangerous and unfortunate precedent. Total
funds for a year's program could, on the other hand, be requested by the Department of State under the Mutual Security
Program. This would undoubtedly prove objectionable to

the Army since it would not only weaken military control over the funds, but also weaken the military principle that civil relief was part and parcel of carrying out successful military operations. If Congress did not exist, there would have also existed the possibility of setting aside funds for a full year's program in both budgets. But Congress did exist with full and furious hatred of budget duplication, well-known to members of the Executive Branch and particularly the staff in the Bureau of the Budget. There was, therefore, only the possibility of splitting up the funds between the two programs with provision for the Army to transfer any unexpended funds and undistributed supplies to UNKRA on a transfer of responsibility. The relationship of this possible budget approach to a truce in Korea and United States relations with the South Korean government does not, however, seem to have been examined at the same time. Or, if it was examined, no one seems to have told the Army Chief of Staff or the President's Special Economic Representative to the Republic of Korea.

1. Supplemental Memorandum of Understanding, March 24, 1952.

2. Minutes of UNC-UNKRA Tokyo Joint Committee Meeting, 5 January 1952.

3. *Ibid.*, 4 February 1952.

4. Letter from J. Donald Kingsley, Agent General, UNKRA, to General James Van Fleet, Commanding General, Eighth United States Army, Korea, dated 6 May 1952, p. 3. (Hereinafter referred to as Kingsley/Van Fleet letter.)

5. These problems are discussed at some length in a report prepared by UNESCO the following year. *Rebuilding Education in the Republic of Korea,* Report of the UNESCO-UNKRA Educational Planning Mission to Korea (Germany: UNESCO, May, 1954). See especially Part II: "Recommendations for Reconstruction, February, 1953," pp. 114–21.

6. Minutes of UNC-UNKRA Tokyo Joint Committee Meeting, 19 May 1952.

7. Exhibit 1 to the Minutes of UNC-UNKRA Tokyo Joint Committee Meeting, 2 June 1952.

8. Mark Clark, *From the Danube to the Yalu* (New York: Harper & Bros., 1954), pp. 143–44. General Clark's inference that he had control over UNKRA funds is, of course, mistaken. If the military turned down an UNKRA project, these funds simply were not used.

9. See paragraph 2 of Article IV of the ECA Agreement of December 10, 1948, with the Republic of Korea, which states: "The Government of the Republic of Korea will insure that the periodic allocation of the foreign exchange by categories of use will be made in consultation with and with the concurrence

# 130 MILITARY POLICY AND ECONOMIC AID

of the United States Aid Representative, and that expenditures of foreign exchange will be made in accordance with such allocations."

10. The make-up of the Meyer Mission was reported in the *New York Times,* April 5, 1952, p. 2.

11. See the text of the Agreement signed by the Mission on May 24, 1952, *Economic Coordination Between the Unified Command and the Republic of Korea,* Treaties and other International Acts Series 2593, Department of State Publication 4895 (Washington: Government Printing Office, 1953).

12. *Ibid.*

13. *Ibid.*

14. Heer, *Report on Relationship of Proposed UNKRA Program to Counter-inflationary Objectives of the Agreement on Economic Coordination,* pp. 8–10.

15. *Ibid.,* p. 8.

16. Letter from Major General T. W. Herren, Deputy Army Commander, Eighth United States Army Korea, to Deputy Agent General Sir Arthur Rucker, dated July 11, 1952 (Kingsley papers).

17. Arthur J. Bloomfield, *Report and Recommendation on Banking in South Korea,* prepared for the UNCACK (Pusan, Korea, March 31, 1952), p. 13.

18. Testimony of Brigadier General G. Honnen, Chief, Budget Division, Department of the Army, Hearings before a subcommittee of the Committee on Appropriations, House of Representatives, 82nd Congress, 2nd Session, *Urgent Deficiency Appropriations for 1952* (Washington: Government Printing Office, 1952), p. 77.

19. Testimony of C. T. Wood and G. Hall, Hearings before a subcommittee of the Committee on Appropriations, House of Representatives, 82nd Congress, 2nd Session, *Mutual Security Appropriations* (Washington: Government Printing Office, 1952), pp. 706–709.

20. Testimony of G. Hall, *ibid.*

21. Testimony of General Reeder, Hearings before a subcommittee of the Committee on Appropriations, House of Representatives, 82nd Congress, 2nd Session, *Urgent Deficiency Appropriations for 1952* (Washington: Government Printing Office, 1952), p. 104.

22. In a speech at Brown University on May 30, 1952, Ambassador Muccio said: "Whether or not peace is restored [in Korea] is now dependent entirely on [the Communists]. In the meantime, with military success won by the UN Forces in Korea, we are in a position, as General Van Fleet said recently, to outfight or outsit the Communists." Reprinted in the Department of State *Bulletin,* XXVI, No. 677 (June 16, 1952), 942.

23. Hearings before the Committee on Appropriations, U.S. Senate, 82nd Congress, 2nd Session, *Urgent Deficiency Appropriation Bill, 1952* (Washington: Government Printing Office, 1952), p. 56.

24. *Ibid.,* p. 57. (Italics added.)

25. Report of the Committee on Appropriations, *Urgent Deficiency Appropriation Bill, 1952,* Senate Report No. 1780, 82nd Congress, 2nd Session (Washington: Government Printing Office, 1952), p. 3.

26. *Congressional Record,* Vol. XCVIII, Part 6, 82nd Congress, 2nd Session, p. 7528.

27. *Ibid.*

28. *Ibid.*

# CHAPTER VI

# THE DICHOTOMY IN AMERICAN POLICY

*The Change in the Military's Position*
*An UNKRA Program in Spite of Itself*
*The End of the Second Year*

# THE DICHOTOMY IN AMERICAN POLICY

## *The Change in the Military's Position*

News of the restrictions on the military program was quick to reach the Far East. While the military member of the Combined Economic Board was, on the one hand, turning down UNKRA projects on the basis of their being inflationary, the UN Command suddenly asked UNKRA to finance a number of its own relief projects for which military funds were not available. In a memorandum dated July 3, 1952, Colonel Hensey, still in charge of the Army's Korea Aid Program, noted:

> Sufficient funds are not available to UNC to finance all of the projects listed in [the military's program for fiscal year 1953. Certain] raw material items and equipment for industrial rehabilitation projects . . . are considered necessary not only from the rehabilitation point of view but also from the standpoint of relief in Korea. Considering the nature of these projects which are directed toward rehabilitation of Korean economy, it is believed that they are vital to successful implementation of immediate UNC operations and UNKRA rehabilitation plans.[1]

The Colonel then went on to ask that UNKRA assist in carrying out the Army program by financing projects totalling approximately $15,000,000. He pointed out that in most cases the projects were follow-ups to previous work and that "since procurement has been initiated and parts of these projects already completed, it is considered advisable that UNKRA make necessary funds available to DA to complete the projects as previously planned." Where a totally new project was involved, he suggested that instead of doing its own purchasing, UNKRA might "turn over to DA sufficient funds to cover the cost of the project plus the cost of transportation." He ended by saying: "This headquarters desires to emphasize that the projects listed above which have been specifically selected for financing by UNKRA are of the industrial rehabilitation and sustaining import types." Thus, "it is considered there should be no objection by UNKRA to financing these projects since they are of the type which UNKRA will ultimately undertake." [2]

While, on the surface, Colonel Hensey's proposals might have seemed like an open invitation for UNKRA to assume the partnership in an integrated program for which the joint committee system had been created, it was, unfortunately, much less from the viewpoint of the UN agency. The Army was prepared to handle the procurement, transportation and distribution of the supplies, and the military civil assistance command in Korea would, as the only operational element in the field, oversee their end-use; UNKRA's participation in the project would thus be limited to handing a check for a number of millions of dollars to the Army Comptroller and eventually receiving and duly noting a receipt and periodic reports on the disposition of the funds. This could hardly be called a partnership in making policy, or even in operating the program. As such, it was virtually impossible for UNKRA to accept the military proposals without question for they would certainly minimize the impact of UNKRA funds through their control by the U.S. Army. This, it will be recalled, was a possibility which had provoked the objections of other contributors to the UN program at the time of the Agent General's visit to Korea in February, 1951, and at the time the Memorandum of Understanding was signed.

The UN Command's weak budget position did, however, provide an opportunity for UNKRA to make a beginning on its own program of reconstruction while taking over part of the military program. It, also, presented an opportunity for real joint planning which still was the only way for UNKRA's position in Korea to be strengthened, but which the UN Command had, thus far, been rich enough to withstand. The Agent General took the position:

"We will not merely substitute our financing for Army's, but are prepared to develop a real joint program . . . . , I should like to develop some programs to which the Army would make a contribution in the same way that we have been doing toward Army programs . . . ."[3]

The move to get a joint program finally under way was undertaken in a situation where guerrilla activity, partially provoked by communist infiltration and partially by robber bandits' taking advantage of the critical economic conditions, presented dangers even as far south as Pusan. It was, thus, simply impossible for the military authorities to allow a civilian agency to operate in these areas without the protection that came from association with area commanders and this was, in all fairness, understood by UNKRA. The security and economic dangers within South Korea, itself, were, moreover, aggravated by the political crisis that had exploded. President Rhee sought to protect his executive powers from legislative restrictions by pushing through a constitutional amendment providing for the election of the President by direct popular suffrage instead of by the National Assembly. When his proposals were turned down by the Assembly, Rhee used the general elections in May to defeat, through a campaign of intimidation and arrest, those members of the Assembly who had opposed his plans. While the elections returned a high pro-Rhee majority to the legislature, they, also, succeeded in adding new strains to a Korea already tense with the dissatisfaction of living amidst war and want. This was clearly the time to use all resources, under a military-civilian partnership, to protect the rear echelons from endangering the relative security that had been produced in the front lines.[4]

Whatever their differences, UNKRA was now proceeding under the same assumptions as the military authorities in Tokyo and Korea: principally, that there was no imminent hope for a truce, that a dangerous security situation existed behind the lines even if the area around the battlefront was now firm, and that inflation and political instability added to the security threat. There was, however, a difference of opinion as to what could be done within the context of this setting. The UN Command concluded that these circumstances called for continued rigid military supervision over the Korean economic life with a restriction on investment until stability was gained. UNKRA, on the other hand, sought to develop a large recovery program in which the inflationary impact of investment projects would be mitigated by substantial importation of consumer goods for sale, thus making a beginning in the reconstruction job, raising Korean morale, and still attacking the deadly inflationary pressures. Whichever was right, both agencies were basing their actions on a realistic evaluation of the situation, unlike the policymakers in Washington who seemed to be cutting off the Army's power to act while doing nothing to strengthen UNKRA's position, thus leaving a vacuum in a most dangerous situation.

The changes that were necessary to get action—a loosening of the military attitude in the Far East and a willingness to allow UNKRA to carry out a large-scale program even though there was no truce—did not, as one might wish, come about through a far-reaching review of American policy in Korea. It came through the bureaucratic process of a cut in the Army budget and a fortunate change of personnel in key military positions in Washington and Tokyo. By early July, command of the Army's Division of Civil Affairs and Military Government had been assumed by Major General William F. Marquat. General Marquat's contribution toward breaking the log jam was in broad acknowledgment that a reconstruction program could be undertaken under military conditions such as those that existed in Korea, and that a civilian agency could participate in the program even though ultimate authority must, for security reasons, rest with the military commander. His thinking might well be summed up in a statement he later made before the House Committee on Appropriations in May, 1953.

The General pointed out that "the concept of long and short-range rehabilitation with respect to military operations is based upon the normal situation where we go into a military operation for a quick decision and the military is not very much interested in the building up of the country in which it operates." Nevertheless, "since the Korean military situation is in the nature of an impasse at present, and there is at least a prospect of the cold war continuing, we are faced with the fact that the country in which we are operating cannot be maintained for a much longer period of time at a mere bare existence level. Therefore, we have modified the basic concept" and "feel that when the military situation will permit, the commander should devote a great deal of attention to a marshaling of the resources at his disposal to build up the economy of the country." In consequence, "we do not separate long and short-range rehabilitation" but "say rehabilitation is an end in itself and, therefore, it should begin at once . . . . Under this special condition all agencies which are constituted to accomplish rehabilitation now or in the future begin to operate immediately in order to begin restoration of the economy of Korea." Finally, General Marquat established that "instead of having a short-range plan and a long-range plan, we have one plan, and we have the military supervising the plan as of now, with the understanding that it will be turned over to the selected agency upon termination of hostilities. We will, in this manner, avoid the development of an impasse or any period of vacuum with consequent loss of efficiency that would result from canceling a short-range and initiating a subsequent long-range program." [5]

Until the reactivation of the Division of Civil Affairs and Military Government (CAMG) in the spring of 1952, the Army's role in the Korean relief and reconstruction operation had normally been handled through the G-4 (Supply) section. There had thus been an understandable emphasis on the logistical problems raised by the participation of UNKRA in a joint program. CAMG seems to have taken hold of the situation from the broader viewpoint of military and foreign policy, particularly when General Marquat assumed command in June. The General's immediate problem, however, was difficult: if the military had to begin thinking of the feasibility of a civilian agency operating in a military theater before the cessation of hostilities, the civilians had to start modifying the rigid interpretation of the "disease and unrest" formula. Any such narrow view was impractical given the broad role the military had to play because of their control of transportation and distribution facilities and their ultimate authority in the area so long as security risks existed. General Marquat did not, however, seem to agree with the extremely broad interpretation assumed by the military authorities in Tokyo. He later told a congressional committee that "we have tried to be very circumspect about holding the Far East Command to the language of the CRIK [Civilian Relief in Korea, the military program] appropriations and not programming to spread out into general relief which is covered in other appropriations which you gentlemen are asked to provide." [6]

In seeking a balanced concept of the "disease and unrest" formula, General Marquat also modified the rigidity of the anti-investment policy of the Combined Economic Board. Again in a later statement before a congressional committee, he emphasized that "the first requirement, of course, is to give the people . . . food and clothing and medicines; and the next one is to give them some future prospect of getting some work and the restoration of, let us say, industries which produce consumer goods—not inflationary industries, but industries which will produce consumer goods—and then there is the education of their children. Those are functions which rightfully belong to long-range economic agencies such as the UNKRA Agency and not in the Army CRIK funds." [7]

Shortly after taking over command of CAMG, General Marquat left for the Far East with what seems to be three purposes in mind: (1) to review the UN Command's civil relief program in the light of the budget restrictions; (2) to work out a basis for an expansion of the "disease and unrest" formula that would make practical use of the military resources and authority in Korea without going to the extreme of emulating a military government setup and excluding UNKRA; and (3) to impress upon the UN Command the desire and need that reconstruction, with active UNKRA participation, begin immediately. Before leaving, he consulted with UNKRA officials on several occasions, a refreshing departure from the lack of contact with the UN agency at the time the Meyer Mission was leaving for Korea.[8] The General was, thus, aware of what UNKRA could do and had a realistic basis for working out a new approach with the UN Command. Part of the reason for the General's trip seems to have been the continuing reluctance of the military in Washington to issue an order to the theater commander, preferring to work out a system that the field would agree to. Whatever General Marquat did, therefore, would have to remain within the framework of the Memorandum of Understanding and the continued operations of the Combined Economic Board. His was a task of persuasion, backed up by the prestige of his position, but not one of ordering a new policy into effect.

## An UNKRA Program in Spite of Itself

The cuts in the military budget might have thrown the UN Command into the humble position of asking UNKRA to finance part of its program. It made no immediate change in the military fear that the South Korean government would take quick and disastrous advantage of any divided authority that might be UNKRA's price for meeting the request for financing. The policy of the military member of the Combined Economic Board was as rigidly anti-investment as ever. Indeed, prior to General Marquat's visit, the Command seemed to make every effort to discourage UNKRA from drawing up long-range plans for Phase 2, lest they stimulate Korean requests that the plans be realized immediately without waiting for an end to hostilities.

In his talks with General Van Fleet and President Rhee in April and May, Mr. Kingsley had discussed his intentions of bringing expert teams to Korea to begin a blueprint for future operations. He had emphasized that "we must get on with comprehensive long-range planning . . . which we have found difficult to carry out effectively in the past due to the severe limitation of staff housing and facilities." He thus announced plans "to enlist the support of the United Nations specialized agencies, of interested governments, and of a top-flight private firm of economic consultants" and "within a matter of weeks to have working here an agricultural planning team from the FAO, a health team from WHO, and a UNESCO Educational Commission, as well as a team of over-all economic planners." [9]

By early July, the specialized agencies had organized their teams and they were ready to leave for the Far East when Kingsley received word that the UN Command would not agree to their operating in Korea. Van Fleet's prior agreement seems to have been based on his concern to lift South Korean morale and to rebuild the national spirit that would be needed to support the South Korean Army he was now training. By July, however, Van Fleet's control over relief and reconstruction activities had ended with the establishment of a Korean Communications Zone (K COM Z) directly responsible to the UN Command in Tokyo. His reasons for supporting Kingsley's request for a substantial UNKRA program became lost in the UN Command's initial rigidity in applying the counterinflationary measures of the Meyer Agreement.

In what seems to be an accurate reflection of military reaction in Tokyo, the surveys proposed by Kingsley and agreed to by Van Fleet were viewed as questionable as they were complicating. For one thing, it was pointed out that "although Korea has many lacks, it is definitely not lacking in surveys." For another, "CINCUNC cannot allow the prestige of its representative on the Combined Economic Board to be undermined. . . . Nothing could be better calculated to lessen the influence of the CINCUNC representative than to have another agency backed by the prestige of the United Nations making independent surveys and bringing out recommendations which might conceivably conflict with the policies embodied in the Agreement." [10] There was no doubt that the number of surveys made of the Korean economy was almost out of proportion to the problems involved. Most of the survey work had, however, been carried out before the war and had not taken into account the serious destruction and changes that had occurred during the first year of fighting. Moreover,

UNKRA's economic advisers, after several months of intensive research, were later moved to conclude that "though many groups have surveyed Korea since the end of World War II, there is a glaring deficiency of studies dealing with the broad economic problems of the country." [11]

The fear that the UN survey teams would undermine the counterinflationary program the military hoped to push through the Combined Economic Board was completely consistent with their earlier resistance to the idea of UNKRA's participating on the Board. Kingsley was, however, by this time completely committed to the survey teams, having contacted the specialized agencies on his return trip from Korea in May and having followed up by continually urging that the agencies speed up the recruitment of the teams. He, therefore, instructed his Deputy, Sir Arthur Rucker, to point out to the Command that long-range planning was a responsibility of UNKRA under the Memorandum of Understanding and that UNKRA had to have leeway in determining how it was going to carry out this responsibility. By early August, just before the arrival of the public health team organized by the World Health Organization, the military reluctantly agreed to the survey teams on Rucker's assurance that their work would be closely coordinated with the activities of the Civil Assistance Command. This was assurance which was, of course, consistent with the "coordination" clause of the Memorandum of Understanding and essential if the expert teams were going to be allowed to move around Korea with anything like the freedom they needed to conduct surveys of any depth. [12]

The arrival of the survey teams coincided with the arrival of General Marquat in the Far East. In addition to informal meetings, the General participated in the monthly meetings of the joint committees in both Pusan and Tokyo. Without imposing any formula on the UN Command, he made it very clear that the Department of the Army was in favor of a joint UN Command/UNKRA program on the practical basis of making use of all funds available for work in Korea, particularly in view of the reduction of the military budget for relief.

He left it up to the field, however, to develop a program and to decide the precise role UNKRA was to undertake in its operation.[13]

The integrated program that was the only way for UNKRA to have any real status in Korea, no matter what the terms of formal understandings called for, now seemed to be in the making. The increasing stability along the battlefront and instability in the rear echelons, the restrictions on the Army's budget for Korean relief and the high level military support impressed upon the UN Command by General Marquat, and the presence of a full cadre of experts, now all converged to form a more sympathetic environment than had ever existed. Moreover, the risk that an UNKRA program might still be delayed in the process of clearance was minimized as military responsibility for relief and reconstruction was assumed, shortly after General Marquat's visit, by Admiral Byron Hanlon, first, as General Clark's personal representative on the Combined Economic Board and, then, as the chief of the UN Command's J-5 section.[14]

An integrated economic recovery program, however, needed more than cooperation; it needed a framework of political policy if it was going to be developed on any long-range basis. What kind of Korea did the recovery program have to support? The question was only in the process of being answered in the autumn of 1952. On UNKRA's side, the WHO team was soon joined by teams from the Food and Agricultural Organization and the UN Educational, Scientific and Cultural Organization, as well as a private firm of economic consultants.[15] On the UN Command's side, the military training program undertaken the previous summer by General Van Fleet now began to supply some idea of the size of an army that the South Koreans could handle. In the meanwhile, immediate needs had to be viewed from a short range. The UNKRA program that was approved during this period was, in the light of the current situation, a mixed program that augmented the Army's program of importing consumer goods, but still provided the first stage in an investment program for Korean reconstruction.

The Republic of Korea was brought into the picture through the organization of a Coordinating Committee, made up of representatives of the government, the UN Command, and UNKRA. For all intents and purposes, the Coordinating Committee, practically, if not formally, superseded the joint committees in Korea and Tokyo. These presumably continued to exist under the terms of the Memorandum of Understanding, but there were no meetings after early October when the Coordinating Committee was formed. With the government and UN Command members, Minister Paik Too Chin and Admiral Hanlon, also representing their agencies on the Combined Economic Board, the Coordinating Committee brought UNKRA into relationship with the Board just as it brought South Koreans into what was, in fact, the joint committee system in simplified form.

The Coordinating Committee, thus, for the first time, provided a mechanism for quick decision. The Committee was actually constituted at a meeting held in Pusan on October 20, at which time UNKRA presented a Plan of Expenditure calling for the expenditure of $70,000,000 for approval.[16] At its second meeting, three days later, the Committee approved all of the projects in the program that were not already in operation.[17] While the projects approved by the Committee had been worked up through the staffs of all three agencies and already informally reviewed by all parties, they did not have to be referred to any other committee outside Korea or to the South Korean government as was the case when the Korea Joint Committee had been operating. The lack of Korean participation which had weakened the joint committee system had been made up. Moreover, American support of UNKRA seemed, through the back door of the restrictions on the military budget, to have been finally impressed on the UN Command during General Marquat's visit.

With the approvals of the UN Command and the South Korean government in hand, Kingsley presented the program to his Advisory Committee in November. There was, by now, a tendency for the members of the Committee (other than the United States) to be cautious in the light of a growing disillusionment with the possibility of multilateral programming in Korea and with the Rhee government. They were, however, presented with a *fait accompli* and almost had to approve the program.[18] Any possibility that the program might be rejected by the Committee was avoided by having cleared the major features with the State Department in Washington while the projects were being prepared for submission to the Coordinating Committee in the field. Such a strategy insured U.S. concurrence when the program came up for a vote and U.S. support against objections from other members.

The mixed nature of the program was evident in that $20,000,000 of the total $70,000,000 was set aside for the importation of grains and fertilizers. The extensive project of commodity imports had a threefold purpose: (1) to provide grains to help meet the food shortage brought on by a poor harvest in 1952; (2) to provide fertilizers to be used in the hope of producing a successful crop in 1953; and (3) to drain money off the market by offering these commodities for sale and, thus, assisting in the counterinflationary program. In addition to the commodity imports, the program included a number of projects of a social or investment nature: the rehabilitation of medical schools and hospitals; the restoration of libraries and the equipping of schools; the construction and equipping of agricultural experiment stations and veterinary laboratories; the construction of a textbook printing plant; the rehabilitation of secondary railroads in the rice-growing areas; the rehabilitation of textile mills; and a program of housing construction using manually operated earth block machines that would make maximum use of indigenous materials. Investigatory projects were to be undertaken to lay the groundwork for major capital investment through the construction of cement, fertilizer and flat glass plants. Finally, provisions were included for the continued research of the public health, agricultural, educational and economic survey teams to prepare a blueprint for a more comprehensive recovery program to be undertaken at a later stage.[19]

The approvals of the South Korean government, the UN Command and the UNKRA Advisory Committee were, as long and involved as they may have been, but steps in the actual launching of the program. UNKRA still needed financing. Despite pledges totalling $205,590,806, the agency had only received slightly more than $18,000,000 by mid-September of 1952.[20] With the approval of the $70,000,000 program by the Advisory Committee in November, Kingsley approached the governments to make good on their pledges in order that the agency be in a position to commit funds. The United States pledge still stood at $162,500,000, or sixty-five per cent of the originally proposed initial program of $250,000,000; only $10,000,000 had, however, actually been contributed to UNKRA under the restrictions of the agency's limited program and the cautious warnings in the language of the appropriations bills. By the end of 1952, however, sufficient funds had been appropriated to enable the United States to make quick payment to UNKRA in meeting its share of the $70,000,000 program. The act of actually turning substantial sums over to the UN agency for the first time seems to have stimulated several basic policy questions.[21]

The easiest question to resolve was whether the UNKRA program should include funds for the importation of grains. If the military were to be restricted to relief operations under the "disease and unrest" formula, should not UNKRA be restricted to "reconstruction" if a confusing overlapping of responsibility and funding was to be avoided? As desirable as a clear-cut differentiation between "relief" and "reconstruction" may have been, it was recognized that there had to be flexibility in the very unclear period of truce negotiations. Moreover, the inability of the Army to meet the commodity needs completely was considered justification for using

UNKRA to fill the gap after good evidence was presented that available South Korean and military resources were being used to the maximum in the total commodity import program.

It was more difficult to answer whether the proposed UNKRA program was consistent with the counterinflationary program that had been the purpose of the Economic Coordination Agreement negotiated by the Meyer Mission. The commodity import project had the additional advantage of giving UNKRA the means to earn local currency through the sale of grains and fertilizer, and thus pay the expenses of its program without new won drawings. Indeed, the program had been intentionally designed to comprise a self-paying unit so that its total effect would not be inflationary. Also, since the commodity import project could be put into operation earlier than the investment projects where plans and procurement had a longer lead time, the immediate effect of the program would be counterinflationary. Yet as well-intentioned as the program may have been, there was no guarantee that its total effect would be counterinflationary when taken in relationship with the programs being undertaken by the Republic of Korea and the UN Command. The perfect answer (if there was one) lay, of course, in a completely integrated program. But if the mechanism for achieving such a program had finally been established in the Coordinating Committee in Korea, the program itself was only in the process of development and would still take time. UNKRA could, of course, continue to be kept under limitations until an integrated program could be presented. Nevertheless, pressures for the program were being exerted by the Koreans and the military authorities in the Far East, as well as UNKRA. The fact that it was geared to pay for itself was thus accepted as the best response to the inflationary issue under existing conditions.

Consideration of an integrated program going beyond the relief formula of the earlier military programs and beyond the initial small investment projects of the present UNKRA proposals, posed in itself far-reaching questions that Washington now began to examine for the first time in two years. What was the possible magnitude and shape of the long-range program? At the time UNKRA had been established, a tentative program of $250,000,000 had been planned for the first year of operations. It was clear, then, and clearer now in 1952 that the total cost of Korean reconstruction would be four or five times the amount of the first program. Yet, after almost two years of negotiations, pledges to the UNKRA program had only reached slightly over the $200,000,000 mark and it was seriously questioned whether more than $150,000,000 could actually be collected. Stated rather bluntly, this meant that UNKRA was not going to have the money to carry out the program of Korean reconstruction unless the United States made up the difference between total costs and contributions from other governments even if this meant that the United States would wind up paying ninety or more per cent of the bill. Stated equally bluntly, there was no question but that Congress would never appropriate funds to permit a contribution greater than sixty-five per cent of the total.[22] It was only logical to conclude, therefore, that UNKRA was never going to be able to do the job of reconstructing Korea.

If the magnitude of the long-range program posed an insurmountable problem, the shape that the program seemed destined to take loomed equally menacingly in the path of the multilateral approach. Despite the decision to go to the aid of the desperate Republic of Korea in June, 1950, and the subsequent commitment of several hundred thousand ground troops, Korea remained, as it had in 1949, a poor place for the United States to fight a war. Since the weak South Korean Army proved an equally weak deterrent to aggression, the United States, as soon as the tide of battle had been turned back, had started an intensive training program. In the late spring of 1951 Generals Ridgway and Van Fleet began to build up an effective South Korean force that could assume the major ground responsibility in holding back another communist threat. By the fall of 1952, the South Korea Army had been increased from the 65,000 limit the United States was supporting at the time of the communist invasion, to 14 combat trained divisions of about 14,000 troops each, and provision had already been made for the United States to train and support an additional 6 divisions for a total 20-division South Korean Army.[23]

The long-range economic aid program that the United States military authorities in the Far East were, at last, beginning to put together (and that the Rhee government was demanding) was, therefore, based on support for this substantial defense establishment. With economic aid principally a defense support effort, a UN agency could not, by its very nature of being a creation of the UN General Assembly, assume major responsibility for the program even if it could muster the necessary financial resources. Thus, UNKRA might very well become added baggage that the United States could ill afford to carry. Yet if UNKRA were allowed to begin to operate the $70,000,000 program, it would become so intricately involved in the real work of reconstruction as to complicate the larger defense support program that was certain to get under way sooner or later. By withholding payment of its contribution to the $70,000,000 program, the United States could instantly kill off the agency before it started and avoid the complications that were sure to arise in the future.

The decision was nevertheless made to contribute despite the conclusion that the agency was not going to be able to undertake the long-range program of reconstruction. It seems to have been based on the premise that the United States could not acknowledge, at this stage at any rate, that the whole Korean conflict was not a UN affair. As long as the United States was committed to the halting of communism on the Korean peninsula, reluctantly or not, it had sought since 1947 to internationalize its commitment and could not now retreat. A refusal to support the present UNKRA program despite the logic of doing so, would have meant more than the death of a UN agency. It would have exposed the weaknesses of achieving international support for the American commitment in Korea before a truce had been gained and the future of the peninsula determined.

Early in January, 1953, the United States, therefore, transferred sufficient funds, within the sixty-five per cent/thirty-five per cent ratio, to enable UNKRA to move ahead with its $70,000,000 program. This action did nothing, however, to remove the obvious dichotomy that was now fast developing in American policy: support for a UN Korean Reconstruction Agency, on the one hand, and a South Korean defense support program on the other. During this same month, Dwight D. Eisenhower was inaugurated as the first Republican president in twenty years.

## The End of the Second Year

The dilemma of American reconstruction policy in Korea by the time of the Presidential election had gained almost unsolvable proportions. It consisted fundamentally in seeking to internationalize an American commitment. The allies of the United States were, however, beginning to balk at the costs of sharing a burden that was not a matter of their immediate concern and that the United States would have to assume even if they refused to meet their quota. Moreover, the establishment of a large South Korean defense force under the domination of the Rhee government seemed hardly what they had bargained for in following the United States into the Korean conflict.

In doing little more than holding the line in reconstruction and keeping the allies pledged to contribute to the program, the United States unwittingly allowed the course of events to overtake its policy. By the end of 1952, there was little hope that Korean reconstruction could ever be a UN responsibility even if it remained in the interest of the United States that it be so. And yet a deep reassessment of policy during the course of the year might well have exposed its very weakness and jeopardized the whole idea of collective action that seemed, with the possible avoidance of World War III, a major achievement worthy of the frustrations of the truce negotiations.

From the time of the Memorandum of Understanding, therefore, the problems of Korean reconstruction were handled on a day-to-day basis even at the risk of temporary contradictions. In such a situation, the focus of power in Korean economic affairs became fixed in the military authorities in the Far East. As the needs of Korea became ever more critical, the mandate and facilities available to the UN Command offered them the opportunity to fill the vacuum created by the cautious reluctance to finance a civilian-directed program while a threat of new hostilities hovered over the truce negotiations. Yet, while their mandate was strengthened and broadened by the economic agreement finally signed with the South Korean government in May, military facilities were suddenly weakened and narrowed by the terms of their budget.

The contradiction of extending the military's responsibility and then restricting their means was perhaps exceeded by the more fundamental contradiction of continuing to support the idea of a UN reconstruction program while simultaneously supporting plans for an extension of the South Korean army. There is nothing illogical in an economic aid program supporting the development of native ground troops friendly to the United States. The logic was based on several factors: that the Republic of Korea was in danger, that the danger was a threat either to American security or to American global interests, and that it was preferable, from the point of view of military strategy, that the danger be, initially at any rate, met by South Korean rather than United States ground troops. But it should have been more readily recognized that the development of substantial South Korean military forces was fast destroying the environment that any kind of UN program needed either for the settlement of political disputes or the reconstruction of the economy.

American policy in support of a reconstruction policy for Korea had been based on the political and military situation that existed before the Chinese Communists entered the conflict. Nevertheless, after making the decision to fight a limited war and live with a divided and potentially dangerous Korea, nothing was done to change that policy or to seek to adjust the political and military factors in the new situation so as to provide an environment in which the original policy could be realized. Thus, the narrow perspective of a military-dominated reconstruction program and the political force of a growing South Korean Army soon created a situation in which it was impossible to follow a multilateral policy effectively.

1. Memorandum from Colonel Walter R. Hensey, Jr., Assistant Chief of Staff, G-5, CINCUNC to Sir Arthur Rucker, Deputy Agent General, UNKRA, dated July 3, 1952 (Kingsley papers).

2. *Ibid.*

3. Cable from Agent General Kingsley to Deputy Agent General Rucker, dated July 9, 1951 (Kingsley papers).

4. See *New York Times* report on the Agent General Kingsley's evaluation of the situation upon his return from Korea in early June; *ibid.,* June 4, 1952, p. 2.

5. Hearings before a subcommittee of the Committee on Appropriations, House of Representatives, 83rd Congress, 1st Session, *Department of the Army Appropriations for 1954* (Washington: Government Printing Office, 1953), pp. 613–14.

6. *Ibid.,* p. 584.

7. Hearings before a subcommittee of the Committee on Appropriations, House of Representatives, 83rd Congress, 1st Session, *2nd Supplemental Appropriation Bill for 1953* (Washington: Government Printing Office, 1953), pp. 577–78. General Marquat was, at this time, defending the Army request for CRIK for the second half of the fiscal year from January 1 through June 30, 1953, the assumption that the UN Command would transfer full responsibility to UNKRA at the end of 1952 having proved wrong (as, indeed, everyone should have realized at the time it was made).

8. See above, p. 117.

9. Kingsley/Van Fleet letter, May 6, 1952, pp. 1–2.

10. Heer, *Report on Relationship of Proposed UNKRA Program to Counter-inflationary Objectives of the Agreement on Economic Coordination,* pp. 13–14.

11. Preliminary Nathan Report, Letter of Transmittal, p. 2.

12. When the WHO team arrived in Korea, UNKRA, at the request of the military authorities, sent the members a memorandum which, *inter alia,* cautioned that "it is obviously of great importance to avoid any risk of the UN Agencies in Korea speaking to the Government with two voices . . . . No difficulty should arise if discussions with the Government are confined in general to long-range planning and if UNKRA, and through them the military authorities concerned, are kept currently informed of the progress of such discussions . . . ."

13. Minutes of UNC-UNKRA Joint Committee Meeting, Tokyo, August 21, 1952.

14. *New York Times,* September 8, 1952, p. 2.

15. Robert R. Nathan Associates, Inc., of Washington, D.C.

16. Minutes of the 1st Meeting of Coordinating Committee (ROK-UNKRA-UNC), Pusan, Korea, October 20, 1952.

17. Minutes of the 2nd Meeting of Coordinating Committee (ROK-UNKRA-

UNC), Pusan, Korea, October 23, 1952. The Plan of Expenditure was for the financial year from July 1, 1952 through June 30, 1953, already commenced, and thus included the few projects that had already been cleared through the joint committees. Although several projects were reconsidered at later meetings, the general approval of the 2nd meeting gave some indication of action that could be taken given the authority and attitude Admiral Hanlon obviously possessed.

18. The difficulties in finding UN financing for the program were more clearly apparent the following year.

19. UN General Assembly, Seventh Session, *Official Records,* Supplement No. 19A (A/2222/Addenda 1 and 2), pp. iv and 1–3. The commodity import program was originally approved at $14,000,000, but shortly afterwards increased to $20,000,000 at the request of the Agent General, see p. 2.

20. *Ibid.,* Supplement No. 19 (A/2222), p. 38.

21. The inter-departmental discussions that went on in Washington in November and December, 1952, have been summarized from a series of interviews conducted in October, 1956; in a cable to the Deputy Agent General on November 18, 1952, Mr. Kingsley pointed out the two immediate problems that had been raised in Washington (and which, subsequently, provoked more fundamental problems of policy): whether the commodity imports should properly be in an UNKRA program; and whether the United States contribution could exceed two-thirds of the total contribution in hand at any time unless there was firm assurance that the other third was being met (Kingsley papers).

22. The problem of dwindling contributions became critical by late 1953, as had been feared a year earlier.

23. Captain Robert Sawyer, *U.S. Military Advisory Group to the Republic of Korea,* Parts I & II, pp. 62, 161–62. Also, for information of the South Korean troop development program, see the testimony of General James A. Van Fleet, following his return from Korea, before the Committee on Armed Services, House of Representatives, 83rd Congress, 1st Session (Washington: Government Printing Office, 1953), particularly pp. 331–35, 342.

CHAPTER VII

# THE SHIFT TO A BILATERAL POLICY

*The Presidential Election of 1952*
*Training the South Korean Army*
*The Change in Agents General*
*The Armistice Is Signed*

# THE SHIFT TO A BILATERAL POLICY

## The Presidential Election of 1952

The Korean conflict raised more questions for the American people than it answered. What was wrong with the most powerful nation in the world that it allowed itself to get pinned down in a part of the world that its military experts said was a poor place to fight? What was the use of having power if it could not be used? Behind the questions, there seemed to be a real yearning for direction, almost a nostalgia for wars that had an ending.

Long before the presidential campaign of 1952, the Republican party too had started to ask questions—questioning the consistency of having maintained that the Republic of Korea was outside the U.S. "defense perimeter" and having then sent troops into the peninsula to fight; and questioning whether it was to the interest of the United States to restrict its independence of action in Korea through participation in a collective enterprise under United Nations auspices. Except for an initial emotional response, neither the party nor the American people, however, went so far as General MacArthur in suggesting that "when all other political means [fail], you then go to force; and when you do that, the balance of control, the balance of concept, the main interest involved, the minute you reach the killing stage, is the control of the military . . . when men become locked in battle . . . there should be no artifice under the name of politics, which should handicap your own men, decrease their chances for winning, and increase their losses." [1]

In a remarkable and fortunate demonstration of what must be the basic sanity of the American people even in the midst of confusion and frustration, the Republican party chose General MacArthur to be its keynote speaker, but not its presidential candidate. Nevertheless the rejection of the extreme

155

MacArthur position did not completely eliminate the deep desire to pursue a direct, controlled course in settling the Korean conflict. An anti-MacArthur Republican like Senator Flanders understood that the whole concept of a limited war leaves the people with "a sort of vacuum." He went on to explain that "it is my strong belief that the attractiveness of General MacArthur's program is . . . that he proposes something to put in [this aching void] . . . and nobody else does." [2]

While there may be some doubt as to whether a presidential campaign offers the best forum for a clear-cut review of foreign policy, the candidates must justify what was done and promise what will be done. In the process, they must deal with the major issues and thus stimulate public opinion to indicate the broad policies it will sustain even if the details remain obscured in the vagaries of campaign oratory.[3] Moreover, a political campaign demonstrates how "domestic" problems of American foreign policy usually are.[4] This was particularly true of the Korean issue.

Senator Robert A. Taft had begun what was to be his last attempt to gain the Republican nomination for the Presidency long before General Eisenhower returned from his military assignment as head of the NATO forces to don his political mantle. Taft was deeply concerned with what seemed to him a growing tendency for the power to declare war to be taken out of the hands of Congress and placed in the Presidency. While recognizing that the President undoubtedly had "the ability to involve the United States in war," Taft questioned whether he had "the right" to do so, not only under the terms of the Constitution but under the fundamental tenets of the theory of the separation of powers of which the Constitution was the most eloquent expression. "In the case of Korea," Taft was firm in holding that "we had no right to send troops to a nation, with whom we had no treaty, to defend it against attack by another nation, no matter how unprincipled that aggression might be, unless the whole matter was submitted to Congress and a declaration of war or some other direct authority obtained." [5] Taft's biographer, William S. White, has told us how the Senator yearned for a world where foreign policy did not exist. "I wish I could just stay out of foreign policy," he is quoted as saying, "but of course I can't." And later: "I am charged with moving in on foreign policy; the truth is that foreign policy has moved in on me." [6] So it was with the Korean conflict. Like Taft, the American people undoubtedly would have preferred to stay out of the Korean conflict entirely. But once it had "moved in on" them, like Taft again, "there seemed to be no choice except to see it through."

Almost immediately upon entering the campaign, General Eisenhower, also, had the Korean issue "move in on him." The General, however, was obviously still feeling his way and would only say that he did "not see any prescription for bringing [the conflict] to a decisive end." He could not, for the moment, offer a more constructive program than "to stand firm and to take every possible step we can to reduce our losses and to stand right there and try to get a decent armistice out of it." [7] Within a week, Eisenhower had gone further in developing a policy by asserting that, since "there was no possibility of a decisive victory . . . he favored building up the South Korean fighting force to a point where the United Nations could withdraw." [8] By now, too, Taft seems to have concluded that anything as decisive as driving the Chinese out of Korea and asking the United Nations to set up a Korean Republic, as he had once advocated, was out of the question. The next best move was to "drag our feet in the Korean truce talks until American arms production got rolling and then arm the South Koreans and withdraw the United Nations forces fighting there." [9]

By the time the Republican convention met, both major candidates had thus agreed that the moment for decisive military action had passed (if, indeed, it ever existed after the Chinese Communists entered the conflict except under the risk of opening World War III). They also agreed that the best solution was to try to get a settlement that would enable the United States to withdraw its military forces from Korea while developing a South Korean army to fill the gap. This

development tended to coincide with the national desire for
an honorable, even if inconclusive, end to a most unsatisfying
war and commitment. But it was more in keeping with political
tradition that the platform adopted by the convention charged
that "[the Democratic administration] plunged us into war
in Korea without the consent of our citizens through their authorized representatives in Congress and . . . carried out
that war without will to victory." [10] If the Republican platform seemed to emphasize Taftian accusations and fears, the
convention's choice of Eisenhower as the party's candidate
was more in meeting the less complicated national mood.

The Eisenhower wing of the Republican party sought to
play down the who-brought-on-the-Korean war battle. But
the obvious concession to Taft in drawing up a foreign policy plank that directly pinned responsibility on the Truman
Administration was too stinging a blow to be ignored by the
Democrats. They, in the way of politics, had to defend the conduct of their party in office. They rose to counterattack under
the leadership of Senator Paul Douglas in the pre-nominating
days of the Democratic convention. Senator Douglas reminded
his audience (if they needed reminding, or were, in the manner of convention audiences, even listening) that General Eisenhower, as Army Chief of Staff and General MacArthur, as
Chief of the Far East Command, had both concurred in the
opinion of the Joint Chiefs of Staff that the withdrawal of
United States troops from the Korean peninsula (finally completed in mid-1949) was strategically necessary. The commitment of ground forces on the Asian continent would have
been a disastrous handicap in the event of the outbreak of a
major war. Douglas went on to point out that placing the
Korean peninsula outside the "defense perimeter" of the United
States had not placed the Republic of Korea outside the concern of the United States. The Truman administration had
been prepared to support a South Korean army and assist in
the development of a viable South Korean economy. This was
thwarted by the short-sighted opposition of the Republicans
in Congress who delayed passage of the Korean Aid Bill in

1949 and 1950 while the Soviet Union was building up a strong force north of the 38th parallel.[11]

Both the Democratic platform committee and candidate, however, like General Eisenhower, seemed to sense the public yearning for a solution to fill the "empty void" rather than a re-hash of old accusations. In the foreign policy plank in their platform, the Party thus claimed that "Korea has proved once and for all, that the United Nations will resist aggression" and urged "continual effort, by every honorable means, to bring about a fair and effective peace settlement in Korea in accordance with the principles" of the United Nations Charter. The convention's choice, Adlai Stevenson, in turn, defended the Administration's intervention in the Korean conflict as "the only thing we dared to do," but cautioned against being "stampeded into a new set of objectives which might well mean heavier involvement in war in the Far East." [12]

If it can be said that political conventions seek to come up with candidates and promises that will meet the mood of the people, then the moderation with which Eisenhower and Stevenson both seemed to approach the Korean issue, indicated a measure of success. If the nation had rejected the risky heroics of the MacArthur plan, then it most certainly had also rejected any unheroic withdrawal and retreat that the Old Guard Republicans might have suggested. Both candidates refused to consider backing down, but were equally sure that the electorate sought a way out without losing whatever moral achievement had been gained in leading a collective effort to resist communist aggression. It was the task of the campaigners to come up with ideas on how this could be done.

In coming around to offer a solution, Eisenhower soon tore into what he called "the incompetence of political leaders which made military action [in Korea] necessary." He suggested that Acheson's "defense perimeter" speech was an example of the incompetence he had in mind.[13] For the future, he saw "no sense in the United Nations, with America bearing the brunt of the thing, being constantly compelled to man [the] front lines." He insisted that "if there must be a war [in Korea], let it be Asians against Asians, with our support on the side of freedom." [14] If the General's way of expressing what was already in the process of being carried out shocked the sensibilities of many, President Truman soon disclosed that the policy of training South Koreans to "man the front lines" was "one of the major achievements of our policy in Korea—and one of the major achievements of our armed forces during the last eighteen months." [15]

The President, obviously stung by the accusation that his Administration had been doing nothing to meet the demand to reduce American manpower commitments in Korea, went so far as to disclose that:

> The United States is now supporting Republic of Korea military forces totaling approximately 400,000 men. Our training schools are turning out 14,000 South Korean soldiers a month. There are 50 per cent more South Korean troops in the battle lines today than there are Americans.
>
> . . . . . . . . . . . .
>
> It takes a long time to make good officers. It takes a good while to train men to handle modern weapons and to service them. But we are making excellent progress.
>
> . . . . . . . . . . . .
>
> Ultimately, it is our objective to have a Korean Republic completely able to defend itself. But this will not be possible so long as the offensive power of the Communist conspiracy is concentrated on South Korea.[16]

The party hammering to get in can deal in generalities and leave impressions of what should be done. The party in power, politically accountable for the past conduct of government, must deal with the facts of its policy or risk being tripped up by someone who knows the facts. How did the record in Korea substantially differ from advocating that "it be Asians against Asians, with our support on the side of freedom?" Certainly, training South Koreans was preparing Asians to fight "against Asians;" and supporting the Rhee government was, in the eyes of most politicians in 1952, supporting "the side of freedom," if only, some might dare admit, comparatively speaking. If there was little difference between what the Republicans were urging and the Democrats were doing, then the choice had to be made on the basis of who could do it best and quickest; and on this score the Democrats were at a disadvantage, having had the power but not having done it. Here Eisenhower ran over the top when he offered the impression that he would do it personally and immediately by going to Korea if he were elected.[17] Here was the dramatic proof of how a fresh new approach could solve old problems! Eisenhower carried the day.

There is no adequate way to measure the influence of the Korean issue on the Eisenhower victory except, perhaps, to rely on experienced insight. For example, Arthur Krock ranked Korea high on the list of reasons for Eisenhower's election and explained that: "The trend in favor of a change was solidified and expounded by the military stalemate in Korea, and by the charges of Administration critics that incompetent statecraft permitted the war to break out and indecisive policy accounted for the stalemate and the continuing casualties." [18]

Yet, in the case of Korea, it must be made clear that the change was not going to be in basic policy, but only in the way that policy would be carried out. Eisenhower had never, during the campaign, charged the Democratic administration with not doing the right thing once involved in the conflict; he was in favor of holding the present battleline, continuing the negotiations with the communist side, training South Korean troops, and withdrawing American units as quickly as local units could be put into the line. What he charged was that none of these things was being done very well. Indeed, during the final days of the campaign, he had released a personal letter from General Van Fleet which emphasized a lack of support from Washington in training the South Korean Army:

. . . The ROK Army is in apple pie order . . . . Thank goodness, I have insisted on high standards in the ROK school system and replacement training centers, and have a goodly number of replacements in the pipeline.

I have done this on my own responsibility with very little encouragement and never an approval for any increases. I am confident that approval will be granted post haste for an increased ceiling in the ROK Army . . . .

You know that I have felt all the time that we should be preparing strenuously all during the past year for what may eventually be required, and that my plans include doubling the size of the ROK Army—twenty divisions instead of ten. I said, "Give me six and I would release two United States divisions; or, give me four and I would release one United States division." It finally got down to a two-division increase, but still no approval to this date.[19]

Secretary of Defense Lovett immediately pointed out that General Van Fleet had been given all the support he needed; Van Fleet, however, wanted to build up the South Korean Army faster than the Pentagon and Generals Ridgway and Clark thought practical or wise.[20] In this battle of the experts, the lay public was completely at the mercy of the last, most convincing speaker. The greatest expert of them all, General Eisenhower had, by bringing the subject up in the first place, made it very clear that the training of the South Korean Army and the consequent withdrawal of American troops from the fighting front, could be handled more quickly than it was. And the people elected him to do just that.

In the sprawling way that is the process of democracy, the people had now spoken. They had not repudiated the United Nations for, except for the lunatic fringe, both political parties were committed to the continued support of the United Nations and had said so in their platforms. But they had made it quite evident that little would be accepted as an excuse to delay the return of American soldiers from Korea. It was, thus, equally evident that an economic aid program for South Korea had to be based on the support of the largest military force that country could sustain and that such a basis all but eliminated the feasibility of operating the program through the United Nations. There, other governments that did not have such a keen interest in the development of a South Korean army might be in a position to influence its course.

## Training the South Korean Army

The President-elect spent several days in Korea early in December. For whatever could have been accomplished in a closely guarded, tightly timed trip of this kind, there is no reason to doubt that it did both him and the American people considerable good. If anything, Eisenhower learned from American military leaders on the spot that building up the South Korean Army into a first class fighting force was still going to take considerable time no matter what he may have grown to believe in the passion of the campaign wind-up. Even the South Korean leaders who, however irritating they may have been in negotiations with the UN Command, had always come out very impressively in their willingness to fight their own battles if given the weapons, had to admit that they could not yet hold the line against the communists. They asked for quicker and more military and economic aid.[21]

This was not the first time that the development of a South Korean army had been a major preoccupation of the United States. As early as 1946, General Hodge had been interested in the need to develop a Korean army in the area under United States control. But he was cautioned not to build up a local force that might complicate the union of the American and Russian zones into a single Korean nation. American efforts from then on were concentrated on the creation of a constabulary force for internal policing purposes with a simultaneous de-emphasis on this force being used to foster or defend national aims.[22] As the United States began to look to the withdrawal of its own troops, however, some thought had to be given to conversion of the constabulary to a more formidable national defense force if it was going to assume any of the responsibility for keeping the communists north of the 38th parallel. Late in 1947, therefore, General Hodge, in response to a request from the Joint Chiefs of Staff, suggested that a South Korean army of six divisions could be trained and equipped in one year. In transmitting Hodge's recommendations to Washington, however, General MacArthur warned against establishing a South Korean army prematurely.[23] Several months later, MacArthur again argued against a South Korean army "because of the limited training facilities in Korea, the lack of competent Korean leadership, and the diminishing capabilities of XXIV Corps (General Hodge's Command) to foster such an army." He suggested that the South Korean constabulary be increased to 50,000 and equipped from U.S. Army sources in Korea. In April, 1948, the Department of the Army, following MacArthur's advice, authorized General Hodge to train and equip a South Korean constabulary of 50,000 in order "to create conditions so that American forces could be withdrawn from Korea at the end of 1948." [24]

At the time the National Security Council recommended to the President in early 1949 that a complete withdrawal of United States forces was "politically and militarily desirable," it also recommended that military aid be based on a South Korean force further increased to 65,000 men.[25] Nevertheless, the observation has been made that "before the Communist invasion, United States military assistance to the Republic of Korea was predicated upon the policy that the South Korean military establishment was an internal security force"; and further that: "equipment furnished by the United States was to permit the development of an organization that could maintain security within the borders of the Republic of Korea, while, incidentally, deterring attacks from north of the thirty-eighth parallel." [26] United States military aid was not only limited to supporting a force level of only 65,000, but also excluded items of heavy equipment such as tanks and 155mm. howitzers. These limits were justified on military practicality given the terrain factors in Korea and Korean inexperience; but, secondarily, it would seem, on the fear that Syngman Rhee might take off on military adventures of his own.[27] Nevertheless, not even the light equipment to have been provided under the Military Defense Assistance Program for fiscal year 1950 had reached Korea when the communists struck.[28]

The South Koreans were in no condition to meet the planned, trained drive from the north and their meager forces were quickly split under the force of the attack.[29] But the importance of the South Koreans' taking a major role in their defense quickly became a matter of political if not military concern. Undoubtedly moved by the frantic cry for arms from the Rhee government, Ambassador Muccio, as soon as the remnants of the South Korean Army were regrouped and UN forces took the line, called for the United States to arm "as many able-bodied South Koreans as possible without regard to the pre-war limitation." [30] General MacArthur, however, was fighting a war and showed little patience for untrained irregular troops. By the time he had launched the Inchon landings, the Joint Chiefs of Staff had started to think about the size and composition of the army Korea would need to consolidate the nation. They went so far as to request and receive the views of MacArthur "that postwar Republic of Korea ground forces should consist of ten infantry divisions with necessary nondivisional combat and technical and administrative services to support a total strength of approximately 250,000 men." [31] The intervention of Chinese Communists into the conflict, however, suspended any future planning in the turmoil of the immediate crisis.

In January, 1951, President Rhee now sent a direct call for arms to man the front with Korean youth. But it was, again, MacArthur's brutally realistic appraisal that the weapons at his disposal would be best put into the hands of the Japanese Police Reserve than used to create new South Korean units and that inexperienced Korean manpower could be better used to replace losses in existing units. The General went on to note that: "the long-range requirements for or desirability of arming additional ROK personnel appeared to him to be dependent upon determination of the future United States military position with respect both to the Korean campaign and the generally critical situation in the Far East." [32] The General's comment was undoubtedly meant to underscore what he considered a lack of firm Far Eastern policy and to remind the Joint Chiefs that they had to make such decisions, not the theater commander.

The Department of the Army then proceeded to carry out a preliminary study to determine the future force level of the South Korean Army the United States would have to support once the UN Command had stabilized the ground action, the South Koreans had taken over the major task of containing the enemy and the Chinese Communists had begun what would eventually be complete withdrawal. After several weeks of work, the Army asked the General for his comments on its plans to support a South Korean Army of ten infantry divisions, totaling 300,000 men. MacArthur, just a few days before his dismissal, informed the Department that he considered his earlier proposal of ten divisions totaling 250,000 men "still sound." On April 18, therefore, Army Chief of Staff, General Collins, approved the MacArthur level as a basis for future planning. He sent General Van Fleet to take on the immediate job of training South Korean troops against this force level, as well as to assume command of the Eighth Army as General Ridgway moved over to Tokyo.[33]

By early summer Ridgway and Van Fleet had worked out a training plan which would "require at least three years to develop an effective ROK Army [or two years] if fighting stopped in Korea." In relaying details of the plan to Washington, however, Ridgway emphasized that "the United States could not afford to enter an armament race with the Soviet Union through the medium of United States–equipped Republic of Korea divisions versus Russian-equipped North Korean or Chinese Communist divisions." He suggested alternatively that "the ROK Army's effectiveness should be based on its strength of ten divisions, rather than on the estimated requirements of a ROK Army capable of withstanding future Communist aggression." [34] General Ridgway's precise reasons for cautioning against building up a South Korean army sufficiently powerful to resist future communist aggression are not evident. Nevertheless, an immediate corollary to his scheme was the continued readiness of United States ground units to be thrown into battle to defend the Republic of Korea against further aggression. Ridgway may have viewed the training program in the light of his own shock, later expressed, that "the state of our Army in Japan at the outbreak of the Korean War was inexcusable." [35] It was clear that if the South Korean Army, once developed to its maximum capacity and efficiency, was still not capable of withstanding communist aggression and if the territorial integrity of the Republic of Korea continued to be of concern to the United States, then the United States had no alternative but to maintain force in readiness to come, once again, to the assistance of the Republic. The only choice the United States would seem to have, would be to determine whether the force sent in would be confined to sea and air power, with the possible use of nuclear weapons, or would again consist principally of ground troops with the purpose of keeping the conflict localized.

During the following year, the training program shot ahead under General Van Fleet's guidance and so, indeed, did the South Korean force levels. By the fall of 1952, the South Korean Army had already been increased to fourteen divisions and the size of each division fixed at 14,000 men. [36] Moreover, the target was now fixed at a 20-division ROK army, mainly, it seems, under Van Fleet's urging as well. Nevertheless there was some question as to how quickly the training program could produce the leadership and technical ability for the South Koreans to manage such a large defense establishment. But if there remained questions as to how quickly a 20-division ROK army could be put on its own military feet and exactly what part it might be able to play in United States strategic interests in the Far East, it still provided, for the first time, a practical, agreed basis for planning an integrated long-range economic recovery program. By early November, economists with the UN Command were, in fact, given this very assignment: to draw up a plan for econmic aid to South Korea that would enable that country to restore prewar living standards and support a 20-division army with diminishing outside assistance. By the time President-elect Eisenhower visited Korea in December, 1952, the wheels were already turning to give him the means to meet his campaign promises.

The convergence of military and political pressures was now creating, with almost inevitable sureness, an environment in which multilateral programming for Korean reconstruction would be impossible. President Rhee's persistent calls for arms were now paying off. He was getting a modern, mechanized army trained in battle alongside experienced American military units and in the advanced officer-training institutions in the United States itself. But it was an army that might well be nothing but an embarrassment to what was still the ultimate purpose of the United Nations in Korea, the "peaceful" unification of the peninsula. It was also sure to be a burden to reconstruction. The new President of the United States was getting a native force to fill the gap so that he could withdraw American units in return for military and economic aid. The price was going to be high, but it was a price he had been politically authorized to pay by his overwhelming victory at the polls provided that an honorable truce could be worked out and he made sure that American soldiers were brought home. What was to characterize the transaction, therefore, was the primarily military purpose of the economic aid.

## The Change in Agents General

At the very minimum, American policy on Korean reconstruction was, by early 1953, finally coming back to what must be considered a more realistic basis than had existed since the Chinese Communists had entered the conflict in November, 1950. After more than two years of planning to support a United Nations program for the reconstruction of a unified Korea, the facts of life had now overtaken the theory. Not only was Korea not to be unified, but the nations of the world were no longer willing to meet the commitments of multilateral reconstruction: the finances to meet the program and the military forces to protect the investment. Only the United

States was prepared or, indeed, in a position to meet the expenses. But it was willing to do so only if the South Koreans themselves built up the force to protect the investment.

In the two years that it took for American policy to drop the dichotomy into which it had fallen in the days of the Inchon landings, the relationship between the United States government and UNKRA had not been an easy one. The Agent General considered that the agency and his post were essentially creations and, in large measure, instruments of American policy; he could, therefore, only maintain as strong a position with the Republic of Korea, contributing governments and the American military authorities in the Far East as the U.S. government openly demonstrated it was prepared to support. Since the agency was an instrument of policy, however, he did not consider that it was in a position to initiate American policy even if he himself wanted to. UNKRA could neither tell the military authorities what role the agency was to play in Korea nor tell the South Korean government what they might expect from its program. These, he felt, were matters for the American government to decide. His job was to build up the instrument and have it ready to produce, but it was not within his power to determine when or how, except through counsel and suggestion, unless the United States first made up its own mind.

Thus, while the United States delayed active support of a multilateral program on the basis of a continuing state of hostilities, the Agent General had no alternative but to try to adapt to the fact that the Korean affair was primarily an American military show. Within this framework, the very circumstances under which the United States had been entrusted with full authority for military operations by the Security Council resolution of July 7, 1950, made it necessary to organize UNKRA in Korea in accordance with U.S. Army security regulations for a theater of military operations. While the Army was unusually cooperative in accepting civilians, American and non-American, to work with its emergency relief teams, the requirement that such personnel sign statements agreeing to work under military supervision carried with it a recognition that the UN Command could request their withdrawal for reasons of military security. Nor were there special provisions reducing this control over UNKRA personnel operating independent of the military command.

The special problems involved in having to organize an international program under military security restrictions, help to explain why it was necessary to organize UNKRA independent of the other UN agencies. It will be remembered that it was the United States that insisted that the Agent General report directly to the General Assembly and not through the Secretary-General or through UNCURK. Nevertheless, even in a relationship of virtual equality, UNCURK proved to be a most ill-suited partner in the field. The Commission, for all practical purposes, was outdated within a month after it was created and its primary concern, the political unification of Korea, was frustrated by the Chinese Communist intervention. The Commission, thus, had little power, a condition that became pronounced as the designated governments began to staff the membership with men of no great substance or vision.[37] With no function or force, the Commission could nevertheless not be disbanded because such a step would have been considered a disavowal of the very ideal of unification. But, from Kingsley's point of view, close association with the Commission served no practical purpose. Indeed, it could present disadvantages should the Commission take a stand that was critical of the conduct of the UN Command or the government of the Republic of Korea and seek to have its views promoted by UNKRA. The early proposals of UNCURK in February and March, 1951, that UNKRA undertake an aggressively active program over clearly military opposition, seemed to prove the point.

Similarly, there were problems in associating UNKRA closely with the United Nations Secretariat and, particularly, with the Office of the Secretary-General. It was no secret that Secretary-General Lie was most unhappy with the exclusive

American control of the military operations even to the exclusion of his office. Whether or not one agrees that the United States was correct in following this "solo" course in view of the collective responsibilities it had assumed as a Unified Command, it was a fact that neither Kingsley's concept of UNKRA as an instrument of American policy nor the security problems involved in organizing activities in the field, permitted the agency to be used to develop greater multilateral control over the direction of the Korean enterprise than the United States was willing to accept voluntarily. Moreover, Kingsley was anxious not to allow the operations of what he hoped would be a large-scale reconstruction program to become entangled in the now full-grown bureaucracy of the UN system. He, therefore, from the beginning, developed an organization that was politically and administratively separate from the UN structure, collaborating in general housekeeping and other areas where there was no opportunity for the Secretariat to influence policy.[38]

During the organizational period, the Agent General, too, thus found himself forced into a kind of "solo" role. The future of UNKRA lay, fundamentally, not in conditions that might be created by the agency or by any other UN body, but in the success of the program's being consonant with the interests of the United States in Korea. Because the United States was committed in Korea, whether it liked it or not, it seemed practical to assume that the United States wanted a Republic of Korea that was economically strong. Furthermore, because the United States had, since 1947, pursued a policy of internationalizing the Korean issue, it seemed practical to assume that the United States wanted other nations to participate in the process of making South Korea economically strong. If both assumptions were correct, then from the point of view of the Agent General it was incumbent upon the United States, in the pursuit of its own interests, to press for the conditions under which the UNKRA program could be successful. Indeed, these assumptions seemed confirmed by the refusal of the United

States to put the agency into cold storage when the intervention of the Chinese Communists upset conditions of the original resolution.

What Kingsley was asking for meant taking political risks that the State Department was not prepared to take: to insist on restrictions on the authority of the UN Commander that would permit UNKRA to carry out a reasonably substantial program while the truce negotiations were dragging on; [39] and to limit the military establishment of the Republic of Korea so that a post-truce program could be carried out without the crushing burden of huge defense expenditures and the fear that the Rhee government might upset the truce and, simultaneously, the reconstruction work. As far as Kingsley was concerned, the unwillingness of the State Department to take these risks was defeating its own policy of supporting a UN program.

The views of the Agent General put constant pressure on the State Department to override the dominant military position in Korea, a move which, as we have seen, the Department was as constantly reluctant to make. There thus developed a definite tension between the Department and the Agent General which, as the opportunities for multilateral programming grew more and more remote, drew the agency and the Department farther and farther apart. Yet, in a sense, the split was nothing more than a manifestation of the shift in American policy from a multilateral to a bilateral program. Insofar as total policy was shaping up, it was no longer vital to the interests of American policy to have a strong UNKRA program.

What influence the Agent General could have had under the best of conditions is difficult to determine. Surely, he could have done nothing to change the demands for a decisive, controlled policy that was the mandate given to the new President by the voters in 1952 and, when translated into a solution for Korea, meant a bilateral defense support program. But there was always a feeling among some State Department officials, especially among those working on multilateral programs, among members of other delegations and even among some

UNKRA personnel, that the Agent General might have en-
hanced the chances for the agency's future had he spent more
time in Korea in 1951 and 1952. He might have convinced
the Korean people in particular and public opinion in general of the intentions and capacity of the United Nations to
accomplish the reconstruction mission. Kingsley, himself, took
the position that he was prepared to establish his permanent headquarters in Korea at such time as the way had
been cleared for the agency to operate a program there. Until
then, he considered that he had to deal personally with the
diplomatic, organizational and financial obstacles to the program wherever they existed, whether in Washington, New
York, Tokyo or Korea. Moreover, he considered that the
agency would be irreparably weakened if he were in the position of having to negotiate on a daily basis with the UN Command and the government of the Republic of Korea without
strong and definite American support and a healthy bank account to back him up. The best that the Agent General might
have accomplished by permanent residence in Korea would
have been to gain greater concessions from the UN Command
to an UNKRA program. But whether these would have been
great enough to make a substantial difference in the size and
timing of the program was questionable. He therefore preferred to apply his influence tactically when it could be used to
maximize concessions, rather than get caught up in the day-to-
day battling and politicking going on in Korea. Nevertheless,
as soon as the major contributors had paid in sufficient funds
to implement the $70,000,000 program approved late in 1952,
Mr. Kingsley took charge of the field operation, staying in
Korea almost until the end of his tenure of office the following
spring.

The frequent absence of the Agent General from Korea before this had, however, probably been something of an affront
to the government of the Republic of Korea for both psycho-
logical and practical reasons. As a reaction to the experience
of forty years of Japanese domination and as an assertion of
the strong nationalism brought on by the conflict with the com-

munists, there was a highly emotional insistence that planning
for Korea's future had to be done in Korea under Korean surveillance and leadership. Undoubtedly, Syngman Rhee was
also disappointed in losing a strong personal ally in the Agent
General, constantly at his side in his struggles with the UN
Command over economic controls. His dissatisfaction with the
Agent General and his chagrin that UNKRA was not carrying
out a substantial program probably became related in his
thinking and in his complaints to the diplomatic missions in
Seoul, particularly the American Embassy. In turn, these
complaints must have been reported to their home governments. It thus seems to have been Korean views that were most
strongly reflected in a *New York Times* editorial run in early
May when it was clear that Kingsley's contract was not going
to be renewed and the search was on for a new Agent General:

> . . . [The Agent General] must be a man who will stay in Korea
> and see the job through, leaving the world-wide junkets for the
> purpose of raising money to some subordinate expert in that par-
> ticular field. . . . Furthermore, a primary qualification of the
> man for this post should be his ability to work cooperatively with
> the Koreans and with their government. The rebuilding of Korea
> is not a 'hand-out' operation that can be conducted at arm's length.
> It is not merely a job for the theoretical—and foreign—expert. It
> has human as well as technical requirements.[40]

But Syngman Rhee is a realist and it must have been apparent to him, at least from mid-1952, that it was the United
States, not the United Nations, that had to give him what he
wanted if they denied him a united Korea: an army and the
heavy industry to support a large defense establishment. These
were the fruits that large elements in the UN were bound to
reject, particularly with India having been placed on the
UNKRA Advisory Committee and Great Britain and the
Commonwealth nations showing increasing disenchantment
with Rhee's attempts to consolidate his power. The United
States, however reluctantly, was committed in Korea and could
not get out so long as the cold war continued, but could mini-

mize its commitment of troops by maximizing the contribution
the South Koreans could make. This gave Rhee tremendous
bargaining power with the United States that he would never
have had with UNKRA; all the more reason for agitating for
direct economic aid from the United States even while attempting to use the presence of UNKRA to force his views on American aid officials.

If UNKRA was, indeed, an instrument of American foreign
policy, it represented only one side of the coin, the internationalization of the Korean problem, and this was the side with
which Kingsley had become clearly identified. But as military
and political pressures converged to clear up the dichotomy in
American policy, practical and expedient reasons developed
for relieving him from his post without requiring the new Republican administration to undertake a public reassessment
of U.S. policy in Korea. In early spring of 1953, Kingsley's
contract came up for renewal and when the United States was
asked for counsel by the UN Secretary-General, it chose to
nominate someone else for the post. If nothing more, it could
be simply accepted that the Eisenhower Administration could
not nominate for a position of responsibility in furthering its
Korean policy, about which they had made such positive political accusations and promises, a man who had been closely
connected with the previous Democratic regime. Kingsley had
held a number of important posts under the Roosevelt and Truman administrations, most prominently as Program Coordinator on the White House staff in the late forties.

The United States thus nominated, instead, Lt. General
John B. Coulter, an army officer whose last post before his retirement in 1951 had been Deputy Commander of the Eighth
Army in Korea in charge of Civil Affairs. In this post, General
Coulter had strengthened his knowledge of Korea and renewed a friendship with Syngman Rhee that had developed
while serving as Deputy Commander and, later, as Commanding General of U.S. Army Forces in Korea during 1948 and
1949. Following his retirement, he had acted as chief of
UNKRA's Washington office, thus giving him an understand-

ing of the agency and a working relationship with the U.S. officials responsible for Korean affairs. As a man trained in military traditions, General Coulter was undoubtedly better equipped to accept an essentially military-oriented solution to the Korean question than was Mr. Kingsley. Although General Coulter's political affiliations were not, as in the case of most professional military men, publicly discernible, he nevertheless had a connection with the new Republican administration. Henry Cabot Lodge, Jr., an early Eisenhower supporter and recently appointed chief U.S. delegate to the United Nations with ambassadorial rank and cabinet status, had been a member of the General's immediate staff during part of World War II.

In his final appearance before the Advisory Committee, Mr. Kingsley felt free to discuss what he considered the three main problems for UNKRA, problems he undoubtedly felt that the United States in particular had not really faced up to: the military burden of the Republic of Korea, the large financial needs the agency would have, and the dangers of a large-scale bilateral American program being undertaken alongside the UNKRA program. He pointed out that "The Republic of Korea is now bearing a military burden far beyond its capacity to support and military aid is meeting only a portion of the staggering costs involved." Because this burden was "the root cause" of inflation, he suggested that "every effort should be made to develop a military aid program clearly distinct from the UNKRA program and of sufficient magnitude so that civilian assistance will have to absorb none of the abnormal costs involved." Even under these conditions, the cost of Korean reconstruction was estimated to require "a minimal capital investment of from $1,250,000,000 to $1,500,000,000." This posed enormous financing problems. Kingsley made this clear, but strongly urged that the effort be made entirely on a multilateral basis, emphasizing the risks involved in trying to operate both a multilateral and an exclusively American economic aid program in Korea at the same time: "Divided responsibility is bad at best, and in the Korean situation it can be demonstrably disastrous. The Korean Government is sufficiently inexpert in economic matters and sufficiently sophisticated in the politics of maneuver to render futile any system of divided economic advice. This I am certain of because we have had enough experience to be certain of it. An organ of the United Nations clearly cannot be under the direction and control of a single member state and there would seem to be little merit, on the other hand, in a unilateral program to be controlled and directed by one member nation. In my view, therefore, the governments of the free world, including my own, have come to a point of critical decision respecting the economic rehabilitation of Korea. This is the turning point, when major decisions must be taken and major commitments either accepted or denied." [41]

## The Armistice Is Signed

In mid-March, Ambassador Ellis O. Briggs had informed the Korean National Assembly that, in response to an appeal from Assembly President Shin Hicki to President Eisenhower, a "highly competent civilian" was being sent to help Korea straighten out and build up her economic household.[42] Three weeks later, the President, approving a recommendation of the National Security Council, appointed Dr. Henry R. Tasca as special Representative of the President for Korean Economic Affairs. By the time Dr. Tasca arrived in the Far East, the UN Command had considerably progressed in estimating South Korea's economic needs over a projected five-year period to train and maintain a 20-division army. Also, UNKRA's team of economic consultants had already submitted a preliminary report which was available to the Presidential representative, as were data and materials collected by the specialized agency teams, now in the process of compiling and interpreting them to provide yardsticks for future action. Because of the military data involved in the force level to be supported by the United States, much of the information being collated by the UN Command was, undoubtedly, not passed on to UNKRA; [43] the UN agency had, however, as a matter of necessity and policy, shared the research of its expert teams with the military authorities and the South Korean government on the assumption that the results would provide a basis for an integrated long-range program of reconstruction.

The raw material Dr. Tasca needed was thus available. His principal task was to come up with a plan to carry out the program and offer it as a "package" for political approval to the President who, in turn, could offer it to Congress. Tasca's mission was, in this sense, more political than technical; it was to collate the available data in the UN Command's projected plan and UNKRA's technical reports, and relate them to the new Administration's pledge to reduce the American commitment of ground troops in Korea, to the training of the South Korean Army, and to the counterinflationary objective of the Combined Economic Board. This could, of course, have been accomplished through existing agencies. But the idea of a Presidential mission, headed by a man with experience in dealing with economic/military problems in Germany and in working with General Eisenhower and enjoying his confidence, gave the whole enterprise the sparkle of a fresh, total approach. It was also politically appealing and completely in line with Eisenhower's campaign warning that the Administration that got us into the war couldn't be trusted to get us out.[44]

Just before Dr. Tasca had arrived in Korea, the chances for the United States to get out of the war were increased many fold when General Clark received a favorable reply from the communist side to his proposal for an exchange of sick and wounded prisoners of war. The actual exchanges which were carried out a month later, in April, opened anew the whole question of the repatriation of prisoners of war which had deadlocked the truce talks for months. The previous December, the United States had voted in favor of an Indian-sponsored resolution in the UN General Assembly calling for all prisoners to be released to a neutral repatriation commission. The resolution had emphasized the principle that "force shall not be used against the prisoners of war to prevent or effect their return to their homelands." It provided that any prisoners who had not been repatriated at the end of a specified time period would be transferred to the care of the United Nations.[45] If the Assembly's resolution preserved the principle of voluntary repatriation which the UN side had maintained during the months of truce negotiations, it nonetheless denied North Korean prisoners the "right" to go to South Korea by keeping them under UN "care." This was a compromise that the United States, if not Syngman Rhee, was prepared to make to arrive at some kind of armistice agreement.

The communist side continued to refuse to admit that there were prisoners who would refuse to be repatriated. Chinese Premier Chou En-lai nevertheless issued a statement on March 30, suggesting that "negotiations [be undertaken] to repatriate immediately after the cessation of hostilities all those prisoners of war in their custody who insist upon repatriation and to hand over the remaining prisoners of war to a neutral state so as to ensure a just solution to the question of their repatriation." [46] The Chou proposal and the success of "Little Switch," the exchange of the sick and wounded, were sufficient demonstrations by work and deed that provisions might be worked out within the framework of the Indian resolution. Full armistice talks, in recess since the previous October, were now resumed in late April, to the anger of Syngman Rhee.

General Clark has claimed that his relations with South Korea's chief of state "had been excellent right up to the moment the United States indicated clearly it intended to go through with an armistice that might leave his country divided and the northern portion in the hands of Chinese Communist troops. Then I became the whipping boy for his bitterness and frustration." [47] To the General was left the chore of bringing Rhee over to agreeing to abandon his plan that Korean prisoners of war held by both sides be set free at the 38th parallel and allowed to walk southward or northward as they wished.

To the South Korean President, the very act of sitting down at the armistice table had been a disavowal of the purpose of unifying Korea. Yet, so long as the talks continued there was always the chance that the frustrations of negotiating with the communists might become so tense as to provide an incident and an opportunity for his newly trained and equipped troops to spearhead a final, decisive drive to the north. But as the armistice talks now moved into high gear, not only did such a possibility grow more remote, but he was to be deprived of the sight of North Korean soldiers publicly refusing to return to their communist-dominated homes and choosing to come to *his* Korea. The fierce yearning for a settlement that President Eisenhower considered a mandate from the American people, spelled almost complete defeat for the equally fierce yearnings for unification that drove Syngman Rhee.

On May, 25, the day the UN negotiators were working out the final details of the repatriation scheme with the communist side, General Clark and Ambassador Briggs visited Rhee. They sought his assurances that he would not disrupt the armistice plans by pulling the South Korean forces out of the line and sending them off on a defiant offensive of his own. In return for his agreement to comply with the terms of the armistice, they informed Rhee that the nations with forces in Korea would pledge further military support if the communists broke the armistice. Also, the United States would keep troops in and near Korea until peace was firmly established, would build up the South Korean Army to twenty divisions, and provide a billion dollar economic aid program.[48]

General Clark later recalled that he had never seen Rhee so disturbed. For what he and Briggs were telling him was that Korea might never be united in his lifetime. The South Korean President dismissed the possibility of peaceful settlement and told the Americans:

> Your threats have no effect upon me. We want to live. We want to survive. We will decide our own fate. Sorry, I cannot assure President Eisenhower of my cooperation under the circumstances.[49]

Two days later Rhee wrote directly to Eisenhower:

> I earnestly wish I could see my way clear to make a public statement, as requested, pledging to accept any armistice you may

deem necessary. But we are fearfully aware, on the other hand, that to accept any armistice arrangement which would allow the Chinese Communists to remain in Korea would mean to the Korean nation, in terms of eventualities, an acceptance of a death sentence without protest. It is a hard thing for a nation to do.

Rhee then went on to put forward his own proposal:

We propose a simultaneous withdrawal of both the communist and United Nations forces from Korea, on the condition that a mutual defense pact between our two governments precede it. . . .

[Under the Mutual Defense Pact], the United States will agree to come to our military aid and assistance immediately without any consultation or conference with any nation or nations, if and when an enemy nation or nations resume aggressive activities against the Korean Peninsula.

The Security Pact should include the United States help in the increase of the ROK armed forces. . . .

Adequate supplies of arms, ammunition, and general logistic materials will be given Korea with a view to making it strong enough to defend itself without needing American soldiers to fight in Korea again.

The United States air and naval forces will remain where they are now so as to deter the enemy from attempting further aggression.

And finally:

In case the idea of simultaneous withdrawal is found unacceptable to either or both of the negotiating parties, I beg of you to allow the Koreans to continue the fighting, for this is the universal preference of the Korean people to any decisive armistice or peace. . . .[50]

What Rhee was proposing was not, of course, a basis for an armistice agreement. It was American protection for his own forceful unification of the Korean nation, protection unfettered by international affiliation and carrying the risks of getting the United States plunged into the war its government had dared the wrath of many of its great military leaders to avoid. Within a few days, Eisenhower replied to Rhee that "we would not be justified in prolonging the war with all the misery that it involves in the hope of achieving, by force, the unification of Korea." But the American President reaffirmed that

> we believe that in Korea there should be a more perfect union and . . . we shall seek to achieve that union by all peaceful methods. We believe that there should be domestic tranquillity and that can come from the end of fighting. There should be provision for the defense of Korea. That will come from the mutual security treaty which we are prepared to make. The general welfare should be advanced and that will come from your own peacetime efforts and from economic assistance to your war-torn land. Finally, a peaceful settlement will afford the best opportunity to bring to your people the blessings of liberty.[51]

Rhee, however, was not satisfied that the goals of the American constitution could so easily be realized in his own troubled nation while the communists dominated the northern half. It was almost two weeks later that he replied, emphasizing that "when [your generous offers] come as a price for our acceptance of the armistice as we know it, they cannot but have little inducement, because, as I have said before, to accept such an armistice is to accept a death warrant." Frantically seeking to impress upon Eisenhower the immensity of his error in trusting to an agreement with the communists, Rhee warned that "The terms of the armistice being what they are, the Communist buildup will go on unhampered until it is capable of overwhelming South Korea with one swoop at a moment of the Communists' own choosing." "What is to follow for the rest of the Far East?", he asked, "and the rest of Asia? And the rest of the free world?" [52]

This time Rhee's warnings were not all words. On the day before he had replied to Eisenhower, June 18, 25,000 anti-communist North Korean prisoners of war had broken out of their camps with the obvious connivance of their South Korean guards. The armistice was immediately thrown into jeopardy. President Eisenhower no longer depended on letter writing himself; he immediately sent Assistant Secretary of

State Walter S. Robertson to Seoul to confer with Rhee. Robertson carried with him not only further assurances of military and economic aid and a Mutual Security Pact, but also a pledge that the United States would join the Republic of Korea in withdrawing from the political conference called for in the armistice proposals if there were no concrete results after 90 days.

Robertson spent almost a week in intense, secret talks with the South Korean leader. Outside, the Rhee propaganda machine stirred the populace into an anti-armistice frenzy. Hysterical school girls sat in the streets, weeping and crying, "Don't sell Korea." In the conference room, Rhee wanted more than just a pledge to withdraw from the political conference if nothing was achieved; he wanted a pledge to resume the war. But Robertson held firm; the United States could not agree to getting involved in further military action that was not provoked by outright aggression. The most he would do would be to assure Rhee that the United States would meet with South Korean officials at a high level in order to work out joint objectives before the political conference met.[53] Finally, Rhee succumbed. Robertson immediately returned with a letter from Rhee to Eisenhower promising that the South Korean government would not obstruct the armistice. The next day the chief UN negotiator informed the communists at Panmunjom that "in consequence of negotiations just completed . . . you are assured that the [UN Command], which includes the ROK forces, is prepared to carry out the terms of the armistice." [54] The communists asked further guarantees, mainly that the UN Command was not pledged to support aggression by Syngman Rhee, and got them. By July 19, the communists, too, announced they were prepared to conclude an armistice.[55] The agreement was signed at Panmunjom on July 27, after over three years of fighting and two years of negotiating.

The terms of the armistice and the agreement with Syngman Rhee now crowned the pressures moving the United States toward a bilateral policy for economic aid to Korea. Surely, the pledge of economic aid had been made by the United States in its own name and not in the collective name of the Unified Command or as leader of a UN coalition. With Korea remaining divided, with the threat of aggression from north or south still very real, with the United States pledged to support a large defense establishment in South Korea, there seemed little that would permit large-scale operations by a United Nations agency. And yet the Memorandum of Understanding called for UNKRA to take over responsibility for all relief and rehabilitation activities within 180 days. It was getting ever more difficult to bet on both sides of the coin.

1. *Military Situation in the Far East,* Part I, p. 45. Although General MacArthur's theory might be considered the epitome of the military view, it is considerably narrower than Clausewitz' view that "war can never be separated from political intercourse, and if . . . this occurs anywhere, all threads of the various relations are, in a certain manner, broken, and we have before us a senseless thing without an objective, [a war that would be] entirely war, entirely the unbridled element of hostility." (Quoted in Alfred Vogts, *Defense and Diplomacy* [New York: King's Crown Press, 1956], p. 469.) It should, perhaps, be pointed out that MacArthur, stimulated by newspaper criticism of his statement, modified it the next day in explaining that "at no time in our system of government is there any question of the civil administration being in complete control. What I said was meant to convey the idea that there should be no non-professional interference in the handling of troops in a campaign." (*Military Situation in the Far East,* Part I, p. 289.) What the General seemed to neglect is that "the handling of troops in a campaign" (e.g., whether or not they are to cross the 38th parallel) is, in itself, very often a matter of considerable political (i.e., non-professional military) concern.

2. *Ibid.,* Part I, p. 649.

3. An excellent essay on this subject is Dexter Perkins, "Foreign Policy in Presidential Campaigns," *Foreign Affairs,* XXXV, No. 2 (January, 1957), 213. Specifically Professor Perkins notes that "the election of 1952—whatever else it did or did not do—made it crystal clear that the American people did not desire the resumption of the Korean War, that they wished the struggle there to be brought to an honorable end if that were at all possible."

4. Professor Morgenthau has expressed this idea by saying that "American foreign policy and, through it, the weight of American power in international affairs is to a peculiar degree dependent upon the moods of American public opinion, as they express themselves in the votes of Congress, election results, polls, and the like." (Hans J. Morgenthau, *Politics Among Nations* [New York: Alfred A. Knopf, 1950], p. 101.)

5. Taft's views on the relationship between the President and Congress in foreign policy are best summarized in his own book, *A Foreign Policy for Americans* (Garden City, New York: Doubleday & Co., Inc., 1952), pp. 21–36.

6. William S. White, *The Taft Story* (New York: Harper & Bros., 1954), p. 148.

7. From transcript of General Eisenhower's first press conference at Abilene, Kansas, *New York Times,* June 6, 1952, p. 10.

8. *New York Times,* June 13, 1952, p. 13.

9. *Ibid.,* June 13, 1952, p. 1.

10. *Ibid.,* July 27, 1952, Section IV, p. 5.

11. *Ibid.,* July 22, 1952, p. 15.

12. *Ibid.,* July 27, 1952, Section IV, p. 5.

13. *Ibid.,* September 23, 1952, p. 16.

14. *Ibid.,* October 3, 1952, p. 16.

15. *Ibid.,* October 18, 1952, p. 12.

16. *Ibid.,* October 18, 1952, p. 12.

17. *Ibid.,* October 25, 1952, p. 8.

18. *Ibid.,* November 9, 1952, Section IV, p. 3.

19. *Ibid.,* October 30, 1952, p. 26.

20. *Ibid.,* October 31, 1952, p. 1.

21. *Ibid.,* December 9, 1952, p. 6.

22. Captain Robert Sawyer, *U.S. Military Advisory Group to the Republic of Korea,* Parts I and II, p. 29.

23. Although General MacArthur, as he so often reminded everyone during the hearings on his dismissal, did not have the Military Government group in Korea under his Command, the Joint Chiefs seem to have chosen to send their request for recommendations for a Korean army strength level through the Far East Command because of the relationship to the whole problem of military security in the Far East, and particularly in relation to the security of Japan.

24. Sawyer, *op. cit.,* pp. 43–46.

25. *Ibid.,* pp. 62, 161–62.

26. *Ibid.,* p. 160; see also the testimony of General Bradley, *Military Situation in the Far East,* Part II, pp. 994–95.

27. The South Koreans, nevertheless, proceeded to distribute equipment for 65,000 to over 100,000 men, and to utilize it with little sense of conservation or efficiency. *Ibid.,* p. 163.

28. *Ibid.,* pp. 167–73.

29. General MacArthur noted, on a trip to the front several days after the attack: "It was quite apparent . . . that the South Korean Army had been so hard hit that it was completely disintegrated and in full flight."—*Military Situation in the Far East,* Part I, p. 231.

30. Sawyer, *op. cit.,* pp. 263–64.

31. *Ibid.,* pp. 263–65.

32. Paraphrase of message from General MacArthur to the Joint Chiefs of Staff on January 6, 1951; read by General Bradley, *Military Situation in the Far East,* Part II, p. 1116.

33. Sawyer, *op. cit.,* pp. 269–71; Bradley, *op. cit.,* Part II, p. 1222.

34. Message of July 22, 1951, from CINCUNC to DA, quoted in Sawyer, *op. cit.,* pp. 283–84.

35. Matthew B. Ridgway, *Soldier* (New York: Harper & Bros., 1956), p. 191.

36. See General Van Fleet's testimony before the Committee on Armed Services, House of Representatives, 83rd Congress, 1st Session (Washington: Government Printing Office, 1953), pp. 331–35, 342.

37. The members of the Commission were Australia, Chile, Netherlands, Pakistan, Thailand, and Turkey; but rarely were all the members represented in the field after the first year.

38. The specialized agencies had, at first, looked upon the Korean situation as a wonderful opportunity to demonstrate their value and ability. Moreover, the resolution of December 1, 1950, had recommended that the agencies be used in the UNKRA program. To meet the security requirements and to avoid the confusion and delay of overlapping jurisdictions, Kingsley had to make it understood that, in Korea, personnel from the agencies would have to work on the basis of technical experts under general UNKRA supervision. For the view of the Food and Agricultural Organization, see *New York Times,* September 20, 1950, p. 14, and September 21, 1950, p. 3.

39. Kingsley never sought to undertake a comprehensive program before a truce was achieved since he realized that until port and transportation space could be fully released, UNKRA could not meet the supply requirements of major reconstruction projects.

40. *New York Times,* May 11, 1953, p. 26.

41. United Nations Press Release KOR/380, May 13, 1953.

42. *New York Times,* March 18, 1953, p. 3.

43. Here was a technical reason why a defense support program could not be handled through a UN agency. Military security would not have permitted information concerning the South Korean Army to be passed on to UNKRA staff.

44. So powerful a political move had this been that, on the eve of the elections, Stevenson had been forced to say: "The Korean war and the miserable stalemate there must be freshly reviewed by fresh minds"—a remark more designed to get votes than the friendship of the Truman administration (*New York Times,* November 4, 1952, p. 25).

45. General Assembly Resolution 610 (VII), December 3, 1952.

46. Quoted in Mark Clark, *From the Danube to the Yalu,* p. 244.

47. *Ibid.,* pp. 257–58.

48. *Ibid.,* p. 269.

49. *Ibid.,* pp. 270–71.

50. Letter from President Rhee to President Eisenhower, May 30, 1953. Reprinted in Appendix II to Hearings before the Committee on Foreign Relations, U.S. Senate, 83rd Congress, 2nd Session, *Mutual Defense Treaty with Korea* (Washington: Government Printing Office, 1953), pp. 52–53.

51. Letter from President Eisenhower to President Rhee, June 6, 1953, *ibid.,* pp. 53–55.

52. Letter from President Rhee to President Eisenhower, June 19, 1953, *ibid.,* pp. 55–56.

53. Clark, *op. cit.,* pp. 287–88. See also Representative Walter Judd's version of Mr. Robertson's confidential oral report to a small group of congressmen on his return. Hearings before the Committee on Foreign Affairs, House of Representatives, 83rd Congress, 2nd Session, *Mutual Security Act of 1954* (Washington: Government Printing Office, 1954), p. 456.

54. Clark, *op. cit.,* p. 291.

55. *Ibid.,* p. 292.

# CHAPTER VIII

# THE ORGANIZATION OF BILATERAL ASSISTANCE

*The Pattern of the New Program*
*Organization of the Program in the Field*
*The Withering Away of UNKRA*

# THE ORGANIZATION OF
# BILATERAL ASSISTANCE

## *The Pattern of the New Program*

By the time the armistice was signed, the United States had spent $1,170,250,000 in economic and military aid to South Korea since World War II, and this did not include the costs of maintaining troops on the peninsula during the early occupation or during the hostilities after June, 1950.[1] Nevertheless, the day after the armistice was signed, President Eisenhower asked Congress to authorize the expenditure of another $200,000,000 in economic aid as a first installment in a billion dollar Korean aid program.[2] It was not beyond the realm of possibility that Congress would balk at increasing this already enormous investment in a part of the world where United States military leaders hoped never to have to fight again. Yet with philosophic realism, Congress did not question the billion dollar aid program in detail, but simply and swiftly accepted it as the price which the United States had to pay to stop the war and bring its soldiers home.[3]

Before going before Congress, the President had already had the recommendations of the Tasca Mission for a month. The Administration was thus in the happy circumstance of having a plan of operations in hand when Congress authorized it to act. As a matter of fact, the Tasca report had already been circulated to the interested departments and an interdepartmental working group had prepared firm recommendations, generally patterned after those in the report, for presentation to the National Security Council.[4] The essence of the Tasca recommendations confirmed the political promises already made to Syngman Rhee by calling for a bilateral program of defense support and reconstruction over a period of four to five years at an estimated cost of $1,000,000,000.[5] The emphasis of the program was to be on the reconstruction of

189

agricultural and industrial production facilities in order to achieve a stable economy capable of bringing living standards back to the prewar level and, at the same time, to support an efficient defense force without outside aid. The defense support program to be administered by the Mutual Security Administration (soon to be renamed the Foreign Operations Administration, FOA, with the amalgamation of Technical Cooperation, or Point IV, functions) should, it was suggested by the Tasca Report, be one part of a tripartite system. It was argued that until there was a full political settlement (or, presumably, until the ROK Army was sufficiently built up to hold its own), U.S. military units would have to remain in Korea. They would, therefore, continue a program of emergency relief to insure stability behind the front lines in case of a fresh outbreak of hostilities.[6] In addition, the Tasca report recommended that the UNKRA program also be continued in order to preserve the multilateral approach on which the UN military operations had been based.

If every possible influence was working toward a bilateral reconstruction policy, there were also strong pressures to maintain at least a semblance of international cooperation in Korea. Even if the Tasca Report had not recommended that the UNKRA program be continued (although the report never discussed how the program was to continue without funds), President Eisenhower had already made it quite clear that he was not prepared to destroy the concept of collective action still kept alive by the presence of the forces of sixteen nations in Korea. Like the Truman Administration before him, he was bound to admit that the allies were not materially necessary in the pursuit of American policy in Korea itself. But he nonetheless viewed the existence of an alliance in Korea as important to the global strategy of the United States in developing a world system to deter the further expansion of communism. Late in May, Senator Taft, in his last foreign policy address, had suggested that the United States have one try at reaching an armistice and, if unsuccessful, forget the United Nations so far as the Korean War was concerned and go it alone.⁷ The President quickly made it clear, in a press conference two days later, that he did not agree. He admitted "that there arise occasions when if one—any one nation or any one authority—were acting singly, possibly the decision in that point would be better than to subject it to all of the trimmings and compromises that come out of the effort to achieve some kind of unanimity of opinion." Nevertheless, "you can't have cooperative action in these great developments and processes in just the spots of the globe or in just the particular problems that you would like to select" and "if you are going to go it alone one place, you of course have to go it alone everywhere." ⁸

There may, of course, be too much black and white in the President's generalization; it may be very possible to go-it-alone in one part of the world and still maintain the anti-communist alliance elsewhere. But the alliance having been put into action in Korea, any denial of its cohesiveness and determination after three years of battle strains would undoubtedly have been a most undesirable admission of weakness. Thus, on the day the armistice was signed, the sixteen nations that had contributed troops to the UN side during the war, affirmed, presumably under United States inspiration, that "if there is a renewal of the armed attack, challenging again the principles of the United Nations, we should again be united and prompt to resist." At the same time they warned that "the consequences of such a break of the armistice would be so grave that, in all probability, it would not be possible to confine hostilities within the frontiers of Korea." ⁹

In his message to Congress requesting authority to spend $200,000,000 to begin a program of Korean recovery, the President had not, however, made it clear exactly how the program would be administered nor what role UNKRA might play. Indeed, the new Agent General, Lt. General John B. Coulter, had to acknowledge to newsmen that "no United States officials had consulted or informed him about the $200,000,000 request." At UN Headquarters there was not "one word from Washington to indicate whether all, or in fact any part, of the

$200,000,000 will be given to the United Nations agency or whether the United States will retain complete control." [10]

Nevertheless, several days earlier, before the armistice agreement had actually been signed and with the recommendations of the Tasca report still confidential and under review, Mr. Stassen, the new Administrator of the Mutual Security Program, had appealed to the economy-mindedness of the Congress by offering practical reasons of the dollars-and-cents variety why the United States should continue to support the UNKRA program. He pointed to the fact that "a United States dollar contributed to UNKRA constitutes only 65 per cent of the UNKRA budget, the remaining 35 per cent being made up by contributions from other governments." And proceeded to ask "just how would a deliberate refusal to save 35 cents on every dollar be satisfactorily explained to the taxpayer?" [11] (on the assumption, of course, that, one way or another, aid had to be granted). Mr. Stassen also reminded the Senate Committee on Appropriations that "the program of rehabilitation of war damage in Korea has always been considered a collective United Nations responsibility" and still further asked: "Is the United States now prepared to so reduce its payments on the pledge which its representatives in the United Nations made nearly two years ago as to virtually abandon its leadership in this field of United Nations activity with consequent probable loss of interest by other governments?" [12]

With little consideration that a UN program could hardly operate successfully under the conditions existing in Korea at the time of the armistice, the United States, come Republicans or Democrats, continued to refuse to acknowledge publicly that UNKRA could not work. Indeed, at a meeting of the sixteen nations that had participated in the Korean action, Secretary of State Dulles expressed the "hope that the governments of the allied nations would contribute economically to [Korea's] rehabilitation." He went on to tell the meeting that the Tasca report "envisages the expenditure of from $800,-000,000 to $900,000,000 over a period of three or four years for Korean rehabilitation," [13] as if to challenge them to increase the range of their pledges under the UNKRA program.

The memoranda on United States organization for economic aid activities in Korea, presented for the President's approval by the Bureau of the Budget and the National Security Council in the first week of August, thus followed the pattern recommended by the Tasca Mission: a tripartite system with UNKRA carrying on in coordination with a much larger bilateral defense support program.[14] There were certain underlying principles that, it was deemed, had to be followed if the system were to be successful in getting an integrated U.S./ UN/ROK recovery program into operation:

1. The Commander-in-Chief of the United Nations Forces had to continue to have "over-all responsibility for all United Nations and United States activities" so long as he had responsibility "for the security of Korea."

2. In order to avoid "wasteful duplications," a "clear-cut division of activities should be established . . . among the United Nations Korean Reconstruction Agency, civilian relief (i.e., the military's program) and United States rehabilitation."

3. In order to achieve this "clear-cut division of activities" and integrated planning, "a single individual, under CINCUNC, should be delegated the function of programming for and supervising the implementation of such activities."

In theory, the continuance of the authority of the UN Commander after the armistice may have seemed an aberration from the Memorandum of Understanding which UNKRA had signed with the Command in December, 1951. The Memorandum, however, had stipulated that Phase 2, the period when UNKRA would assume responsibility for all relief and rehabilitation activities, "shall commence . . . at the termination of the period of 180 days following the cessation of hostilities in Korea, as determined by the [Unified Command], *unless it is determined by the [Unified Command], in consultation with the Agent General, that military operations do not permit the commencement of Phase 2 at that time.*" [15] The armistice had left the political questions unanswered and thus permitted the Unified Command to rationalize, as it did, that "military operations do not permit the commencement of Phase 2" at this time. Moreover, the new Agent General, given the dependence of UNKRA on United States support if for no other reason, was in no position to disagree when consulted. The concept of the ultimate authority of the theater commander thus provided the United States with an excellent mechanism for maintaining a multilateral program in Korea, but keeping it under the surveillance of the head of its own bilateral program who would enjoy the prestige and authority of the theater commander himself. It was possible to keep the symbol of collective action alive while making sure that it did not compromise the basic objectives of the defense support program.

It was the defense support program, however, which was most prominently mentioned in a joint statement issued by President Rhee and Secretary of State Dulles as they completed negotiations on the Mutual Security Pact which, like the rehabilitation program, had been part of the bargain for Rhee's cooperation in reaching the armistice agreement. The two statesmen confirmed that

> . . . the projected three to four year program for the rehabilitation of the war-ruined Korean economy shall be coordinated through the combined economic board, under the joint chairmanship of the Korean and American representatives. This program contemplates the expenditure of approximately one billion dollars of funds, subject to appropriations thereof by the United States Congress. Two hundred million dollars has already been authorized, out of prospective defense savings.[16]

In essence, the United States would develop a defense support program for South Korea and UNKRA would be assigned a certain segment to operate. The size of UNKRA's share would be determined by the contributions UNKRA could collect with the help of the United States and within the limits of the United States share not exceeding 65 per cent of the total. Undoubtedly, the projects which UNKRA would undertake would have to be determined not only by its financial resources, but also, because of its connection with the United Nations, by emphasis on nonmilitary areas of the economy.

The absorption of the UN program of Korean reconstruction into the larger orbit of American defense support was not an isolated phenomenon. After a world-wide survey of the United States technical assistance program in September, the *New York Times* concluded that "the [U.S.] Point Four Program [of technical assistance to underdeveloped countries] . . . is fast becoming an instrument of America's 'cold war' policy." As such, "its original identity and [humanitarian] purpose are being absorbed in one way or another into the United States military assistance program and the counter-offensive against Communist encroachment which the aid effort represents." [17] Undoubtedly, the Korean conflict and the accompanying demand for a more direct, a more controlled, a more controllable foreign policy contributed to the greater integration of military, economic and technical assistance efforts with the almost inevitable subordination of economic and technical assistance to military demands. Why should anyone have thought that in Korea itself the trend should be in any other direction? It was the "New Look" policy of building up native ground forces, while relying on mobile American sea and air power as deterrents to aggression and subordinating economic and technical aid to this over-all strategic concept. The Korean case was the first and best example of how the Eisenhower Administration was bent on achieving an effective, controllable and economical system of military security for the free world. [18]

## Organization of the Program in the Field

The recommendations of the National Security Council were quickly implemented after the President's approval by the appointment of Mr. C. Tyler Wood of the Foreign Operations Administration (FOA) to the post of economic advisor to the

Commander-in-Chief of the UN Command. Actually, Mr. Wood was appointed to three posts. First, he was the FOA Administrator of the bilateral defense support program. Second, as economic advisor to the UN Commander, he was given authority and responsibility for dealing with the government of the Republic of Korea on questions of financial policy, including the perennial favorites, the government's policy on bank credit and rates of exchange. Finally, in his capacity as Economic Coordinator, he was responsible for seeing that the UNKRA and Army programs were meshed with defense support efforts to make up one integrated recovery plan.[19]

Mr. Wood's first order of business was to establish working relationships with the military authorities, UNKRA, and the South Korean government. Although he was subordinate to the UN Commander, his appointment was subject to specific duties spelled out in the National Security Council recommendations of August 7 and confirmed by the President. Thus, while the ultimate authority of the theater commander was not impaired by the new organizational arrangements, the Economic Coordinator came armed with precise duties which the theater commander could not question. In point of fact, policy in Korean economic affairs had now been taken out of military hands for the first time since the outbreak of hostilities. While the primacy of the theater commander's position was acknowledged, it did not necessarily subject United States policy to military control.[20] Even though the Tasca Report had indicated that there would, for some time, be a continuing civilian relief need for the Army to meet, with the signing of the armistice there seems to have been little expectation that this program could go very much beyond a strict interpretation of the "disease and unrest" formula. There was, therefore, little incentive for the military to seek a more important policy-making role in economic affairs, especially since the principle of the ultimate authority of the theater commander had already been preserved by the subordination of the Economic Coordinator to General Clark.

The arrangements with UNKRA had equally smooth sailing. The new Agent General quickly informed Mr. Wood that, in order that "the relief, rehabilitation and stabilization programs . . . be coordinated . . . as component parts of an over-all program, . . . the coordinating function should be exercised by the Economic Coordinator." General Coulter, therefore, expressed willingness to accept "determinations made by the Economic Coordinator" on (1) "over-all requirements and priorities," (2) "the allocation of responsibility" within the over-all program, (3) economic policies, and (4) "negotiations with the Korean government on broad policy and on broad program matters." While these matters were to be subject to mutual consultation and consistent with the "mission" of UNKRA, no independence of action was preserved by the UN agency.[21] Under the coordinated approach, UNKRA assumed responsibility for the rehabilitation work in specified areas: industries, fisheries, mining (with the exception of tungsten mines),[22] education, housing and flood control, reclamation, irrigation and forestry projects in the field of agriculture. UNKRA was also to assist in certain public health and welfare projects that were primarily to come under the Army relief programs. The Army's Korea Civil Assistance Command (formerly UNCACK), in addition to administering relief projects and handling all reception and distribtuion services, was to act as the operating arm of the bilateral United States program in assuming field responsibility for transportation, communications, public works, national defense, police and general agriculture projects.[23]

In practice, UNKRA actually had a considerable amount of influence in program determinations at the working level. Although the Economic Coordinator had the final decision on requirements lists and priorities, he necessarily based his decisions on recommendations which, in the fields of their responsibility, were originally formulated and supported by UNKRA staff. UNKRA planning officers worked closely with Mr. Wood's staff and, as would be expected, in the first months were of immeasurable assistance in sharing the data and experience they had accumulated.[24] The technical work of programming was, however, carried out within the broad policies laid down by the Economic Coordinator. These, in turn, were determined by the objectives of American policy in Korea, objectives which may not necessarily have been the same had they been formulated by an organ of the United Nations.[25]

Negotiations with the government of the Republic of Korea traveled a more hazardous road. Following his August meeting with Secretary of State Dulles during which the Mutual Security Pact had been negotiated, President Rhee issued an exuberant statement, particularly intended for home consumption. In it, he claimed full recognition from the United States for the rights of Koreans to share in the administration of the aid program. This time he did not dwell on the arguments over the government's right to control bank credit and rates of exchange, but sought a more direct way of impressing his victory on his people. He proclaimed that "In the past, the United States has regarded aid to Korea as a kind of two-edged sword, with purchases being made in Japan to bolster the Japanese economy, with the goods later being used for the Koreans' benefit." "Now," he warned, "Korean patriotism, which looks upon Japan as a traditional enemy, will try to prevent the spending of Korean rehabilitation funds in Japan." [26] When Rhee agreed not to obstruct the armistice agreement in return for an army, a defense pact, consultation on political conference objectives and an aid program, he did not agree to accept whatever kind of aid program the United States offered. Almost from the moment the armistice was signed, the Rhee government started on a propaganda campaign the ultimate purpose of which was to gain exclusive Korean control over aid funds. First, Rhee sought to consolidate his own people behind his scheme by constant complaints that the United States was just using Korea to strengthen Japan. Later, he moved to seek the support of American public opinion and, it is presumed, the American Congress, by recklessly accusing the American field administrators of mismanagement and waste and their Washington counterparts of bureaucratic red tape and misguidance. "China received bil-

lions of dollars' worth of goods and materials," Rhee cried,
"but most of it was wasted. Whoever may have been responsible, we do not want Korea criticized as China was." [27]

At the time the Economic Coordinator first arrived in Korea,
the government had, during the previous eight months, made
real efforts, on its own, without the support of large aid expenditures, to undertake a stabilization program. In February,
1953, the government had undertaken a monetary reform on
its own initiative, calling in "won" and issuing a new currency,
"hwan," set at a rate of sixty to the dollar. The reform had
two primary purposes: first, to eliminate large accumulations
of the old currency which individuals would not be willing to
disclose to the government for fear of provoking tax evasion
investigations and which, therefore, would be eliminated from
the market; second, to limit the initial drawings of the new
currency and thus, also, limit the total currency on the market.
The tight controls originally set up had to be relaxed under
political pressure during the next few weeks. The net effect of
the currency reform, however, coupled with the importation
and distribution of large quantities of consumer goods, had
been a comparative stabilization of prices for the first time in
years.[28]

Shortly after the currency reform, the South Korean government also showed a most reasonable attitude in agreeing on
a rate of exchange for the repayment of advances to the UN
Command. In negotiating with Admiral Hanlon in May, while
the military authorities were still responsible for economic
affairs, Prime Minister Paik concurred in relating the rate of
exchange to the index of wholesale prices. Under this system,
the rate was, at that time, set at 180 hwan to $1.00, three times
the government-pegged rate of 60 hwan to $1.00 and reason-
ably close to the black market rate which was fluctuating between 190 hwan and 265 hwan to $1.00.[29] The rate of 180
hwan to $1.00 was in fact accepted by all parties for transac-
tions during the first year of the defense support program
which was, thus, freed from the contentions that had so often
hampered United States/Korean cooperation in the past.[30]

The most serious problem in dealing with the Rhee government involved, rather, the procurement of goods and equipment in Japan, the rate of capital investment, and gaining valid assurances that the government would maintain a tight credit policy. By procuring supplies and equipment in Japan, the United States could get goods into Korea more quickly and cheaply and, by balancing the program between the consumer goods imports and investment projects, the inflationary impact of the program would be minimized. Rhee was, however, dead set against the Korean aid program's being operated in any way that would bolster the Japanese economy. He also sought the use of aid funds to build up the heavy industry that South Korea lacked to support a large defense establishment. Thus, between September and December, Rhee tore up agreement after agreement that Mr. Wood had painstakingly negotiated at a Cabinet level.[31] Not until December 14 was an understanding reached to provide a basis of United States/Korean cooperation in implementing the defense support program.[32]

The Combined Economic Board which had been established under the Meyer Agreement of May, 1952, was maintained as a mechanism for insuring an integrated program and providing for Korean participation. It was, moreover, carefully stated that: "As in all the relations between the Republic of Korea and the United States of America, the program will be carried out with the full mutual respect for sovereign rights." While a main purpose of the program was "to raise the planned investment . . . to the highest level consistent with financial stability," nothing precise was said about what this level was. Moreover, considerable emphasis was placed on the obligations of the South Korean government to take anti-inflationary measures which would enhance economic stability and, accordingly, by reducing the need for consumer goods to absorb hwan through sales, release aid funds for investment projects. Specifically, it was "estimated that the total credit expansion which can take place through the banking system without endangering financial economic stability would be at the rate of hwan 11 billion in the coming 12 months." Some satisfaction, however, must have been gained by the Rhee government in the announcement that "mutually satisfactory procurement arrangements" were being developed.

The chairman of a congressional committee that visited Korea in October admitted, after three days of hearing testimony on the organization of the relief and rehabilitation program, that "the further I get into this thing, the more confused I get." [33] Tyler Wood himself agreed almost three years later that when he first arrived he was somewhat shaken at "the possibilities of duplication, of over-lapping, of confusion inherent in [the situation]." He admitted that "we did not succeed entirely [in reducing duplication]. On the other hand, I am amazed myself as to how well this very complicated organization has worked which had inherent in it all sorts of possibilities for jurisdictional jealousies and real confusion." [34]

Accepting Mr. Wood's conclusion that, at least, the FOA/ UN Command/UNKRA coordinating mechanism was successful, some attempt may be made at explaining why. First and foremost, there was an undeniable assertion of wisdom in the original suggestion to place the coordinating function in a "single individual." With all the benefits to be derived from committee work, the tabling of various and varying attitudes, the give-and-take that finds holes in arguments and may also find a way to fill them, sooner or later a decision must be made and no substitute has yet been found for entrusting decision-making in an operating program to a "single individual." All the benefits of committees can, as a matter of fact, be had through conscientious and effective staff work that presents the alternatives, the risks and the possible effects of specific action. At this point, it is a matter of making a choice, not continuing the debate on why certain choices should not be made; and the single administrator, within the limits of a system of bureaucratic, political and professional responsibility, is in a position to do so. No such possibility for getting action had ever existed under the joint military/UNKRA committee system that had operated in 1952.

Secondly, the Economic Coordinator, the "single individual," was undoubtedly able to do his job because the military authorities were not bent on interfering despite the primacy of their authority in the area. There were, of course, advantages derived from the fact that active hostilities were over, from the confidence which the UN Commander must have had in the Economic Coordinator and from the fact that the Economic Coordinator was heading an American, and not a United Nations, operation. It may, nevertheless, still be concluded that the organizational arrangements demonstrate that there is not necessarily anything inherent in the military system which requires that the Army "take over" all activities in an area of acute military concern. The positive terms of reference the Economic Coordinator carried with him from Washington were checks on the authority of the theater commander who could take no action that might affect the Coordinator's duties adversely despite the omnipotence of his position otherwise. The civilian side of the government had, in effect, given the military the limits of their responsibility and authority for economic affairs in Korea and had assumed responsibility themselves for everything beyond those limits. Whether any such limits should have been made prior to the armistice is, of course, deeply debatable; but there may be good justification for estimating that had positive and reasonable limits been set and consequent risks assumed by the civilian side of the government, they would have been accepted by the military, even if they might have advised against it.

Finally, the Economic Coordinator's task was simplified by the complete subordination of the UNKRA effort to the defense support program. Moreover, the problems of tying the UNKRA projects into the integrated plan became less and less a chore as UNKRA funds began to dry up until, finally, the agency could not afford to undertake new projects even within the specified fields where the Agent General had assumed responsibility under the original agreement with the Economic Coordinator.

## The Withering Away of UNKRA

Quickly after the signing of the armistice agreement, the General Assembly had reaffirmed the intention of the United Nations to carry out a program of relief and rehabilitation in Korea.[35] Indeed, at the Assembly's Eighth Session in the fall of 1953, the Agent General received general authorization to implement a program of $85,000,000 for the financial year ending June 30, 1954, and $110,000,000 for the financial year from July, 1, 1954, to June, 30, 1955. The details of the programs which were additional to the $70,000,000 program inaugurated almost a year earlier, were, however, to be worked out with the United Nations Command and subject to final approval by the UNKRA Advisory Committee. Unfortunately, the Assembly could not, at the same time, provide the funds that would make these programs possible, but only "urge" that contributions be made.[36]

During the debate in the Assembly's Second (Economic and Financial) Committee, the American delegate repeated that his government "was definitely committed to the concept of cooperative action" in Korea. He warned, however, that while the United States expected to continue to contribute to UNKRA, the rate of its contributions would depend on the rate of payments of other countries since the United States had only undertaken to provide 65 per cent of the total original target of $250,000,000.[37] A concerted fund-raising campaign was soon set into motion, officially through the Assembly's Negotiating Committee on Extra-Budgetary Funds and, simultaneously, through normal diplomatic channels by the United States government.

The Special Negotiating Committee which the Assembly had established at its Fifth Session in 1950 to work out contributions to UNKRA had been re-established each year and charged, not only with the task of contacting governments to encourage voluntary contributions to the Korean program, but also lately with similar responsibilities for the UN Expanded Program of Technical Assistance, for the United Nations Relief and Works Agency for Palestine Refugees in the Near East (UNRWAPNE) and for the United Nations Children's Fund (UNICEF). When the Committee took up its efforts on behalf of UNKRA after the Eighth Session, pledges to the agency totaled $207,622,000. In its report to the Assembly at the Ninth Session in 1954, the Committee announced that despite a slight increase in pledges to $210,075,323, only $112,189,865 had actually been paid and prospects for further payments were extremely doubtful. It was the sad experience of negotiating for funds for UNKRA, particularly, that led the Committee to suggest

> . . . that proposals for target figures for extra-budgetary programmes should . . . be referred, before final approval, to an appropriate body for a realistic appraisal of the amounts of money that are in fact likely to be available for the programme. . . . While such a procedure may mean that a smaller target figure is fixed for a programme in its early stages, it would undoubtedly avoid the later embarrassment and administrative complication that arise when a programme, designed according to a large target figure, is forced in fact to operate on a far smaller sum of money.[38]

The United States had assisted the work of the Negotiating Committee during the early months of 1954 by privately approaching other governments through its diplomatic representatives in foreign capitals.[39] In Europe, little excitement could be roused not only because the major nations, Britain and France, had other commitments in Asia which they considered came before Korea, but also because the Korean affair had never had the same emotional appeal it had had in the United States. The American defense support program had, in addition, underscored the fact that Korea was an area of primary concern to Washington and only of secondary importance to other governments. Moreover, the uncertainty of Korea's future despite the armistice, the burden of European defense that was being accepted under the unifying effect of the Korean conflict and American pressure, and the reluctance to

support the Rhee government, all contributed to make it virtually impossible to gain substantial fresh funds for UNKRA.

For the countries of Latin America and Asia, interest in
UNKRA had centered on its being a pilot project for an expanded program of international technical and economic assistance. The uncertainties of the political and military situation, however, continually frustrated the furtherance of this
theme and dulled the interest of these nations which had to be
more conscious of their own needs for economic development.
The growing neutralist bloc could not, moreover, be expected to
contribute to UNKRA after its subordination to the defense
support program of the United States. An attempt had been
made in 1950 to gain the support of this group by placing
India on the UNKRA Advisory Committee. The Indian delegation, however, had never taken an active role on the Committee
and during the Eighth Session the Indian representative on the
Second Committee had considered it adequate to note his
government's support for reconstruction while reminding
everyone "that relief should be given to the whole peninsula." [40]
Finally, those nations, such as the Philippines, Thailand and
Turkey, that might be expected to assist, had largely exhausted
their potential contributions to the Korean problem by their
contributions to the military operations and the emergency
relief program.

The political conference on Korea held in the spring of 1954
did not, unfortunately, create a more sympathetic environment for pleading for contributions to UNKRA. Although
the armistice agreement had required that a political conference be held within three months of the signing, it was not until
the Berlin Conference of February, 1954, that arrangements
for the meeting were made. At Berlin, the Foreign Ministers
of the United States, the United Kingdom, France and the
Soviet Union finally reached agreement on a conference to be
held in Geneva in April to discuss both the Korean and Indo-
Chinese questions. Agreement on Korea, however, never got
very far once the conference met. Discussions quickly came
down to two Allied requirements on which it proved impossible

to get communist accord: recognition of the authority and competence of the United Nations in Korea; and procedures for carrying out free elections throughout Korea under UN supervision.[41] The communist side refused to recognize UN authority and termed the Security Council and General Assembly resolutions on Korea between 1950 and 1953 illegal, charging that the United States had used the United Nations as a cover for waging a war of aggression. On the question of elections, the communists countered with a proposal for a meeting of an all-Korean Commission in which North Korean governmental participants would have a virtual veto although they represented a minority of the total Korean population. In the face of these objections, the nations which had contributed military forces to the United Nations Command announced that "further consideration and examination of the Korean question . . . would serve no useful purpose." [42]

The Geneva Conference did little more than confirm the political division of the Korean peninsula. The problem of free elections which had plagued the efforts at unification in 1946 had not lost any of its imponderable implications. Korea was to remain divided for a long time and any enterprise connected with Korea had to accept this as a fact of life. If anyone had expected that the circumstances under which UNKRA had originally been created might still come to pass, his argument would be even less convincing after Geneva. Nor was there any chance now that the United States would abandon its defense support program and try to create a new set of circumstances, centering on the neutralization of Korea, which would enable UNKRA to work. Syngman Rhee had kept his peace, as agreed, but he certainly would not now give up his new army. [43]

For the United States, UNKRA now became only a symbol of collective action in Korea.[44] The agency would be supported so long as other governments contributed and the United States' share did not exceed 65 per cent of the total. Accordingly, at the Ninth Session of the General Assembly, additional contributions of $14,500,000 were announced by the governments of Australia, Canada, the United Kingdom and the United States, with the United States matching the other contributions in order to keep its share at the agreed ratio.[45] In announcing his government's contribution, however, the British delegate declared that "Her Majesty's Government has decided to make this final contribution in common with other governments which have contributed so generously to the funds of the Agency in the hope that members of the United Nations which have not hitherto contributed, or which are in a position to make further contributions, will now be as generous as possible in subscribing funds to enable the Agency to complete its excellent work." [46]

The end of contributions from the United Kingdom and the British Commonwealth governments meant, in fact, the end of contributions from the United States as well. The British and Commonwealth contributions represented the only source of substantial funds for UNKRA after the United States. As of June, 30, 1955, by which time the contributions announced at the Ninth Session of the Assembly had been received, of a total of $138,465,474 received by the agency, $92,902,615 had been contributed by the United States and $38,427,369 by the United Kingdom, Australia, Canada and New Zealand, almost 100 per cent of the original pledges of the latter governments.[47] In an effort to stimulate contributions from other sources, the Chairman of the Negotiating Committee immediately after the closing of the Ninth Session of the General Assembly addressed a last appeal to all governments:

> The General Assembly has set the target figure for the UNKRA program at $266 million and . . . expressed the desire that the implementation of the programs of UNKRA . . . be achieved to the maximum extent possible. If this wish of the General Assembly is to be met, prompt and substantial pledges and payments from the majority of states will be required. If such contributions are not forthcoming, the program will have to be drastically curtailed . . . .[48]

The appeal was a failure and the Committee reported to the next session of the Assembly that "[it] does not believe that

## TABLE 2 *

STATEMENT OF GOVERNMENT PLEDGES AND CONTRIBUTIONS TO THE UNITED NATIONS
KOREAN RECONSTRUCTION AGENCY AS AT 30 JUNE 1957
(In U.S. Dollar Equivalent)

| Member States | Amount Pledged | Received in Cash | Received in Kind † | Total Received | Balance Outstanding |
|---|---|---|---|---|---|
| Argentina | 500,000 | ...... | 500,000 | 500,000 | ...... |
| Australia ‡ | 3,616,446 | 3,616,446 | ...... | 3,616,446 | ...... |
| Austria | 179,474 | 139,474 | 40,000 | 179,474 | ...... |
| Belgium | 600,000 | 600,000 | ...... | 600,000 | ...... |
| Burma | 49,934 | ...... | 49,934 | 49,934 | ...... |
| Cambodia | 1,000 | 1,000 | ...... | 1,000 | ...... |
| Canada | 7,413,021 | 7,413,021 | ...... | 7,413,021 | ...... |
| Chile | 250,000 | 250,000 | ...... | 250,000 | ...... |
| Denmark | 860,000 | 336,615 | ...... | 336,615 | 523,385 |
| Dominican Republic | 10,000 | 10,000 | ...... | 10,000 | ...... |
| Egypt | 28,716 | ...... | 28,716 | 28,716 | ...... |
| El Salvador | 500 | 500 | ...... | 500 | ...... |
| Ethiopia § | 40,000 | 40,000 | ...... | 40,000 | ...... |
| France | 142,857 | 142,857 | ...... | 142,857 | ...... |
| Greece | 18,063 | ...... | 18,063 | 18,063 | ...... |
| Guatemala ‖ | 7,704 | 7,704 | ...... | 7,704 | ...... |
| Honduras | 2,500 | 2,500 | ...... | 2,500 | ...... |
| Indonesia | 143,706 | 143,706 | ...... | 143,706 | ...... |
| Israel | 36,100 | ...... | 36,100 | 36,100 | ...... |
| Italy | 2,014,933 | 320,000 | 1,694,933 | 2,014,933 | ...... |
| Lebanon § | 50,000 | 50,000 | ...... | 50,000 | ...... |
| Liberia | 15,000 | ...... | 15,000 | 15,000 | ...... |
| Luxembourg | 50,000 | 50,000 | ...... | 50,000 | ...... |
| Mexico | 40,000 | ...... | ...... | ...... | 40,000 |
| Netherlands | 1,052,632 | 1,052,632 | ...... | 1,052,632 | ...... |
| New Zealand | 836,850 | 836,850 | ...... | 836,850 | ...... |
| Norway | 1,725,323 | 1,698,846 | 26,477 | 1,725,323 | ...... |

TABLE 2 *(continued)*

| | Amount Pledged | Received in Cash | Received in Kind † | Total Received | Balance Outstanding |
|---|---|---|---|---|---|
| *Member States (continued)* | | | | | |
| Pakistan | 315,000 | 315,000 | . . . . . . . . | 315,000 | . . . . . . . . |
| Panama | 3,000 | . . . . . . . . | . . . . . . . . | . . . . . . . . | 3,000 |
| Paraguay § | 10,000 | 10,000 | . . . . . . . . | 10,000 | . . . . . . . . |
| Saudi Arabia | 20,000 | 20,000 | . . . . . . . . | 20,000 | . . . . . . . . |
| Sweden | 966,518 | 374,926 | . . . . . . . . | 374,926 | 591,592 |
| United Kingdom of Great Britain and Northern Ireland ‡ | 26,840,002 | 26,840,002 | . . . . . . . . | 26,840,002 | . . . . . . . . |
| United States of America ‡ | 92,902,615 | 92,902,615 | . . . . . . . . | 92,902,615 | . . . . . . . . |
| Venezuela | 100,000 | 30,000 | 70,000 | 100,000 | . . . . . . . . |
| Total | 140,841,894 | 187,204,694 | 2,479,223 | 139,683,917 | 1,157,977 |
| *Non-Member States* | | | | | |
| Liechtenstein | 465 | 465 | . . . . . . . . | 465 | . . . . . . . . |
| Monaco | 1,144 | 1,144 | . . . . . . . . | 1,144 | . . . . . . . . |
| Switzerland | 313,954 | 290,698 | 23,256 | 313,954 | . . . . . . . . |
| The Vatican | 10,000 | 10,000 | . . . . . . . . | 10,000 | . . . . . . . . |
| Viet-Nam | 10,000 | 10,000 | . . . . . . . . | 10,000 | . . . . . . . . |
| Total | 335,563 | 312,307 | 23,256 | 335,563 | . . . . . . . . |
| Grand total | 141,177,457 | 187,517,001 | 2,502,479 | 140,019,480 | 1,157,977 |

* Source: UN General Assembly, Twelfth Session, *Official Records*, Supplement No. 17 (A/3651), p. 33.

† These contributions in kind have been made available to the Unified Command for use in the Emergency Programme for Civilian Relief in Korea.

‡ Previous contribution statements have shown pledges of $4,001,726 for Australia, $28,000,000 for the United Kingdom, and $162,500,000 for the United States. At the time these pledges were made, the governments concerned stipulated that payment of the full amounts was conditional upon certain matching contributions, being received from other governments, and in the case of Australia and the United States upon certain percentage limitations. In this statement these amounts have been adjusted to reflect the maximum contributions of these governments in accordance with the terms of their pledges, on the basis of total contributions made by other governments to the programme.

§ Offered to Emergency Programme but made available to UNKRA.

‖ The contribution from the government of Guatemala represents the proceeds of sale by the government of 15,000 pounds of coffee.

any further efforts it might make on behalf of UNKRA would be likely to produce further substantial contributions." [49]

In his report to the Tenth Session, the Agent General told the Assembly that the projects that had been set into operation more than two years earlier had now begun to have a real impact on the Korean economy. Nevertheless, he was obliged to face up to the hard facts of a dwindling purse. He, therefore, announced that "a time-table has been established which calls for the completion of most of [the projects] by the end of 1956, although a few of the larger construction projects [and certain technical assistance projects] will carry over into 1957 and possibly into 1958." [50] In the same tone, the Assembly, for the first time in five years, did not urge governments to contribute to UNKRA, but simply stressed "the desire that the approved programmes of the Agency be expeditiously implemented to the maximum extent possible within available funds." [51]

In the final accounting, thirty-eight governments contributed to UNKRA in either cash or kind (see Table 2). Over 90 per cent of total contributions, however, came from four governments—the United States, Great Britain, Canada, and Australia—and were paid against pledges made at the time UNKRA had been established. The United States, moreover, constantly maintained that if it were to increase its contribution beyond the 65 per cent limitation, the multilateral character of the agency would be lost and it would no longer even be a symbol of international cooperation.[52] What was ignored was the fact that American influence would be over-riding in any case and that the multilateral character of the program depended more on the restraint of the United States than on the initiative of other governments. Nevertheless, the United States had done little, after 1950, to make contributions to UNKRA attractive to other governments from the point of view of their own interests. Thus when, by 1955, the United States had paid 65 per cent of the disappointing total that could be expected, "there was no alternative," as Assistant Secretary of State Robertson explained, ". . . but to agree that an orderly liquidation of UNKRA should follow." [53]

# BILATERAL ASSISTANCE 211

1. Appendix to Hearings before a Subcommittee of the Committee on Government Operations, House of Representatives, 83rd Congress, 2nd Session, *Relief and Rehabilitation in Korea* (Washington: Government Printing Office, 1954), p. 171. Hereinafter referred to as *Brownson Committee Hearings.*

2. For the text of the President's message to Congress, July 27, 1953, see the Department of State *Bulletin,* XXIX, No. 737 (August 10, 1953), 193–94.

3. As Representative Judd (R. of Minnesota), a frequent critic of the Truman Administration's Far Eastern Policy, said in telling of Mr. Robertson's briefing of Congress on his return from negotiating with Rhee in late June: "The President was as anxious as our chairman (of the House Committee on Foreign Affairs) to get the boys out of Korea and that is one of the prices we paid for it. He had to accede to this or continue the war or see Korea go over to the enemy. . . ."—Hearings before the Committee on Foreign Affairs, House of Representatives, 83rd Congress, 2nd Session, *Mutual Security Act of 1954* (Washington: Government Printing Office, 1954), p. 456.

4. See the testimony of G. Hall, Hearings before a subcommittee of the Committee on Appropriations, House of Representatives, 83rd Congress, 1st Session, *Mutual Security Appropriations for 1954* (Washington: Government Printing Office, 1953), pp. 596–97.

5. See the text of the Relief and Rehabilitation recommendations of the Tasca Report in the Department of State *Bulletin,* XXIX, No. 741 (September 7, 1953), 313–15.

6. Even though the Tasca Report was written before the armistice was actually a fact, this argument was nonetheless valid since the agreement signed on July 27 left the major political problems to a subsequent conference.

7. *New York Times,* May 27, 1953, p. 6.

8. *Ibid.,* May 29, 1953, p. 4.

9. UN Doc., S/3079 (August 7, 1953).

10. *New York Times,* July 28, 1953, p. 7.

11. Hearings before the Committee on Appropriations, U.S. Senate, 83rd Congress, 1st Session, *Mutual Security Appropriations for 1954* (Washington: Government Printing Office, 1953), pp. 922–23.

12. *Ibid.*

13. *New York Times,* August 2, 1953, p. 1.

14. *Memorandum for the President,* from the Director of the Bureau of the Budget, Joseph M. Dodge, dated August 6, 1953, subject: *United States Organization for Economic Aid Activities in Korea;* also, *Memorandum on the United States Organization for Economic Aid Activities in Korea,* submitted to the President for approval by the National Security Council, dated August 7, 1953. Reprinted in *Brownson Committee Hearings,* Appendix pp. 230–32. For purposes of convenience and clarity, these two documents are handled as one in the discussion of their contents. If some differentiation is necessary, it can be said that the NSC Memorandum was of a "policy" nature and that of the Bureau of the Budget of a "management" nature.

15. Italics added.

16. Statement by Secretary of State Dulles and President Rhee, August 7, 1953. Reprinted in Senate Document No. 74, 83rd Congress, 1st Session, *The United States and The Korean Problem,* Documents 1943–1953 (Washington: Government Printing Office, 1953), pp. 125–26.

17. *New York Times,* September 24, 1952, p. 1.

18. See text of Secretary Dulles' speech of January 12, 1954, before the Council on Foreign Relations in New York, Department of State *Bulletin,* XXX, No. 761 (January 25, 1954), 107–10.

19. The triple duties of Mr. Wood's post had been spelled out in considerable detail in the National Security Council's recommendations of August 7, 1953.

20. Mr. Wood's own explanation of the position is found in *Brownson Committee Hearings*, pp. 15–19.

21. For exchange of letters between General Coulter and Mr. Wood, see *Brownson Committee Hearings*, Appendix, p. 233.

22. The entire tungsten production is sold to the United States and supervision of this activity was thus maintained under exclusive United States management.

23. The division of responsibility was set out in a memorandum from the Office of the Economic Coordinator dated September 8, 1953. For text, see *Brownson Committee Hearings*, Appendix, pp. 234–37.

24. As an example, see memorandum dated September 26, 1953, from the Office of the Economic Coordinator to KCAC and UNKRA, subject "Preparation of Project Listings," reprinted in *Brownson Committee Hearings*, Appendix, pp. 228–29.

25. The program objectives in Korea were thus expressed by the Economic Coordinator in a briefing document prepared for the Brownson Committee in October 1953: "The over-all objective of the proposed program is to develop a viable economy capable, without outside assistance, of (a) supporting a standard of living approximating that of 1949–50, and (b) supporting a military force adequate to deter external aggression and repel invasions by other than a major military power."—*Brownson Committee Hearings*, Appendix, p. 208.

26. *New York Times,* August 11, 1953, p. 4.

27. *Ibid.,* June 9, 1954, p. 10.

28. *Brownson Committee Hearings,* Appendix, pp. 200–201.

29. *Ibid.,* Appendix, pp. 204–5.

30. When the rate was again reviewed in June, 1954, however, the controversy broke out anew and was not settled until President Rhee had gone so far as to take the matter up with President Eisenhower during his visit to Washington in July. Tense negotiations over the next few months finally resulted in the signing of a new agreement on November 17, 1954. The new agreement provided that the rate of exchange would be that available through the sale of United States dollars to private traders at open auction. This soon resulted in a rate of exchange of 500 hwan to $1.00.

31. *New York Times,* December 15, 1953, p. 2.

32. For text of agreement, see House Report No. 2574, Twenty-Third Intermediate Report of the Committee on Government Operations, House of Representatives, 83rd Congress, 2nd Session, *Relief and Rehabilitation in Korea* (Washington: Government Printing Office, 1954), Appendix IV, pp. 68–69 (hereinafter referred to as *Brownson Committee Report*).

33. *Brownson Committee Hearings,* p. 136.

34. Hearings before the Committee on Foreign Affairs, House of Representatives, 84th Congress, 2nd Session, *Mutual Security Act of 1956* (Washington: Government Printing Office, 1956), pp. 355–56.

35. General Assembly Resolution 711 (VII), *The Korean Question,* August 28, 1953.

36. General Assembly Resolution 725 (VIII), *The Korean Question: Report of the Agent General of the United Nations Korean Reconstruction Agency,* December 7, 1953.

37. UN General Assembly, Eighth Session, 2nd Committee, *Official Records,* 283rd meeting (December 2, 1953), pp. 195–96.

38. UN Doc. A/2730, *Report of the Negotiating Committee on Extra-budgetary Funds* (20 September 1954).

39. *New York Times,* February 4, 1954.

40. UN General Assembly, Eighth Session, 2nd Committee, *Official Records,* 283rd Meeting (December 2, 1953), p. 197.

41. See the *Korean Problem at the Geneva Conference, April 26–June 15, 1954,* Department of State Publication 5609, International Organization and Conference Series II (Far Eastern), 4 (Washington: Government Printing Office, 1954).

42. UN Doc. A/2786, *Report to the United Nations on the Korean Political Conference* (11 November 1954).

43. In July, President Eisenhower invited Rhee to Washington and, in what must be considered a move to placate the Korean leader after the dismal failure of the Geneva Conference (which Rhee had predicted), reaffirmed the principles behind the defense support program. See *New York Times,* July 31, 1954, p. 2, for the joint statement issued at the completion of the talks.

44. See the testimony of Deputy Assistant Secretary of State for Far Eastern Affairs, Everett F. Drumright, Hearings before the Committee on Foreign Affairs, House of Representatives, 83rd Congress, 2nd Session, *The Mutual Security Act of 1954* (Washington: Government Printing Office, 1954), p. 451.

45. Press Release KOR/459, 4 January 1955, issued by the United Nations, Department of Public Information, pp. 2–3.

46. UN General Assembly, Ninth Session, Plenary Session, *Official Records,* 511th Meeting (December 14, 1954), pp. 481–82.

47. This did represent 100 per cent in the cases of Canada and New Zealand. UN General Assembly, Tenth Session, *Official Records,* Supplement No. 18 (A/2936), p. 25.

48. For text of appeal, see Press Release KOR/461, 31 January 1955, issued by the United Nations, Department of Public Information.

49. UN Doc. A/2945, *Report of the Negotiating Committee for Extra-budgetary Funds* (30 August 1955), p. 3.

50. UN General Assembly, Tenth Session, *Official Records,* Supplement No. 18 (A/2936), p. 22.

51. General Assembly Resolution 920 (X), *Report of the Agent General of the United Nations Korean Reconstruction Agency,* 25 October 1955.

52. See, for example, Mr. Stassen's testimony before the Committee on Appropriations, U.S. Senate, 83rd Congress, 2nd Session, *Mutual Security Appropriations for 1955* (Washington: Government Printing Office, 1954), pp. 155–56. At the time, the United States contribution to the UN Expanded Program for Technical Assistance amounted to 55 per cent of the total. The UNKRA 65 per cent thus bore a relationship to United States policy on this and other voluntary UN programs. For a good discussion of the problems of financing UN programs and a summary of the United States position, see *Budgetary and Financial Problems of the United Nations,* Staff Study No. 6, Prepared for the Subcommittee on the United Nations Charter, Committee on Foreign Relations, U.S. Senate, 83rd Congress, 2nd Session (Washington: Government Printing Office, 1955), Document No. 164, particularly pp. 167–70.

53. Hearings before a subcommittee of Committee on Appropriations, House of Representatives, 84th Congress, 1st Session, *Mutual Security Appropriations for 1956* (Washington: Government Printing Office, 1955), p. 362.

# CHAPTER IX

# SUMMING UP

# SUMMING UP

When Mr. Robertson concluded that the United States had no alternative but to agree to the liquidation of UNKRA, Congressman Gary, Democrat from Virginia, assured him that "you will find that is very agreeable to [the Appropriations] committee." The congressman explained that "we have never been too sold on UNKRA" because "we did not feel the other countries were making a comparative contribution and we felt that if we were going to do the job we might as well do it ourselves and in our own way and have control over the funds rather than put the money up and someone else spend it." [1]

Mr. Gary was voicing a not unusual congressional concern that money handed over to an international agency passes beyond the fiscal controls of the government and, indeed, beyond any system of accountability that will insure that it will be used to further American interests.[2] The State Department, on the other hand, had objected to exceeding the sixty-five per cent of the total contributed because it would mean that the United States would have *too much* control over UNKRA and the program would lose its international character. The Department, however, had always been most aware of congressional interest that the United States have a proper say in UNKRA affairs. At the time General Coulter was appointed as head of the Agency, for example, a State Department spokesman confided to the House Committee on Appropriations that "[a] point that I trust is of interest to the committee is what degree of participation does the United States have in determining UNKRA policy." He went on to tell the committee that "the present Agent General of UNKRA who was appointed by the Secretary-General of the United Nations on May 16, 1953, is Lieutenant General Coulter, United States Army retired, who had had 3 years of both military and diplomatic experience in Korea and thereafter has served a year as

217

the Chief of the Washington Office of UNKRA before this appointment." As if this wasn't enough, he confirmed that General Coulter "was sponsored by the United States." [3]

Between the insistence on the part of Congress that the United States protect its investment and the State Department's difficulty in seeing that this is done without possibly frustrating what might be different, although not opposing, interests of other nations, lies a fundamental problem in United States participation in international agencies: How much of a "say" is proper? The absolute dependence of any agency on its American contribution throws the controlling mechanism into imbalance, for financial oversight is nothing more than political control when it begins to be concerned with how much can be spent for what and where. In the case of UNKRA, American influence was also strengthened by the control that its military leaders held over all activities in South Korea. Even if UNKRA had been able to develop independent means of income, it could not have operated without the support of a directive to the theater commander from his Washington superiors.

If UNKRA were not an instrument of American foreign policy, as had been maintained by the first Agent General, it certainly depended on the United States whether the agency would be active or inactive, whether, in fact, it would operate or go into liquidation. What is most distressing about the UNKRA experience, therefore, is that if the American government had wanted to pursue the Korean recovery program through the United Nations after the armistice agreement was signed, if it had been judged to be in the national interest of the United States to do so, it might well have been politically impossible. The long period of inactivity and frustration had killed enthusiasm for UNKRA on the part of nations that would have to contribute to its support. It had also embittered the men in Congress who saw large administrative costs and no operations, and, thus, their worst fears justified. The long, drawn-out, indecisive fighting and the impact of the charges of guilt and neglect debated during the presidential election of

1952, aggravating the already grave national trauma produced by the loss of China to communism, the MacArthur dismissal, and the irresponsible search for scapegoats conducted principally by Senator McCarthy, had left little public patience for solutions that did not hasten the withdrawal of American troops from Korea, and, superficially at any rate, reduce American involvement in the Far East. Finally, the build-up of the South Korean Army and the bargain with Syngman Rhee to keep him from destroying the truce, not to mention Rhee himself, were obligations of the United States alone, obligations that other nations could hardly be expected to share.

The United States had been so instrumental in setting up UNKRA in 1950 that it must be assumed that, at the time, it was in the national interest to support a reconstruction program through the United Nations. Reconstruction policy could not, however, be formulated in isolation, but had to be related to political and military objectives. UNKRA, of course, was planned in that brief period of enthusiasm when the military objective of the United States and of the United Nations was to create conditions permitting the unification of the Korean peninsula and the holding of free elections in North Korea under UN supervision.[4] But UNKRA also belonged to the period of limited objectives, of stopping communist aggression at the 38th parallel and leaving the unification of Korea to a future conference table. For in an announcement that was never made, President Truman had planned late in March, 1951, with the knowledge and consent of other nations with troops in Korea, to suggest to the communists that a cease-fire be arranged. The President had intended to urge that "the Korean people are entitled to the assistance of the world community in repairing the ravages of war . . . assistance which the United Nations is ready to give and for which it has established the necessary machinery. . . . What is needed is peace, in which the United Nations can use its resources in the creative tasks of reconstruction."[5]

Mr. Truman did not make his announcement. Several days

earlier General MacArthur had issued an unauthorized ultimatum to the communist side warning that "the enemy . . . must by now be painfully aware that a decision of the United Nations to depart from its tolerant effort to contain the war to the area of Korea, through an expansion of our military operations to its coastal areas and interior bases, would doom Red China to the risk of imminent military collapse." [6] After the shock of MacArthur's threat to expand the war, the President felt than an offer to end the fighting would be too confusing for friend and foe alike and so he did the next best thing: he dismissed General MacArthur from his command and recalled him from the Far East.

UNKRA began life in Korea under the storm that broke over the MacArthur dismissal. But if support for the agency was still consonant with the limited objective the United States was now pursuing in Korea, it was only the tail and could not be expected to wag the dog. Mr. Truman was no longer in a position to call for the peace in which UNKRA could operate without risking an accusation of appeasement amid the passions of the public hearings on MacArthur's case. The call had to come from the other side and when it did, on the heels of the communist set-back in their May and June drives to recapture Seoul, it had to be handled with caution and care, with an awareness of the danger that it might be a booby trap to delay the fighting while the communists regrouped, refreshed and restrengthened their military power. Under such circumstances it was politically and militarily hazardous to weaken the authority of the theater commander in order to begin an internationally supervised reconstruction program.

Nevertheless, by the time the truce talks started in July, the basic elements of a stalemate were apparent even though the fighting did not entirely stop. Secretary of State Acheson had responded to the communist demand that all foreign forces leave Korea immediately by promising that "[even] if there is an effective armistice, a United Nations force must remain in Korea until a genuine peace has been firmly established and the Korean people have assurance that they can work out their

future free from the fear of aggression." He added that "the
size of the United Nations force remaining in Korea will depend upon circumstances and, particularly, upon the faithful-
ness with which an armistice is carried out." [7] The determination to maintain forces under UN sponsorship in Korea was
still American policy almost nine years later.

In many ways the truce talks were not the end, but only the
beginning, the beginning of a period of "suspended operations." "Nevertheless," as a very wise observer remarked, "a
period of suspended operations, even though the crucial issues
behind the war are also held in suspense, is a period of political
opportunity. And one way of using the time to advantage is to
make a start, if possible a dramatic start, on the rehabilitation
of South Korea." [8] Unfortunately, the United States did not
make a dramatic start! The whole field of relief and reconstruction was left to the military who operated from the short-
range of immediate military needs. For over a year nothing
was done in the area of reconstruction for fear that a fresh out-
burst of fighting would dissipate the investment. The military, in its handling of relief—supplying food, clothing and
shelter—happily performed miracles. The military were also
given the task of checking economic instability, an undertaking
in which they were considerably less successful.

If the continuance of hostilities made it imperative that the
Army be left with responsibility for dealing with sensitive
political and economic problems, there were at least three by-
products of deep significance. First, the agreement of the
State Department to allow the military to conduct negotiations on an economic aid agreement and to settle matters of
important economic relations between the Republic of Korea
and the United States, was a virtual abdication of political
responsibility. The delegation of authority to a theater commander has distinct advantages when the ultimate objective
of the United States is military victory and all other aims are
subordinated to the actual conduct of the fighting: responsibility is clear, as are objectives, and "the man in charge" is given
authority to do his job. But there may be decided disadvan-

tages to any such unqualified delegation when purely military objectives are not overriding and military considerations tend to frustrate political objectives. By the summer of 1951, the military objective of the United States in Korea was to repel aggression and restore peace and security, and the political objectives were to facilitate peaceful unification of the peninsula and carry out a program of relief and reconstruction under international supervision. At the same time, aggression had been repelled and unification was wisely left to a conference dependent on an early truce, the result of a political decision imposed upon the theater commander. But an international program of relief and reconstruction was not permitted to begin, even within the limits of available shipping and facilities, for fear of weakening the authority of the theater commander. Where the political arm of government assumed responsibility in one area, it renounced responsibility in another, with little estimate of its importance.

Second, however broad-gauged our military leaders become under the widening range of responsibilities the armed forces are undertaking in the peacetime mobilization for cold war, their essential objectives, training and approach are centered on the demands of combat. This was especially true in an area such as Korea where fighting, though under wraps, was still going on. The field command was thus inflexible in its negotiations with the South Koreans, narrow in the interpretation of how far UNKRA could assume responsibilities, rigidly logical in determining that almost any project, no matter how innocent, was ultimately related to the conduct of the fighting, and cautiously conservative in estimating what limited transportation facilities could be diverted to non-military needs. But it is important to remember that the field commanders were only doing what they had to in order to accomplish their mission from a military point of view. They were never instructed to allow UNKRA a wide range of authority in a specified area, to see that additional port and distribution space was cleared so that a reconstruction program could begin during the gray period of truce negotiations, or to arrange for the protection of reconstruction projects because it was in the interest of the United States that such projects be started. Where they themselves were irresponsible was in the intensity with which they emphasized why the announced political objective of an internationally organized reconstruction program could not begin. Indeed, they practically disavowed their own military responsibilities if a political decision was taken against their advice. Nevertheless, the basic decision to lift American reconstruction policy out of the restrictions of the military operations was not theirs to make, but was the responsibility of the political arm of the government.

Third, with the military leaders in the Far East in charge of Korean economic affairs, the problems were handled without guidance from Washington that would relate them to broad American objectives in Asia. Instead they were left within the limited objectives of the military command in Korea. The decision to go to the aid of the attacked Republic of Korea, however, had been made despite the fact that Korea was still a military handicap in case of a major war. The United States had intervened in Korea and was determined to stay, even after deciding to limit the fighting, primarily for reasons of global strategy, to demonstrate to the Soviets that it would oppose aggression with force and, by so doing, deter the Soviets from attempting aggression elsewhere. Once having committed itself, the United States could not retreat. But neither, now, could it move ahead with force. One alternative would have been to begin to transform the essential military liability it had in Korea into political advantage in the cold war, and begin to turn the Republic of Korea itself toward some kind of viable system in which its weak military and economic position would be absorbed and strengthened through association. Instead, Korea was left to the military who had to seek more limited solutions to satisfy the immediate security requirements of their troops.

Despite uncritical acceptance of the military argument that reconstruction could not be started while hostilities were still on, there seems to have been a persistent belief in Washington during the entire period of military domination that UNKRA would begin large-scale operations under the terms of the original resolution as soon as a truce agreement was concluded. This thinking seems to have been based on a reliance on paper arrangements rather than a realistic appraisal of the actual situation taking shape. On paper, pledges to UNKRA totalled over $200 million and UNKRA was to take over from the military 180 days after the cessation of hostilities. In reality, other nations were getting increasingly dubious of assuming direct responsibility for the Korean problem. Moreover, it was becoming clear that a cessation of hostilities was not going to bring with it a peaceful, unified peninsula, but rather tense division, rival armies trained and supported by the United States and the Soviet Union, and domestic political demands that the United States minimize its own ground troops in Korea. Only when, late in 1952, the moment came to transfer substantial sums of money to UNKRA for the first time, did it suddenly strike home to those in Washington who had been handling UNKRA affairs for two years that the agency was not going to be able to take on the job of Korean reconstruction.

Nevertheless, by the time UNKRA was completely liquidated it had spent $146,000,000, undertaken projects at 4,235 different sites in South Korea and had existed for over eight years.[9] It has, therefore, had some effect on the South Korean economy and certainly on the South Korean people who have become accustomed to see UNKRA experts, bags of grain, school textbooks, textile machinery, industrial machinery, housing projects and agricultural tools. What was finally accomplished through UNKRA, however, is a far cry from Mr. Acheson's projection in September, 1950, that what the United Nations did in Korea could help "set a pattern of co-ordinated economic and social action in other places where the need is for development rather than for rehabilitation." Yet, if the circumstances following the intervention of the Chinese Communists set off a chain of complications for a multilateral program in Korea, the need for economic and social develop-

ment elsewhere continues to be as pressing and important as it
was in 1950. Thus, despite all the changes in the circumstances
of UNKRA's establishment, Korean reconstruction might still
have been a superb opportunity for the United States to surge
forward in the struggle for the mind of Asia during the "period
of suspended operations" which was also a "period of political
opportunity."

By the time the armistice was signed, however, there were
clear and almost unsurmountable barriers which kept the
United States from following a multilateral approach to the
problem of Korean reconstruction no matter what advantages
there might have been in such a policy. A large South Korean
army had been trained and equipped; Syngman Rhee had
held the future of the truce in his hands and continued to hold
an incredibly strong bargaining position with the United
States government; American public opinion was clamoring
for the return of United States forces in the UN Command;
and the new Republican administration was unfolding a national strategy that emphasized the military requirements of
foreign aid. These were powerful and unrelenting pressures for
a bilateral policy of defense support for the Republic of Korea. The multilateral policy had to give way.

1. Hearings before a subcommittee of the Committee on Appropriations,
House of Representatives, 84th Congress, 1st Session, *Mutual Security Appropriations for 1956* (Washington: Government Printing Office, 1955), p. 362.

2. It may be only coincidence, but the highest financial officer of most United
Nations agencies has almost always been a United States national, especially
if the executive head of the agency has been the national of another Member
State.

3. Hearings before a subcommittee of the Committee on Appropriations,
House of Representatives, 83rd Congress, 1st Session, *Mutual Security Appropriations for 1954* (Washington: Government Printing Office, 1953), p. 592.
Another example occurred in 1951 when the State Department, through similar
explanation, assured the Senate Committees on Foreign Relations and Armed
Services that "there is every reasonable assurance that United States appropriated funds will not be used by the United Nations to support a government
in Korea which is hostile to the United States or incompatible with United
Nations objectives in Korea as conceived by the United States" (Hearings before the Committee on Foreign Relations and the Committee on Armed Services, U.S. Senate, 82nd Congress, 1st Session, *Mutual Security Act of 1951*
[Washington: Government Printing Office, 1951], p. 679).

4. The high point of this "brief period of enthusiasm" was the passage of the

October 7, 1950, resolution of the General Assembly, authorizing the UN forces to cross the 38th parallel into North Korea.

5. Harry S Truman, *Memoirs,* II, 439–40.

6. Quoted in *ibid.,* pp. 440–41.

7. *New York Times,* July 20, 1951, p. 2.

8. Anne O'Hare McCormick, *New York Times,* July 16, 1951, p. 20.

9. UN General Assembly, Eleventh Session, *Official Records,* Supplement No. 12 (A/3195).

APPENDIXES: DOCUMENTS

# GENERAL ASSEMBLY RESOLUTION 410 (V), 1 DECEMBER 1950, RELIEF AND REHABILITATION OF KOREA [1]

## A

The General Assembly,

Having regard to its resolution of 7 October 1950 on the problem of the independence of Korea,

Having received and considered a report of the Economic and Social Council submitted in accordance with that resolution,

Mindful that the aggression by North Korean Forces and their warfare against the United Nations seeking to restore peace in the area has resulted in great devastation and destruction which the Korean people cannot themselves repair,

Recognizing that as a result of such aggression the people of Korea are desperately in need of relief supplies and materials and help in reconstructing their economy,

Deeply moved by the sufferings of the Korean people and determined to assist in their alleviation,

Convinced that the creation of a United Nations programme of relief and rehabilitation for Korea is necessary both to the maintenance of lasting peace in the area and to the establishment of the economic foundations for the building of a unified and independent nation,

Considering that, under the said resolution of 7 October 1950, the United Nations Commission for the Unification and Rehabilitation of Korea is the principal representative of the United Nations in Korea and hence must share in the responsibility for the work undertaken by the United Nations in furtherance of the objects and purposes mentioned in the said resolution,

Considering that it is nevertheless desirable to set up a special authority with broad powers to plan and supervise rehabilitation and relief and to assume such functions and responsibilities related to planning and supervision, to technical and administrative matters, and to questions affecting organization and implementation as are to be exercised under the plans for relief and rehabilitation approved by the General Assembly, such authority to carry out its responsibilities in close co-operation with the Commission,

A. Establishment of the United Nations Korean Reconstruction Agency for the Relief and Rehabilitation of Korea

1. Establishes the United Nations Korean Reconstruction Agency (UNKRA) under the direction of a United Nations Agent General, who shall be assisted by one or more deputies. The Agent General shall be responsible to the General Assembly for the conduct (in accordance with the policies established by the General Assembly and having regard to such general policy recommendations as the United Nations Commission for the Unification and Rehabilitation of Korea may make) of the programme of relief and rehabilitation in Korea, as that programme may be determined from time to time by the General Assembly;

2. Authorizes the United Nations Commission for the Unification and Rehabilitation of Korea:

(a) To recommend to the Agent General such policies concerning the United Nations Korean Reconstruction Agency's programme and activities as the Commission may consider necessary for the effective discharge of the Commission's responsibilities in relation to the establishment of a unified, independent and democratic government in Korea;

(b) To determine, after consultation with the Agent General, the geographical areas within which the Agency shall operate at any time;

(c) To designate authorities in Korea with which the Agent General may establish relationships; and to advise the Agent General on the nature of such relationships;

(d) To take such steps as may be needed to support the Agent General in fulfilling his task in accordance with the policies established by the General Assembly for relief and rehabilitation;

(e) To consider the reports of the Agent General to the General Assembly and to transmit any comments thereon to the Economic and Social Council and the General Assembly;

(f) To call for information on those aspects of the work of the Agent General which the Commission may consider necessary for the proper performance of its work;

3. Authorizes the Commission to consult from time to time with the Agent General in regard to the provisional programme adopted by the General Assembly on the recommendation of the Economic and Social Council and especially with regard to the adequacy of that programme to meet the needs of Korea as defined in the statement of general policy, and to make recommendations thereon to the Economic and Social Council;

4. Directs the Agent General:

(a) To co-ordinate his programme with measures taken by the United Nations Commission for the Unification and Rehabilitation of Korea to carry out the recommendations of the General Assembly relating to the establishment of a unified, independent and democratic government in Korea, and to support the Commission in fulfilling this task;

(b) To commence the operation of the programme in Korea at such time as may be agreed upon by the United Nations Unified Command, the United Nations Commission for the Unification and Rehabilitation of Korea and the Agent General;

(c) To consult with and generally be guided by the advice of the United Nations Commission for the Unification and Rehabilitation of Korea on the matters set forth under paragraph 2 (a) and be governed by its advice on the matters covered in paragraphs 2 (b) and 2 (c);

5. Further directs the Agent General, in the carrying out of his functions:

(a) To ascertain, after consultation with the designated authorities in Korea, the requirements for supplies and services for relief and rehabilitation made necessary by the consequences of armed conflict in Korea;

(b) To provide for the procurement and shipment of supplies and services and for their effective distribution and utilization within Korea;

(c) To consult with and assist the appropriate authorities in Korea with respect to measures necessary for the rehabilitation of the Korean economy and the effective distribution and utilization within Korea of supplies and services furnished;

(d) To submit reports to the General Assembly through the Secretary-General, transmitting copies simultaneously to the United Nations Commission for the Unification and Rehabilitation of Korea, and to the Economic and Social Council;

(e) To be guided in matters of administration, to the extent consistent with the special requirements of the programme, by the rules and regulations established for the operation of the Secretariat of the United Nations;

Specifically he shall:

(1) Select and appoint his staff in accordance with general arrangements made in agreement with the Secretary-General, including such of the staff rules and regulations of the United Nations as the Agent General and the Secretary-General shall agree are applicable;

(2) Utilize, wherever appropriate, and within budgetary limitations, the existing facilities of the United Nations;

(3) Establish, in consultation with the Secretary-General and the Advisory Committee on Administrative and Budgetary Questions, and in agreement with the Advisory Committee established under paragraph 6 below, financial regulations for the United Nations Korean Reconstruction Agency;

(4) Arrange, in consultation with the Advisory Committee on Administrative and Budgetary Questions, for the rendering and audit of the accounts of the Agency under procedures similar to those applicable to the rendering and audit of the accounts of the United Nations;

6. Establishes an Advisory Committee consisting of representatives of five Member States to advise the Agent General with regard to major financial, procurement, distribution and other economic problems pertaining to his planning and operations. The Committee shall meet on the call of the Agent General but not less than four times a year. The meetings of the Committee shall be held at the Headquarters of the United Nations except in special circumstances, when the Committee, after consultation with the Agent General, may meet elsewhere if it deems that this would be essential to the proper performance of its work. The Committee shall determine its own methods of work and rules of procedure;

7. Requests the Secretary-General, after consulting the United Nations Commission for the Unification and Rehabilitation of Korea and the Advisory Committee, to appoint the United Nations Agent General for Korean Reconstruction, and authorizes the Agent General to appoint one or more Deputy Agents General in consultation with the Secretary-General;

8. Authorizes the Secretary-General to establish a special account to

which should be credited all contributions in cash, kind or services, the resources credited to the account to be used exclusively for the programme of relief and rehabilitation and administrative expenses connected therewith; and directs the Secretary-General to make cash withdrawals from the account upon request of the Agent General. The Agent General is authorized to use contributions in kind or services at his discretion;

9. Recommends that the Agent General in carrying out his functions:

(a) Make use at his discretion of facilities, services and personnel that may be available to him through existing national and international agencies and organizations both governmental and non-governmental;

(b) Consult with the Secretary-General and the heads of the specialized agencies before appointing his principal subordinate personnel in their respective fields of competence;

(c) Make use of the advice and technical assistance of the United Nations and the specialized agencies and, where appropriate, request them to undertake specific projects and special tasks either at their own expense or with funds made available by the Agent General;

(d) Maintain close contact with the Secretary-General for the purpose of ensuring fullest co-ordination of efforts of the organs of the United Nations and the specialized agencies in support of the programme;

10. Authorizes the Agent General to enter into agreements with such authorities in Korea as the United Nations Commission for the Unification and Rehabilitation of Korea may designate, containing terms and conditions governing measures affecting the distribution and utilization in Korea of the supplies and services furnished, in accordance with the statement of general policy on Korean relief and rehabilitation contained in Section B of the present resolution;

11. Requests the Secretary-General to make available to the maximum extent possible, and subject to appropriate financial arrangements, such facilities, advice and services as the Agent General may request;

12. Requests the specialized agencies and non-governmental organizations to make available to the maximum extent possible, and subject to appropriate financial arrangements, such facilities, advice and services as the Agent General may request;

13. Requests the Economic and Social Council to review the reports

of the Agent General and any comments which the United Nations Commission for the Unification and Rehabilitation of Korea may submit thereon, and such other data as may be available on the progress of relief and rehabilitation in Korea and to make appropriate reports and recommendations thereon to the General Assembly;

14. Calls upon all governments, specialized agencies and non-governmental organizations, pending the beginning of operations by the United Nations Korean Reconstruction Agency, to continue to furnish through the Secretary-General such assistance for the Korean people as may be requested by the Unified Command;

15. Invites countries not Members of the United Nations to participate in financing the programme of relief and rehabilitation in Korea;

B. Statement of General Policy on Relief and Rehabilitation in Korea

16. Approves the following statement of general policy:

1. The United Nations programme of relief and rehabilitation in Korea is necessary to the restoration of peace and the establishment of a unified, independent and democratic government in Korea.

2. To this end, it is the objective of the United Nations to provide, subject to the limit of the resources placed at its disposal for this purpose, relief and rehabilitation supplies, transport and services, to assist the Korean people to relieve the sufferings and to repair the devastation caused by aggression, and to lay the necessary economic foundations for the political unification and independence of the country.

3. The United Nations programme of relief and rehabilitation for Korea shall be carried out in practice in such a way as to contribute to the rapid restoration of the country's economy in conformity with the national interests of the Korean people, having in view the strengthening of the economic and political independence of Korea and having in view that, in accordance with the general principles of the United Nations, such assistance must not serve as a means for foreign economic and political interference in the internal affairs of Korea and must not be accompanied by any conditions of a political nature.

4. The United Nations programme is to be a supplement to the general recovery effort that will be undertaken by the Korean people on their own initiative and responsibility, through the most effective utilization of their own resources as well as of the aid which is rendered under the programme.

5. Whilst the programme should be consistent with the pattern of long-term economic development in Korea, it is itself necessarily limited to relief and rehabilitation, and contributions and supplies furnished under this programme shall be used exclusively for that purpose.

6. First priority shall be given to the provision of the basic necessities of food, clothing and shelter for the population of Korea and measures to prevent epidemics. Second highest priority shall be given to projects which will yield early results in the indigenous production of basic necessities; this will include the reconstruction of transport and power facilities. As the programme develops, emphasis should be shifted to the provision of other materials, supplies and equipment for the reconstruction or replacement of war-damaged facilities necessary to the economic life of the country.

7. The necessary measures shall be taken to ensure that distribution shall be so conducted that all classes of the population shall receive their equitable share of essential commodities without discrimination as to race, creed or political belief.

8. Subject to adequate control, the distribution of supplies shall be carried out, as appropriate, through public and cooperative organizations, through non-profit-making voluntary organizations such as the Red Cross, and through normal channels of private trade. At the same time, measures shall be taken to ensure that the cost of distribution and the profit from the sale of supplies are kept to the minimum. Measures shall be taken to ensure that the special needs of refugees and other distressed groups of the population are met through appropriate public welfare programmes, and accordingly the sale of relief supplies will take place only in justifiable cases and under conditions agreed upon with the United Nations Commission for the Unification and Rehabilitation of Korea.

9. The local currency proceeds derived from the sale of relief and rehabilitation supplies or, at the discretion of the Agent General, an amount commensurate with the value of goods and services supplied, shall be paid into an account under the control of the Agent General. The Agent General, after consultation with the United Nations Commission for the Unification and Rehabilitation of Korea, and in agreement with the Advisory Committee referred to in paragraph 6 of Section A of the present resolution, shall use these funds for appropriate additional relief and rehabilitation activities within Korea, for the local currency expenses of the relief and rehabilitation operations of the United Nations, or for measures to combat inflation. The proceeds shall not be used for any other purpose.

10. The necessary economic and financial measures shall be taken by the authorities in Korea to ensure that the resources provided under the United Nations programme, as well as Korean resources, are effectively employed to aid in laying the economic foundations of the country. Among these, special attention should be given to measures to combat inflation, to sound fiscal and monetary policies, to the requisite pricing, rationing and allocation controls (including the pricing of goods imported under the programme), to the prudent use of Korean foreign exchange resources together with promotion of exports, and to the efficient management of government enterprise.

11. Import taxes shall not be imposed on relief and rehabilitation supplies received under the United Nations programme.

12. The authorities in Korea should maintain such records and make such reports on the receipt, distribution and use of relief and rehabilitation supplies as may be determined by the Agent General after consultation with them.

13. All authorities in Korea shall freely permit the personnel of the United Nations to supervise the distribution of relief and rehabilitation supplies, including the examination of all storage and distribution facilities as well as records.

14. The personnel of the United Nations shall be accorded within Korea the privileges, immunities and facilities necessary for the fulfillment of their function.

15. All authorities in Korea and the Secretary-General shall use their best efforts to inform the people of Korea of the sources and purposes of the contributions of funds, supplies and services.

16. In determining Korea's needs for relief and rehabilitation, in drawing up programmes and plans, and in implementing such programmes and plans, the Agency created to administer the relief and rehabilitation programme should consult with and utilize, to the greatest extent feasible, the services of Korean authorities.

# B

The General Assembly

1. Requests the President to appoint a Negotiating Committee composed of seven or more members for the purpose of consulting, as soon as possible during the current session of the General Assembly, with Member and non-member States as to the amounts which governments may be willing to contribute towards the financing of the programme for the relief and rehabilitation of Korea;

2. Authorizes the Negotiating Committee to adopt procedures best suited to the accomplishment of its task, bearing in mind:

(a) The need for securing the maximum contribution in cash;

(b) The desirability of ensuring that any contribution in kind is of a nature which meets the requirements of the contemplated programmes; and

(c) The degree of assistance which can be rendered by specialized agencies, non-member States and other contributors;

3. Requests that, as soon as the Negotiating Committee has ascertained the extent to which Member States are willing to make contributions, all delegations be notified accordingly by the Secretary-General in order that they may consult with their governments;

4. Decides that, as soon as the Negotiating Committee has completed its work, the Secretary-General shall, at the Committee's request, arrange, during the current session of the General Assembly, an appropriate meeting of Member and non-member States at which Members may commit themselves to their national contributions and the contributions of non-members may be made known.

1. Source: UN General Assembly, Fifth Session, *Official Records*, Supplement No. 20 (A/1775), pp. 31–35.

# AGREEMENT BETWEEN UNKRA AND THE UNIFIED COMMAND, JULY 11, 1951 [1]

## DEPARTMENT OF STATE

11 July 1951

Mr. J. Donald Kingsley
*Agent General*
*United Nations Korean Reconstruction Agency*

*Sir:*

Reference is made to my letter of March 29, 1951 and to your reply of April 16, 1951 regarding an understanding to govern relations in the present phase between the United Nations instrumentalities in Korea, the United Nations Command, and the United Nations Korean Reconstruction Agency.

As a result of your letter of April 16 and further consideration of the problem of the Unified Command, it is now proposed that relations between the United Nations Command and the United Nations Korean Reconstruction Agency be established in accordance with the following provisions:

1. The responsibility of the United Nations Command for the operation of the United Nations Command programs of relief and short-term economic aid will continue until such time as the military operations will permit the transfer of this responsibility to UNKRA. The time for this transfer will be determined in accordance with the General Assembly resolution of December 1, 1950, namely, by agreement of the Unified Command, the United Nations Commission for the Unification and Rehabilitation of Korea and the Agent General. It is not possible to estimate at this time when this transfer will take place but with a view to making the transfer as smooth as possible, it is desired to introduce UNKRA into the entire operation as it progresses.

2. Two phases are envisaged:

239

(1) The period starting upon your acceptance of these proposals during which the responsibilities of the United Nations Command and UNKRA will be defined below.

This period will terminate when military operations permit and as agreed by the Unified Command, the United Nations Commission for the Unification and Rehabilitation of Korea and the Agent General.

(2) The period starting at the termination of phase (1) when UNKRA has assumed responsibility and is possibly being assisted by the United Nations Command, principally in the field of procurement and transportation.

3. During phase (1) the United Nations Command will have sole responsibility for all relief and short-term economic aid essential to the military operations. UNKRA will have responsibility for long-range planning and high level technical assistance to the Korean Government and for any program of economic aid additional to the United Nations Command program which the military situation may permit UNKRA to implement.

4. In phase (2) UNKRA will have responsibility for all United Nations relief and rehabilitation activities, being assisted possibly by the United Nations Command in the field of procurement and transportation.

5. During phase (1) UNKRA personnel operating in Korea would consist of two groups as follows:

a. The first group consisting of a small group of governmental economic and industrial technical advisors and personnel engaged in long-range planning who will operate as a group under the direction of the Agent General and be responsible to him.

b. The second group will consist of personnel engaged in programming, short-range planning, determining requirements, and actually supplying for the needs of relief and short-range rehabilitation and reconstruction. Personnel in this group may be integrated in staffs or units of the United Nations Command. The duties of the personnel in this group will be as prescribed by the United Nations Command.

6. The responsibilities of the UNKRA personnel in the first group would be as follows:

a. Technical advice and assistance to the Korean Government.

b. Planning for long-range rehabilitation and reconstruction of Korea.

c. Implementation, to the extent permitted by the military situation, of any program of economic aid additional to the United Nations Command Program.

d. Assisting the operating group by recommendations and in certain cases when called upon, by advice as to specific problems. Close coordination with the second group will be an essential part of the responsibilities of the first group.

e. Such plans or recommendations as may be made will be coordinated with the United Nations Command for determination as to whether or not they affect the mission of the United Nations Command. Any plans or recommendations which, in the opinion of the United Nations Command, affect its mission will be implemented only with the concurrence of the United Nations Command. Approved plans requiring implementation by the United Nations Command will be carried out by its operating agencies in accordance with current procedures.

7. The United Nations Command will be responsible for the logistic support of both groups.

These arrangements are considered workable only if the procedures set forth above for ensuring close coordination and avoiding any action by UNKRA which would conflict with the military necessities are carefully observed. The final authority and control of the Commander-in-Chief, United Nations Command, on the ground during hostilities are not intended to be affected by these arrangements.

If these proposals are acceptable, will you please advise us as soon as possible so that the understanding may be officially communicated to the Commander-in-Chief of the United Nations Command and put into operation promptly.

Very truly yours,

For the Secretary of State:

JOHN D. HICKERSON

*Assistant Secretary of State of the United States of America*

1. Source: KCAC Documents, p. 21.

# MEMORANDUM OF UNDERSTANDING BETWEEN UNKRA AND THE UNITED NATIONS COMMAND, DECEMBER 21, 1951[1]

1. The purpose of this memorandum is to interpret and make effective the existing agreement (hereinafter referred to as The Agreement) governing relations between the United Nations Command (UNC) and the United Nations Korean Reconstruction Agency (UNKRA). The Agreement is that proposed by the Unified Command (UC) as set forth in a letter from the Assistant Secretary of State for United Nations Affairs to the Agent General, UNKRA, dated July 11, 1951, and accepted by the Agent General, UNKRA, by letter dated July 18, 1951, attached as Exhibits A and B respectively.

2. Phase 2 of The Agreement shall commence (subject to such approval by any agent or agency of the United Nations not a party of this Memorandum as may be required at that time by any Resolution of the General Assembly) at the termination of the period of 180 days following the cessation of hostilities in Korea, as determined by the UC, unless it is determined by the UC, in consultation with the Agent General, that military operations do not permit the commencement of Phase 2 at that time, or unless an earlier transfer of responsibility is mutually agreed upon.

3. During Phase 1 of The Agreement:

a. The UNC will have sole responsibility (except in so far as may be otherwise agreed under the terms of sub-paragraph 3f hereinafter) for the operation of all projects of relief and economic aid in Korea.

b. UNKRA liaison with the Government of the Republic of Korea will be conducted only at the Agent General, Deputy Agent General, or Chief of Mission level.

c. UNKRA will maintain Planning Liaison Teams in Tokyo and Korea. The primary duty of these Teams will be to prepare and keep up to date, plans for UNKRA operations to begin at the commencement

243

of Phase 2 of The Agreement. There will be made available to the Planning Liaison Teams full information with respect to plans for, and the operation of, the UNC programs for relief and economic aid in Korea. Also, UNKRA will furnish the UNC with complete information with respect to UNKRA plans for relief and economic aid in Korea.

d. Joint Committees which shall include representatives of the appropriate military authorities and of UNKRA will be maintained in Tokyo and Korea. Such Committees will discuss all matters of common interest related to Korea. The Joint Committee in Tokyo will be the joint forum of UNC and UNKRA for consideration of operations and procedural problems as they relate to mutual responsibilities for Civil Assistance operations in Korea and will prepare from time to time such common implementing directives as may be agreed upon for implementation in the field. The Joint Committee in Korea will be responsible for the exchange of information between UNKRA and UNC and for the preparation of plans for submission to higher authority.

e. As soon as there is a cessation of hostilities in Korea as determined by the UC, the Joint Committee in Tokyo and Korea will prepare plans for the assumption of responsibility by UNKRA at the commencement of Phase 2 of The Agreement. These plans shall include an examination of the kind and approximate amount of goods and services which UNKRA may desire to have made available to Korea for relief and economic assistance, at the commencement of Phase 2 of The Agreement, by any department or agency of the United States acting through the UC.

f. To such extent as may be mutually agreed, UNKRA will undertake, from time to time, relief and rehabilitation projects in Korea, additional to the UNC program. Proposals for such projects will be initiated through the Joint Committee in Tokyo; and arrangements for the operation of agreed projects will be determined by the Joint Committee in Korea or Tokyo as may be appropriate.

g. Except as may be otherwise agreed through the Joint Committee in Tokyo, the technical assistance and advice to be furnished to the Government of the Republic of Korea by UNKRA under the terms of The Agreement will be furnished through the UNC; and technical experts required for this work will accordingly be members of the staff of the United Nations Civil Assistance Command Korea (UNCACK).

h. To such extent as may be mutually agreed, UNKRA will employ and pay civilian technical experts and other civilian staff for service with UNCACK; provided that for the civilian staff now serving with UNCACK, this arrangement will come into effect on January 1, 1952, or, in the case of a staff member whose present contract expires on an earlier date, then on that earlier date. To the maximum extent practicable, the gradings of UNKRA personnel so assigned as members of the staff of the United Nations Civil Assistance Command Korea (UNCACK) will correspond to the existing gradings for similar employment now authorized for UNC personnel.

i. UNKRA personnel attached to and integrated into the staffs and units of the UNC will be under the operational control of the Commander-in-Chief, United Nations Command or a subordinate commander. The duties and rank or precedence of all personnel comprising this group will be prescribed by the Commander-in-Chief, United Nations Command. Such personnel may be reassigned or transferred by the Commander-in-Chief, United Nations Command or appropriate subordinate commander in the same manner as any other member of the United Nations Command and to all intents and purposes, including evaluation and reporting of satisfactory performance of assigned duties, such personnel shall be considered members of the United Nations Command and shall be responsible to the Chief of the Staff or commander of the unit to which attached.

j. UNKRA will cooperate in insuring military security by:

(1) Adopting and implementing the best practicable procedures and safeguards in consultation with appropriate military authorities to insure the loyalty of all its personnel.

(2) Observing the procedures and safeguards prescribed by the Unified Command.

k. UNKRA will maintain in Korea personnel, including administrative personnel, necessary for the implementation of this Memorandum and the UNC will continue to provide logistical support for these staffs.

4. Appropriate directives implementing The Agreement as interpreted by this Memorandum will be issued forthwith.

FOR THE COMMANDER-IN-CHIEF,
UNITED NATIONS COMMAND

C. C. B. WARDEN
*Colonel, AGC*
*Adjutant General*

FOR THE AGENT GENERAL,
UNITED NATIONS RECONSTRUCTION AGENCY

ARTHUR N. RUCKER
Sir Arthur N. Rucker
*Deputy Agent General*

Tokyo, Japan–21 December 1951

1. Source: KCAC Documents, p. 23.

# SUPPLEMENTAL MEMORANDUM OF UNDERSTANDING BETWEEN UNKRA AND THE UNIFIED COMMAND, MARCH 24, 1952

1. The Memorandum of Understanding entered into by and between the United Nations Command (UNC) and the United Nations Korean Reconstruction Agency (UNKRA) in Tokyo on 21 December 1951 is hereby ratified and adopted as a Memorandum of Understanding governing relations between the Unified Command (UC) and UNKRA with respect to the matters set forth therein.

2. In addition to the Joint Committees and to the UNKRA Planning Liaison Teams in Tokyo and Korea as provided for in the Memorandum of Understanding of 21 December 1951:

   *a.* UNKRA will maintain a Planning Liaison Team in Washington with duties as set forth in paragraph 3 c of the aforementioned Memorandum of Understanding with respect to the Planning Liaison Teams maintained in Tokyo and Korea.

   *b.* A Joint Committee shall be maintained at Washington which shall consist of representatives of the UC and of UNKRA. This committee shall discuss all matters of common interest related to Korea and shall be the joint forum of the UC and UNKRA for consideration of major policy questions relating to mutual responsibilities for civil assistance operations in Korea. It will also review such plans and policy recommendations as may be submitted by the Joint UNKRA-UNC Committee in Tokyo. All recommendations of the Washington Joint Committee pertaining to matters set forth above and to projects initiated by the committee in accordance with the provisions of paragraph 3 of the Supplemental Memorandum of Understanding will be forwarded through individual committee members to the principals of such individual members for approval and implementation through UNKRA and/or UNC channels as appropriate.

3. It is mutually understood that while proposals for relief and

247

rehabilitation projects in Korea will normally be initiated through the Joint Committee in Tokyo as provided in paragraph 3 f of the Memorandum of Understanding of 21 December 1951, such projects may be initiated through the Joint Committee in Washington or Korea, and arrangements for the operation of agreed projects will be recommended by the Joint Committee in Washington, Korea, or Tokyo, as may be appropriate. It is further understood that implementing directives prepared by the Tokyo Joint Commitee pursuant to the provision of paragraph 3 d of the 21 December 1951 Memorandum of Understanding will be issued through UNKRA and/or UNC channels as appropriate, after approval by the principals of the committee members.

4. The word "loyalty" as used in paragraph 3 j (1) of the Memorandum of Understanding of 21 December 1951 shall be understood to mean loyalty to the purposes and objectives of resistance to aggression in Korea as expressed in the Resolution of the Security Council of the United Nations adopted 27 June 1950 and in the Resolution of the General Assembly of the United Nations adopted 1 February 1951.

24 March 1952

# AGREEMENT ON ECONOMIC COORDINATION BETWEEN THE UNIFIED COMMAND AND THE REPUBLIC OF KOREA MAY 24, 1952 [1]

WHEREAS by the aggression of Communist forces the Republic of Korea became in need of assistance from the United Nations;

AND WHEREAS the United Nations by the Resolution of the Security Council of June 27, 1950, recommended that members of the United Nations furnish such assistance to the Republic of Korea as may be necessary to repel the armed attack and to restore international peace and security in the area;

AND WHEREAS the United Nations by the resolution of the Security Council of July 7, 1950, recommended that members furnishing military forces and other assistance to the Republic of Korea make such forces and other assistance available to a unified command under the United States;

AND WHEREAS the United Nations by the resolution of the Security Council of July 31, 1950, requested the Unified Command to exercise responsibility for determining the requirements for the relief and support of the civilian population of Korea and for establishing in the field the procedures for providing such relief and support;

AND WHEREAS it became necessary to carry out collective action against aggression on Korean soil;

AND WHEREAS, pursuant to the July 7, 1950, resolution of the Security Council of the United Nations, the Unified Command has designated the Commander-in-Chief, United Nations Command, to exercise command responsibilities in Korea;

AND WHEREAS the Unified Command has already furnished and is furnishing substantial assistance to the Republic of Korea;

AND WHEREAS it is desirable to coordinate economic matters between the Unified Command and the Republic of Korea, in order to insure effective support of the military forces of the United Nations Command, to relieve the hardships of the people of Korea, and to establish and maintain a stable economy in the Republic of Korea; all without infringing upon the sovereign rights of the Republic of Korea;

THEREFORE, the Republic of Korea and the United States of America acting pursuant to the resolutions of the Security Council of the United Nations of July 7, 1950, and July 31, 1950, (hereinafter referred to as the Unified Command) have entered into this agreement in terms as set forth below:

## ARTICLE I

### Board

1. There shall be established a Combined Economic Board, hereafter referred to as the Board.

2. The Board shall be composed of one representative from the Republic of Korea and one representative of the Commander-in-Chief, United Nations Command (CINCUNC). Before appointing its representative each party shall ascertain that such appointment is agreeable to the other party. The Board shall establish such subordinate organization as may be necessary to perform its functions and shall determine its own procedures. It shall meet regularly at an appropriate location in the Republic of Korea.

3. The primary function of the Board shall be to promote effective economic coordination between the Republic of Korea and the Unified Command. The Board shall be the principal means for consultation between the parties on economic matters and shall make appropriate and timely recommendations to the parties concerning the implementation of this Agreement. Such recommendations shall be made only upon mutual agreement of both representatives. The Board shall be a coordinating and advisory body; it shall not be an operating body.

4. The Board and the parties hereto will be guided by the following general principles:

a. The Board will consider all economic aspects of the Unified Command programs for assistance to the Republic of Korea and all pertinent aspects of the economy and programs of the Republic of Korea, in order that each of the Board's recommendations may be a part of a consistent overall program designed to provide maximum support to the military effort of the United Nations Command in Korea, relieve the hardships of the people of Korea, and develop a stable Korean economy.

b. It is an objective of the parties to increase the capabilities of the Republic of Korea for economic self-support so far as is possible within the limits of available resources and consistent with the attainment of fiscal and monetary stability.

c. Successful conduct of military operations against the aggression of the Communists is the primary consideration of the parties. Accordingly, the command prerogatives of the Commander-in-Chief, United Nations Command, are recognized; and the Commander-in-Chief, United Nations Command, shall continue to retain all authority deemed necessary by him for the successful conduct of such operations and the authority to withdraw and to distribute supplies and services furnished under this Agreement in order to meet emergencies arising during the course of military operations or in the execution of civil assistance programs. On the other hand, the prerogatives of the Government of the Republic of Korea are recognized, and the Government of the Republic of Korea shall continue to retain all the authority of a sovereign and independent state.

5. The Board shall make recommendations necessary to insure (a) that the expenses of the Board, and the expenses (i.e., local currency (won) expenses and expenses paid from assistance funds) of all operating agencies established by the Unified Command or the Republic of Korea to carry out assistance programs under this Agreement, shall be kept to the minimum amounts reasonably necessary, and (b) that personnel, funds, equipment, supplies and services provided for assistance purposes are not diverted to other purposes.

## ARTICLE II

### The Unified Command

The Unified Command undertakes:

1. To support the recommendations of the Board to the extent of the resources made available to the Unified Command.

2. To require the Commander-in-Chief, United Nations Command, to designate his representative on the Board and to furnish to the Board such personnel and other necessary administrative support from the United Nations Command as the Board may recommend.

3. To furnish to the Board timely information on all civil assistance programs of the Unified Command and on the status of such programs.

4. Within the limitations of the resources made available by governments or organizations to the Unified Command, to assist the Republic of Korea in providing for the basic necessities of food, clothing

and shelter for the population of Korea; for measures to prevent epidemics, disease, and unrest; and for projects which will yield early results in the indigenous production of necessities. Such measures and projects may include the reconstruction and replacement of facilities necessary for relief and support of the civilian population.

5. To ascertain, in consultation with the appropriate authorities of the Government of the Republic of Korea, the requirement for equipment, supplies, and services for assisting the Republic of Korea.

6. To provide for the procurement and shipment of equipment, supplies and other assistance furnished by the Unified Command; to supervise the distribution and utilization of this assistance and to administer such assistance in accordance with the above cited resolutions of the United Nations.

7. To consult with and to utilize the services of the appropriate authorities of the Government of the Republic of Korea, to the greatest extent feasible, in drawing up and implementing plans and programs for assisting the Republic of Korea, including the employment of Korean personnel and the procurement, allocation, distribution and sale of equipment, supplies and services.

8. To carry out the Unified Command program of assistance to the Republic of Korea in such a way as to facilitate the conduct of military operations, relieve hardship, and contribute to the stabilization of the Korean economy.

9. To make available in Korea to authorized representatives of the Government of the Republic of Korea appropriate documents relating to the civil assistance programs of the Unified Command.

## ARTICLE III

### Republic of Korea

The Republic of Korea undertakes:

1. To support the recommendations of the Board.

2. To designate the representative of the Republic of Korea on the Board and to furnish to the Board such personnel and other administrative support from the Republic of Korea as the Board may recommend.

3. To furnish to the Board timely information on the economy of Korea and on those activities and plans of the Government of the Republic of Korea pertinent to the functions of the Board.

4. While continuing those measures which the Government of the Republic of Korea has endeavored heretofore to make effective, to take further measures to combat inflation, hoarding, and harmful speculative activities; to apply sound, comprehensive, and adequate budgetary, fiscal and monetary policies, including maximum collection of revenue; to maintain adequate controls over the extension of public and private credit; to provide requisite and feasible pricing, rationing and allocation controls; to promote wage and price stability; to make most efficient use of all foreign exchange resources; to maximize the anti-inflationary effect that can be derived from relief and other imported essential commodities through effective programming, distribution and sales; to provide the maximum efficiency in utilization of available production facilities; and to maximize production for export.

5. With reference to assistance furnished under this Agreement:

a. To provide operating agencies which will develop and execute, in consultation with operating agencies of the United Nations Command, programs relating to requirements, allocations, distribution, sale, use and accounting for equipment, supplies and services furnished under this Agreement; to submit to the Board budget estimates of the expenses of such Republic of Korea agencies; to include such estimates in the national budget; to defray those expenses from the resources available to the Government of the Republic of Korea, including, where the Board so recommends, such funds as may be made available under clause 7d(2) of this article; and to insure that such expenses are kept at a minimum. It is intended that such expenses will be defrayed from the general account revenues of the Republic of Korea when the economy of the Republic of Korea so permits.

b. To permit the Commander-in-Chief, United Nations Command, to exercise such control over assistance furnished hereunder as may be necessary to enable him to exercise his responsibilities under the above cited resolutions of the United Nations.

c. To achieve maximum sales consistent with relief needs and to be guided by the recommendations of the Board in determining what equipment, supplies, and services are to be distributed free of charge and what are to be sold.

d. To require Republic of Korea agencies handling equipment and supplies furnished under this Agreement to make and maintain such records and reports as the Commander-in-Chief, United Nations Command, or the Board may consider to be necessary in order to show the import, distribution, sale and utilization of such equipment and supplies.

e. To impose import duties or charges, or internal taxes or charges, on goods and services furnished by the United Nations Command only as recommended by the Board.

f. To permit and to assist the authorized representatives of the Commander-in-Chief, United Nations Command, freely to inspect the distribution and use of equipment, supplies, or services provided under this Agreement, including all storage and distribution facilities and all pertinent records.

g. To insure (1) that the people of Korea are informed of the sources and purposes of contributions of funds, equipment, supplies, and services and (2) that all equipment and supplies (and the containers thereof) made available by the Unified Command to the civilian economy of the Republic of Korea, to the extent practicable, as determined by the Commander-in-Chief, United Nations Command, are marked, stamped, branded, or labeled in a conspicuous place as legibly, indelibly, and permanently as the nature of such equipment and supplies will permit and in such manner as to indicate to the people of the Republic of Korea the sources and purposes of such supplies.

6. With reference to the assistance furnished under this Agreement which is to be distributed free of charge for the relief of the people of Korea, to insure that the special needs of refugees and other distressed groups of the population are alleviated without discrimination through appropriate public welfare programs.

7. With reference to assistance furnished under this Agreement which is to be sold:

a. To sell equipment and supplies at prices recommended by the Board, such prices to be those designed to yield the maximum feasible proceeds.

b. To sell equipment and supplies furnished under this Agreement for cash, unless otherwise recommended by the Board. If the Board should recommend that any such equipment and supplies may be sold to intermediate parties or ultimate users on a credit basis, the amount and duration of such credit shall be no more liberal than that recommended by the Board.

c. To establish and maintain a special account in the Bank of Korea to which will be transferred the balance now in the "Special United Nations Aid Goods Deposit Account" at the Bank of Korea and to which will be deposited the gross won proceeds of sales of all equipment and supplies (1) furnished under this Agreement or (2) locally procured by expenditure of won funds previously deposited.

d. To use the special account established in *c* above to the maximum extent possible as a stabilizing device and as an offset to harmful monetary expansion. To this end withdrawals from this account shall be made only upon the recommendation of the Board, only for the following purposes, and only in the following order of priority:

(1) For defraying reasonable local currency costs involved in carrying out the responsibilities of the Unified Command for relief and support of the civilian population of Korea, provided, however, that such local currency expenses shall not include won advances to the United Nations Command for its bona fide military expenses or for sale to personnel of the United Nations Command.

(2) For defraying such proportion of the reasonable operating expenses of operating agencies of the Government of the Republic of Korea provided under clause 5a above as may be recommended by the Board.

(3) The balance remaining in this special account, after withdrawals for the above purposes have been made and after provision has been made for an operating reserve, shall periodically upon the recommendation of the Board be applied against any then existing indebtedness of the Government of the Republic of Korea to the Bank of Korea or to any other financial institution organized under the laws of the Republic of Korea.

8. To prevent the export from the Republic of Korea of any of the equipment or supplies furnished by the Unified Command or any items of the same or similar character produced locally or otherwise procured, except upon the recommendation of the Board.

9. To make prudent use of its foreign exchange and foreign credit resources and to utilize these resources to the extent necessary first toward stabilization (by prompt importation into Korea of salable essential commodities) and then toward revitalization and reconstruction of the economy of Korea. The use of such foreign credit resources shall be controlled or coordinated as follows:

a. All foreign exchange (both public and private) of the Republic of Korea accruing hereafter from indigenous exports, visible and invisible, except as described in *b* below, shall be controlled solely by the Government of the Republic of Korea.

b. All foreign exchange (both public and private, and from whatever source acquired) now held by the Republic of Korea and that foreign exchange which, subsequent to the effective date of this Agreement, is derived by the Republic of Korea from any settlement for advances of Korean currency to the United Nations Command shall be used only as recommended by the Board.

c. All foreign exchange described in *a* and *b* above shall be coordinated by the Board, in order to integrate the use made of such foreign exchange with the imports included in the Unified Command assistance programs.

10. In order properly to adapt the assistance programs of the Unified Command to the needs of the economy of Korea, and in order to coordinate imports under those programs with imports purchased with foreign exchange, to support the recommendations of the Board in the making of periodic plans for the import and export of commodities and to use such plans as a basis for the issuance of export and import licenses.

11. In order to make most effective use of the foreign exchange resources of the Government of the Republic of Korea in stabilizing the Korean economy:

a. To maximize the won proceeds from the sale of such exchange or from the sale of imports derived from such exchange.

b. To apply such proceeds first against any existing overdrafts of the Government of the Republic of Korea upon the Bank of Korea, except as otherwise recommended by the Board.

c. To hold or spend the balance of such won proceeds with due regard to the effect of such action on the total money supply.

12. To provide logistic support to the armed forces of the Republic of Korea to the maximum extent feasible and to furnish to the United Nations Command timely information concerning the details of this support in order to permit coordinated budgetary planning.

13. To grant to individuals and agencies of the Unified Command, except Korean nationals, such privileges, immunities, and facilities as are necessary for the fulfillment of their function within the Republic of Korea under the above cited resolutions of the United Nations, or as have been heretofore granted by agreement, arrangement or understanding or as may be agreed upon formally or informally hereafter by the parties or their agencies.

14. To insure that funds, equipment, supplies and services provided by the Unified Command or derived therefrom shall not be subject to garnishment, attachment, seizure, or other legal process by any person, firm, agency, corporation, organization or government, except upon recommendation of the Board.

## ARTICLE IV

### Transfer

1. The parties recognize that all or any portion of the responsibilities of the Unified Command may be assumed from time to time by another agency or agencies of the United Nations. Prior to such transfer, the parties shall consult together concerning any modification in this Agreement which may be required thereby.

2. It is the current expectation of the parties that the United Nations Korean Reconstruction Agency (UNKRA), established by resolution of the General Assembly of the United Nations of December 1, 1950, will assume responsibility for all United Nations relief and rehabilitation activities for Korea at the termination of a period of 180 days following the cessation of hostilities in Korea, as determined by the Unified Command, unless it is determined by the Unified Command, in consultation with the Agent General of the United Nations Korean Reconstruction Agency, that military operations do not so permit at that time, or unless an earlier transfer of responsibility is agreed upon.

## ARTICLE V

### Existing Agreements

This Agreement does not supercede in whole or in part any existing agreement between the parties hereto.

## ARTICLE VI

### Registration, Effective
### Date, and Termination

1. This Agreement shall be registered with the Secretary General of the United Nations in compliance with the provisions of Article 102 of the Charter of the United Nations.

2. This Agreement shall enter into operation and effect immediately upon signature hereto. This Agreement shall remain in force so long as the Unified Command continues in existence and retains responsibilities hereunder, unless earlier terminated by agreement between the parties.

Done in duplicate in the English and Korean languages, at Pusan, Korea, on this *24th* day of May, 1952. The English and Korean texts shall have equal force, but in case of divergence, the English text shall prevail.

In witness whereof, the respective Representatives, duly authorized for the purpose, have signed the present Agreement.

For the Government of the United States of America

By CLARENCE E. MEYER
   *Minister and Special Representative*
   *of the President of the United States*

For the Government of the Republic of Korea

By TOO CHIN PAIK
   *Minister of Finance*

1. Source: Treaties and Other International Acts Series 2593, Department of State Publication 4895, 1953.

# MESSAGE FROM THE PRESIDENT TO THE CONGRESS REQUESTING LEGISLATION FOR THE REHABILITATION AND ECONOMIC SUPPORT OF THE REPUBLIC OF KOREA, JULY 27, 1953 [1]

*To the Congress of the United States:*

The signing of the truce in Korea makes it imperative that the United States immediately initiate a program of expanded aid to the Republic of Korea to assist in its rehabilitation and economic support. Such a program, affecting the whole future of the Republic of Korea, must extend over several years, and I shall make further recommendations concerning that program to the Congress at its next session.

At this time I urge upon the Congress the passage of interim legislation which will authorize the President to use, for the rehabilitation and economic support of the Republic of Korea, a sum up to $200 million from the savings in expenditures in the Department of Defense that result from the cessation of hostilities.

The need for this action can quickly and accurately be measured in two ways. One is the critical need of Korea at the end of 3 years of tragic and devastating warfare. The second is the opportunity which this occasion presents the free world to prove its will and capacity to do constructive good in the cause of freedom and peace.

The extent of devastation suffered by the people and the economy of Korea is staggering. Since the outbreak of war in 1950, 1 million South Koreans have been killed; more than $2\frac{1}{2}$ million have become homeless refugees; 5 million depend in whole or in part upon relief to stay alive. Property destruction exceeds $1 billion. This colossal economic disaster has made all the more remarkable the courage and magnitude of the Republic of Korea's military effort.

This Government has been constantly aware that all that has been won by this valiant struggle could be imperiled and lost by an economic collapse. Poverty and despair could inflict wounds beyond the power of enemy guns. Knowing this, we and our allies, throughout the period of hostilities, took necessary measures to keep the Korean economy from buckling under the strain. We were able, through Defense appropriations, to meet minimum relief needs and to contain the threats of disease and unrest. We contributed important support to the program of the United Nations Korean Reconstruction Agency. We provided important incidental benefits to the Korean economy through payments to the Republic of Korea for the local currency requirements of our military forces.

But these measures cannot suffice. They were necessarily designed to meet the immediate exigencies of fighting a war. They cannot be expected either to meet the huge total cost of this effort or to set the foundation for a healthy peacetime economy.

The facing of these needs has been the subject of the most careful study. I directed that a firsthand survey of them be undertaken in Korea more than 3 months ago. The completed survey has been reviewed by the National Security Council. On the basis of its analysis and recommendations, I am convinced that the security interests of the United States clearly indicate the need to act promptly not only to meet immediate relief needs but also to begin the long-range work of restoring the Korean economy to health and strength.

While this program is geared to meeting simply indispensable needs, its precise shape in the future must to some extent be governed by future events. It must take account of the fact that our objectives in Korea are not completely attained so long as Korea remains divided; and the assistance now proposed is carefully designed to avoid projects which would prove valueless in a united country. The implementation of the program will depend upon the continued cooperation of the Government of the Republic of Korea with the United States and the United Nations Command.

There is, as I have said, a second fact beyond the desperate need of Korea, which, I believe, must govern our action at this time. It is the chance—and the need—for the free peoples to give clear and tangible testimony to their awareness that true peace means more than the simple absence of war. It means moral and material health. It means political order and economic progress. It means the living hope, in the hearts of all peoples that tomorrow can bring a more just, a more free, a more productive life than today.

No people on earth has proved more valiantly than the people of Korea their right to hold and cherish this hope. Ours is the task to help and nourish this hope—for the sake of one brave people, and for the sake of all peoples who wait and watch to see if free men can be as wise in the ways of peace as they have proved courageous in the ways of war.

DWIGHT D. EISENHOWER

The White House, July 27, 1953

1. Source: Brownson Committee Hearings, p. 216.

# MEMORANDUM FOR THE PRESIDENT FROM THE DIRECTOR OF THE BUREAU OF THE BUDGET, *UNITED STATES ORGANIZATION FOR ECONOMIC AID ACTIVITIES IN KOREA,* AUGUST 6, 1953 [1]

Concurrently with National Security Council consideration of economic aid for Korea, the Bureau of the Budget has been developing recommendations for the organization for United States and United Nations economic assistance activities in Korea. The attached memorandum prescribing the United States organization for all economic aid in Korea, including the proposed program which would use savings resulting from the truce, was developed by the Bureau with the assistance of the agencies concerned and has the concurrence of those agencies.

The Tasca Mission recommended the continuation of the concept of a Presidential representative for Korean economic affairs, serving under the Commander-in-Chief of the United Nations Command as long as Korea remains a military theater. Although the Economic Coordinator provided for in the attached memorandum would not be a Presidential representative, the other agencies concur with us in the belief that he would have adequate authority, responsibility, and prestige to mold the several assistance activities into an effective program.

The proposed organizational arrangements are designed to give effect to the following conclusions:

1. The present responsibility of the Commander-in-Chief of the United Nations Forces for the security of Korea requires that he have overall responsibility for all United Nations and United States activities in that country, including economic programs for relief and rehabilitation.

2. There will remain in Korea United States military units whose services and facilities can be used in Korean reconstruction. Such re-

sources, insofar as they are available, should be utilized for relief and rehabilitation wherever this is feasible and is advantageous in terms of an efficient or economical operation.

3. A clear-cut division of activities should be established to the maximum feasible extent among the United Nations Korean Reconstruction Agency, civilian relief and United States rehabilitation, so that wasteful duplications are avoided and the operations are closely coordinated.

4. In order to achieve integrated planning and execution of all economic activities in Korea, a single individual, under CINCUNC, should be delegated the function of programming for and supervising the implementation of such activities. This officer should be delegated the function of providing assistance to the Republic of Korea on fiscal and economic matters, and should represent the Foreign Operations Administration in Korea.

5. For these purposes he should have a staff and authority to utilize employees of FOA and Defense, and such UNKRA personnel as may be provided on a non-reimbursable basis.

6. The Foreign Operations Administration, through the Unified Command, should backstop Korean relief and rehabilitation programs in Washington, and should develop integrated programs for submission to the President through the Bureau of the Budget. This is consistent with the recommendations in the Tasca Report.

7. United States procurement should be handled through the existing channels—agency or otherwise—deemed most favorable. Particular emphasis should be given to developing Korean commercial channels.

8. The United States should support the UNKRA program. It is agreed by the agencies concerned that coordination of United States economic activities and UNKRA activities can be achieved best by United States representatives seeking an understanding with the Agent General of UNKRA that the Unified Command, in consultation with UNKRA, will be responsible for:

a. Determination of overall requirements and priorities;

b. Allocation of responsibility for appropriate fields of activity and projects to the various implementing agencies;

c. Determination of policies on pricing and credit and on local currency and its allocation;

d. Negotiations with ROK on broad policy and program matters, and such other matters as may be agreed, on behalf of UNKRA;

e. Deployment of persons made available by UNKRA to avoid duplication in the planning or operation of assistance programs;

and that the Agent General of UNKRA will accept and implement such determinations and negotiations to the maximum extent consistent with the fulfillment of the UNKRA mission as determined from time to time by the General Assembly of the United Nations.

It is recommended that you approve the attached memorandum.

Jos. M. Dodge
*Director*

1. Source: Brownson Committee Hearings, p. 230.

# NATIONAL SECURITY COUNCIL MEMORANDUM ON THE *UNITED STATES ORGANIZATION FOR ECONOMIC AID ACTIVITIES IN KOREA,* AUGUST 7, 1953 [1]

1. The development and supervision in the field of an integrated program of economic aid as a basis for Korean relief, rehabilitation, and stabilization is a responsibility of the Commander-in-Chief of the United Nations Command (CINCUNC) until such date as the Unified Command may determine. During this period, CINCUNC will be responsible for the coordination of military activities with the economic aid operations of the United States Government in Korea, those of the United Nations Korean Reconstruction Agency, and donations from voluntary agencies, and he will, in turn, assure the coordination of the foregoing activities with the activities of the Government of the Republic of Korea pursuant to existing or future agreements. (It is understood that during this period a significant portion of the program will be provided through the utilization of services and facilities of United States military units). With reference to UNKRA, the supervision or coordination referred to above and in 4(a) below shall be consistent with any agreement or understanding between the Agent General of UNKRA and the Unified Command.

2. An Economic Coordinator will be established on the staff of CINCUNC in Korea, as his senior economic staff member.

3. The Economic Coordinator, who will carry the personal rank of Minister, will be appointed by the Director of the Foreign Operations Administration, subject to the approval of the Secretary of State, the Secretary of Defense, and CINCUNC. The salary of the Economic Coordinator will be paid by the Foreign Operations Administration.

4. In the execution of his responsibility, CINCUNC will look to the Economic Coordinator as his economic advisor, and will delegate to the Economic Coordinator functions including but not limited to the following:

a. Development and supervision of integrated programs of relief, rehabilitation, and stabilization, and coordination between military and civilian assistance programs.

b. Representation of CINCUNC on international or joint bodies dealing with Korean economic matters.

c. Representation of CINCUNC in consultations and negotiations with UNKRA and other appropriate United Nations bodies.

d. Representation of CINCUNC and, as may be agreed, the UNKRA in consultations and negotiations with the Republic of Korea on economic matters.

e. Development of United States proposals for economic stabilization, including those which may be necessary conditions to the provision of expanded United States aid to Korea.

f. Collaboration with the Republic of Korea in the implementation of agreed stabilization measures.

g. Development and negotiations of policies for controlling the use of local currency in all aid programs, including priorities and allocations of such currency for the various projects and operating agencies, and the sale of local currency—generating commodities.

h. Development, jointly with appropriate military staffs, of an agreed allocation plan for the use of available transport facilities.

i. Coordination of the procurement channels and delivery schedules for the various commodities and projects. (It is understood that all procurement, funds allocation and expenditure, project, and contractual methods inherent in appropriations language or procedures of the various United States and international agencies will apply as prescribed).

j. Development of policies for the payment of all United States and United Nations local employees, and for any non-monetary assistance given them.

5. The Foreign Operations Administration is designated as the agency of principal interest within the Unified Command for Korean relief, rehabilitation and stabilization, and is assigned the development and direction in Washington of Korean relief, rehabilitation, and stabilization policy and programs, subject to the responsibilities of other departments and agencies as set forth in the President's letter of June 1, 1953. Consistent with paragraph 6, below, FOA also will operate FOA-financed activities under its current instrumentalities and procedures.

6. The Economic Coordinator will be the representative of the Foreign Operations Administration for projects undertaken by that agency in Korea. He will have: (1) the legal responsibility of assuring performance of operations in accordance with the provisions of the Mutual Security Act; and (2) authority to make administrative determinations normally required by FOA of its field representatives.

7. The Foreign Operations Administration will have communications with the Economic Coordinator, using Unified Command channels, except that CINCUNC may comment on any such message.

8. The responsibilities of the Secretary of State and the Director of the Foreign Operations Administration regarding UNKRA and its assistance program shall be those set forth in sections 2 and 4(c) of Executive Order No. 10458, of June 1, 1953, as amended.

9. The Economic Coordinator, in carrying out his responsibilities, shall have full authority to deploy Foreign Operations Administration and Department of Defense Staff, and persons made available by UNKRA, in a manner designed to avoid duplication in the planning or operation of economic assistance programs.

APPROVED:

| Department of State | JOHN FOSTER DULLES |
| Department of Treasury | G. M. HUMPHREY |
| Department of Defense | C. E. WILSON |
| Foreign Operations Administration | HAROLD E. STASSEN |

APPROVED:

D. E. (August 7, 1953)

1. Source: Brownson Committee Hearings, p. 231

# PROPOSALS FROM THE UNKRA AGENT GENERAL TO THE ECONOMIC COORDINATOR UNITED NATIONS COMMAND ON THE COORDINATION OF RELIEF REHABILITATION AND STABILIZATION PROGRAMS UNDERTAKEN IN KOREA, AUGUST 14, 1953 [1]

*Dear Mr. Wood:*

I am prepared to present to the Advisory Committee of the United Nations Korean Reconstruction Agency for its advice my views, which I understand you share, with respect to the following matters.

It is my view that the relief, rehabilitation and stabilization programs being undertaken in Korea by the United Nations Korean Reconstruction Agency, the United Nations Command, and the United States should be coordinated to the maximum feasible extent as component parts of an over-all program. It appears to follow from this view that on the basis of the Memorandum of Understanding between the United Nations Korean Reconstruction Agency and the United Nations Command, as applied to present circumstances in Korea, the coordinating function should be exercised by the Economic Coordinator serving on the staff of the Commander-in-Chief of the United Nations Command.

Accordingly, it is my further view that the Economic Coordinator, in consultation with the United Nations Korean Reconstruction Agency, should be responsible for the determination of over-all requirements and priorities, the allocation of responsibility for appropriate fields of activity and projects to the various implementing agencies, and the determination of policies on pricing and credit and on local currency and its application. It is understood that the local currency resulting from the Agency's program will be deposited in an account, withdrawals from which must receive the approval of the Agent General. In connection with the mentioned responsibilities of the Economic Coordinator, it appears appropriate that, unless otherwise agreed by you, negotiations with the Korean Government on broad policy and on broad program matters be conducted by the Economic Coordinator on behalf of the United Nations Korean Reconstruction Agency; it being understood that the Economic Coordinator will consult concurrently with the Agency with respect to such negotiations. Further, in order to avoid duplication in the planning or operation of assistance programs, the Economic Coordinator should be authorized to manage the deployment of such personnel as may be seconded by the United Nations Korean Reconstruction Agency to the United Nations Command.

I would be willing to accept and implement determinations made by the Economic Coordinator with respect to the matters mentioned above to the maximum extent which I, with the advice of the Advisory Committee of the United Nations Korean Reconstruction Agency, deem to be consistent with the fulfillment of the mission of the United Nations Korean Reconstruction Agency as determined from time to time by the General Assembly of the United Nations.

This letter relates to the relationships between the Economic Coordinator and the United Nations Korean Reconstruction Agency. Of course you and I understand that it is our mutual purpose to work in the closest collaboration with the Government of the Republic of Korea on these matters in assisting that Government to accomplish the rehabilitation of the Republic of Korea.

Sincerely yours,

JOHN B. COULTER

John B. Coulter
*Lt. General, USA (Ret.)*
*Agent General*

Honorable C. Tyler Wood
Economic Coordinator
Room 275
Executive Offices Building
17th & Pennsylvania Avenue
Washington 25, D.C.

1. Source: Brownson Committee Hearings, p. 233.

# BIBLIOGRAPHY

# BIBLIOGRAPHY

In addition to the official United Nations and United States Government publications listed below, I have consulted the records of the debates on the question of Korean reconstruction in United Nations organs from 1950 through 1956. These include the Official Records of the Security Council for the Fifth Year (1950), the Official Records of the Economic and Social Council for the Eleventh Session (Resumed) (1950), and the Official Records of the General Assembly for the Fifth through Eleventh Sessions (1950 through 1956). During the Fifth Session of the General Assembly, the problem of Korean Reconstruction was debated in meetings of the Joint Second and Third Committee, as well as in Plenary Sessions. From the Sixth through the Eleventh Sessions, discussions centered on the annual reports of the Agent General of UNKRA in meetings of the Second Committee and in Plenary Sessions.

I have consulted the *New York Times* extensively. Insofar as possible, I have also consulted the two English language newspapers published in Korea, the *Korea Times* and the *Korean Republic,* both of which reflected the views of the Rhee government, the latter being a semi-official organ of the government. Incomplete files of these newspapers were made available to me in the Division of Research for the Far East of the Department of State, as were files containing daily translations from Korean language newspapers prepared at the American Embassy in Seoul.

For mimeographed records of the Joint (UN Command and UNKRA) and Coordinating (Republic of Korea–UN Command–UNKRA) committees, several sources may be checked: UNKRA, United Nations, New York; UN Command Headquarters, now at Seoul, Korea; and the Division of Civil Affairs and Military Government (CAMG), Department of the Army, Washington, D.C. The minutes which I consulted were as follows:

*Minutes of the Joint UNCACK-UNKRA Committee, Korea:*

| | |
|---|---|
| Minutes of Meeting No. 1 | December 28, 1951 |
| Minutes of Meeting No. 2 | December 31, 1951 |
| Minutes of Meeting No. 3 | February 15, 1952 |
| Minutes of Meeting No. 4 | March 1, 1952 |
| Minutes of Meeting No. 5 | April 1, 1952 |
| Minutes of Meeting No. 6 | May 29, 1952 |
| Minutes of Meeting No. 7 | August 18, 1952 |

*Minutes of the Joint UNC-UNKRA Committee, Tokyo:*

| | |
|---|---|
| Minutes of Meeting No. 1 | January 5, 1952 |
| Minutes of Meeting No. 2 | February 4, 1952 |
| Minutes of Meeting No. 3 | March 3, 1952 |
| Minutes of Meeting No. 4 | April 7, 1952 |
| Minutes of Meeting No. 5 | May 19, 1952 |
| Minutes of Meeting No. 6 | June 2, 1952 |
| Minutes of Meeting No. 7 | August 21, 1952 |
| Minutes of Meeting No. 8 | October 10, 1952 |

*Minutes of the Coordinating ROK-UNKRA-UNC Committee:*

| | |
|---|---|
| Minutes of Meeting No. 1 | October 20, 1952 |
| Minutes of Meeting No. 2 | October 23, 1952 |
| Minutes of Meeting No. 3 | November 3, 1952 |
| Minutes of Meeting No. 4 | December 10, 1952 |
| Minutes of Meeting No. 5 | January 30, 1953 |

*United Nations Publications and Documents*

DEPARTMENT OF PUBLIC INFORMATION. Document ST/DPI/SER.A.79. The Question of Korea (1950–1953). Background Paper No. 79. 10 March 1954.

————. Press Release Series KOR/    . See particularly KOR/461. 31 January 1955.

ECONOMIC AND SOCIAL COUNCIL. E/1851/Rev. 1. *Report of the Secretary-General on Assistance for Civil Population of Korea.* 11th Session (Resumed). 11 October 1950.

————. E/1864. *Report by the Temporary Committee on Provisional Programme for Relief and Rehabilitation Needs of Korea.* 11th Session (Resumed).

————. E/1851/Add. 1. *Suggested Organization for Korean Relief and Rehabilitation Programme of the United Nations,* submitted by the Secretary-General. 11th Session (Resumed). 9 October 1950.

————. E/1852. *Assistance to Civil Population of Korea,* draft resolutions submitted by Australia. 11th Session (Resumed). 9 October 1950.

————. E/1858. *Plans for Relief and Rehabilitation of Korea,* draft resolution submitted by the United States. 11th Session (Resumed). 17 October 1950.

————. E/1858/Rev. 1. *Plans for Relief and Rehabilitation of Korea,* joint draft resolution submitted by the United States and Australia. 11th Session (Resumed). 26 October 1950.

GENERAL ASSEMBLY. Official Records, 5th Session. A/1526. *Special Report of the Advisory Committee on Administrative and Budgetary Questions on Financing Korean Reconstruction.* New York, 1950.

―――. 6th Session. A/1935. *Relief and Rehabilitation of Korea,* Report of the Agent General of the United Nations Korean Reconstruction Agency. 3 November 1951.

―――. Official Records, 7th Session. Supplement No. 19 (A/2222). *Report of the Agent General of the United Nations Korean Reconstruction Agency,* Organization and Work of the Agency from its Activation in February 1951 to 15 September 1952. New York, 1952.

―――. Seventh Session. Supplement No. 19A (A/2222/ Addenda 1 and 2). *Addenda to the Report of the Agent General of the United Nations Korean Reconstruction Agency.* New York, 1953.

―――. Seventh Session. Supplement No. 19B (A/2222/ Addendum 3). *Third Addendum to the Report of the Agent General of the United Nations Korean Reconstruction Agency,* for the period 15 February to 30 June 1953. New York, 1953.

―――. Eighth Session. Supplement No. 14 (A/2543). *Report of the Agent General of the United Nations Korean Reconstruction Agency,* for the period 15 September 1952 to 30 September 1953. New York, 1953.

―――. Ninth Session. Supplement No. 20 (A/2750). *Report of the Agent General of the United Nations Korean Reconstruction Agency,* for the period 1 October 1953 to 1 September 1954. New York, 1954.

―――. Tenth Session. Supplement No. 18 (A/2936). *Report of the Agent General of the United Nations Korean Reconstruction Agency,* for the period 1 September 1954 to 30 June 1955. New York, 1955.

―――. Eleventh Session. Supplement No. 16 (A/3195). *Report of the Agent General of the United Nations Korean Reconstruction Agency,* for the period 1 July 1955 to 30 June 1956. New York, 1956.

―――. Fifth Session. Supplement No. 16 (A/1350). *Report of the United Nations Commission on Korea,* for the period 15 December 1949 to 4 September 1950. Lake Success, New York, 1950.

―――. Sixth Session. Supplement No. 12 (A/1881). *Report of the United Nations Commission for the Unification and Rehabilitation of Korea.* New York, 1951.

GENERAL ASSEMBLY. Seventh Session. Supplement No. 14 (A/2187). *Report of the United Nations Commission for the Unification and Rehabilitation of Korea.* New York, 1952.

――――. Eighth Session. Supplement No. 13 (A/2441). *Report of the United Nations Commission for the Unification and Rehabilitation of Korea.* New York, 1953.

――――. Ninth Session. Supplement No. 15 (A/2711). *Report of the United Nations Commission for the Unification and Rehabilitation of Korea.* New York, 1954.

――――. Tenth Session. Supplement No. 13 (A/2947). *Report of the United Nations Commission for the Unification and Rehabilitation of Korea.* New York, 1955.

――――. Eleventh Session. Supplement No. 13 (A/3172). *Report of the United Nations Commission for the Unification and Rehabilitation of Korea.* New York, 1956.

――――. Ninth Session. A/2786. *The Korean Question,* Report to the United Nations on the Korean Political Conference. 11 November 1954.

――――. Ninth Session. A/2730. *Report of the Negotiating Committee on Extra-budgetary Funds.* 20 September 1954.

――――. Tenth Session. A/2945. *Report of the Negotiating Committee on Extra-budgetary Funds.* 30 August 1955.

UNITED NATIONS RELIEF AND REHABILITATION ADMINISTRATION. *Report of the Director General to the Second Session of the Council.* Council II, Document I. Washington, 1944.

――――. *Report of the Director General to the Council,* for the period 1 January 1945 to 31 March 1945. Washington, 1945.

*United States Government Publications and Documents*

U.S. ARMY, 12TH ARMY GROUP. *Report of Operations* (Final After Action Report). Vol. VII, G-5 Section. Germany, 1945.

U.S. CONGRESS. *Korean Aid Bill.* Hearings before the Committee on Foreign Affairs. House of Representatives, 81st Congress, 1st Session. Washington: Government Printing Office, 1949.

――――. *Mutual Assistance.* Hearings before the Committee on Foreign Relations and the Committee on Armed Services. U.S. Senate, 81st Congress, 1st Session. Washington: Government Printing Office, 1949.

――――. *Foreign Aid Appropriations for 1950.* Hearings before the

Committee on Appropriations. U.S. Senate, 81st Congress, 1st Session. Washington: Government Printing Office, 1949.

U.S. CONGRESS. *Mutual Defense Assistance Act of 1949.* Hearings before the Committee on Foreign Affairs. House of Representatives, 81st Congress, 1st Session. Washington: Government Printing Office, 1949.

————. *Foreign Aid Appropriations for 1950.* Hearings before the Committee on Appropriations. House of Representatives. Washington: Government Printing Office, 1949.

————. *Amend ECA Act.* Hearings before the Committee on Foreign Affairs, 81st Congress, 2nd Session. Washington: Government Printing Office, 1950.

————. *Foreign Aid Appropriations for 1951.* Hearings before the Committee on Appropriations. House of Representatives, 81st Congress, 2nd Session. Washington: Government Printing Office, 1950.

————. *Foreign Aid Appropriations for 1951.* Hearings before the Committee on Appropriations. U.S. Senate, 81st Congress, 2nd Session. Washington: Government Printing Office, 1950.

————. *Military Situation in the Far East.* Hearings before the Committee on Armed Services and the Committee on Foreign Relations. U.S. Senate, 82nd Congress, 1st Session. Washington: Government Printing Office, 1951.

————. *The Mutual Security Program.* Hearings before the Committee on Foreign Affairs. House of Representatives, 82nd Congress, 1st Session. Washington: Government Printing Office, 1951.

————. *Mutual Security of 1951.* Hearings before the Committee on Foreign Relations and the Committee on Armed Services. U.S. Senate, 82nd Congress, 1st Session. Washington: Government Printing Office, 1951.

————. *Mutual Security Appropriations for 1952.* Hearings before the Committee on Appropriations. U.S. Senate, 82nd Congress, 1st Session. Washington: Government Printing Office, 1951.

————. *Mutual Security Appropriations for 1952.* Hearings before the Committee on Appropriations. House of Representatives, 82nd Congress, 1st Session. Washington: Government Printing Office, 1951.

————. *Department of Defense Appropriations for 1952.* Hearings before the Committee on Appropriations. U.S. Senate, 82nd Congress, 1st Session, Washington: Government Printing Office, 1951.

————. *Department of Defense Appropriations for 1952.* Hearings before the Committee on Appropriations. House of Representatives,

82nd Congress, 1st Session. Washington: Government Printing Office, 1951.

U.S. CONGRESS. *Mutual Security Act Extension*. Hearings before the Committee on Foreign Affairs. House of Representatives, 82nd Congress, 2nd Session. Washington: Government Printing Office, 1952.

————. *Mutual Security Act of 1952*. Hearings before the Committee on Foreign Relations and the Committee on Armed Services. U.S. Senate, 82nd Congress, 2nd Session. Washington: Government Printing Office, 1952.

————. *Mutual Security Appropriations for 1953*. Hearings before the Committee on Appropriations. House of Representatives, 82nd Congress, 2nd Session. Washington: Government Printing Office, 1952.

————. *Urgent Deficiency Appropriations for 1952*. Hearings before the Committee on Appropriations. House of Representatives, 82nd Congress, 2nd Session. Washington: Government Printing Office, 1952.

————. *Mutual Security Act Extension*. Hearings before the Committee on Foreign Affairs. House of Representatives, 83rd Congress, 1st Session. Washington: Government Printing Office, 1953.

————. *Mutual Security Act of 1953*. Hearings before the Committee on Foreign Relations. U.S. Senate, 83rd Congress, 1st Session. Washington: Government Printing Office, 1953.

————. *Mutual Security Appropriations for 1954*. Hearings before the Committee on Appropriations. House of Representatives, 83rd Congress, 1st Session. Washington: Government Printing Office, 1953.

————. *Mutual Security Appropriations for 1954*. Hearings before the Committee on Appropriations. U.S. Senate, 83rd Congress, 1st Session. Washington: Government Printing Office, 1953.

————. *Department of the Army Appropriations for 1954*. Hearings before the Committee on Appropriations. House of Representatives, 83rd Congress, 1st Session. Washington: Government Printing Office, 1953.

————. *2nd Supplementary Appropriations Bill for 1953*. Hearings before the Committee on Appropriations. House of Representatives, 83rd Congress, 1st Session. Washington: Government Printing Office, 1953.

————. *Testimony of General James Van Fleet*. Hearings before the Committee on Foreign Affairs. House of Representatives, 83rd Congress, 1st Session. Washington: Government Printing Office, 1953.

———. *Mutual Security Act of 1954.* Hearings before the Committee on Foreign Affairs. House of Representatives, 83rd Congress, 2nd Session. Washington: Government Printing Office, 1954.

———. *Mutual Security Act of 1954.* Hearings before the Committee on Foreign Relations. U.S. Senate, 83rd Congress, 2nd Session. Washington: Government Printing Office, 1954.

———. *Mutual Security Appropriations for 1955.* Hearings before the Committee on Appropriations. House of Representatives, 83rd Congress, 2nd Session. Washington: Government Printing Office, 1954.

———. *Mutual Security Appropriations for 1955.* Hearings before the Committee on Appropriations. U.S. Senate, 83rd Congress, 2nd Session. Washington: Government Printing Office, 1954.

———. *Mutual Defense Treaty with Korea.* Hearings before the Committee on Foreign Relations. U.S. Senate, 83rd Congress, 2nd Session. Washington: Government Printing Office, 1954.

———. *Relief and Rehabilitation in Korea.* Hearings before the Committee on Government Operations. House of Representatives, 83rd Congress, 2nd Session. Washington: Government Printing Office, 1954.

———. *Mutual Security Act of 1955.* Hearings before the Committee on Foreign Affairs. House of Representatives, 84th Congress, 1st Session. Washington: Government Printing Office, 1955.

———. *Mutual Security Act of 1955.* Hearings before the Committee on Foreign Relations. U.S. Senate, 84th Congress, 1st Session. Washington: Government Printing Office, 1955.

———. *Mutual Security Appropriations for 1956.* Hearings before the Committee on Appropriations. House of Representatives, 84th Congress, 1st Session. Washington: Government Printing Office, 1955.

———. *Mutual Security Appropriations for 1956.* Hearings before the Committee on Appropriations. U.S. Senate, 84th Congress, 1st Session. Washington: Government Printing Office, 1955.

———. *Mutual Security Act of 1956.* Hearings before the Committee on Foreign Affairs. House of Representatives, 84th Congress, 2nd Session. Washington: Government Printing Office, 1956.

———. *Mutual Security Act of 1956.* Hearings before the Committee on Foreign Relations. U.S. Senate, 84th Congress, 2nd Session. Washington: Government Printing Office, 1956.

U.S. Congress. *Mutual Security Appropriations for 1957.* Hearings before the Committee on Appropriations. House of Representatives, 84th Congress, 2nd Session. Washington: Government Printing Office, 1956.

——. *Mutual Security Appropriations for 1957.* Hearings before the Committee on Appropriations. U.S. Senate, 84th Congress, 2nd Session. Washington: Government Printing Office, 1956.

——. *Korean Aid Bill.* Report of the Committee on Foreign Affairs. House of Representatives, House Report No. 962. 81st Congress, 1st Session. Washington: Government Printing Office, 1949.

——. *Background Information on Korea.* Report of the Committee on Foreign Affairs. House of Representatives, House Report No. 2495. 81st Congress, 2nd Session. Washington: Government Printing Office, 1950.

——. *Mutual Security Act of 1951.* Report of the Committee on Foreign Affairs. House of Representatives, House Report No. 872. 82nd Congress, 1st Session. Washington: Government Printing Office, 1951.

——. *The Mutual Security Act of 1951.* Report of the Committee on Foreign Relations and the Committee on Armed Services. U.S. Senate, Senate Report No. 703. 82nd Congress, 1st Session. Washington: Government Printing Office, 1951.

——. *The Mutual Security Act of 1951.* Conference Report. House Report No. 1090. 82nd Congress, 1st Session. Washington: Government Printing Office, 1951.

——. *Report to the President submitted by Lt. General A. C. Wedemeyer, September, 1947: Korea.* Printed for the use of the Committee on Armed Services. U.S. Senate, 82nd Congress, 1st Session. Washington: Government Printing Office, 1951.

——. *Substance of Statements made at the Wake Island Conference on October 15, 1950.* Compiled by General Bradley from notes kept by the conferees from Washington. Prepared for the use of the Committee on Armed Services and the Committee on Foreign Relations. U.S. Senate, 82nd Congress, 1st Session. Washington: Government Printing Office, 1951.

——. *Urgent Deficiency Appropriations Bill, 1952.* Report of the Committee on Appropriations. U.S. Senate, Senate Report No. 1780. 82nd Congress, 2nd Session. Washington: Government Printing Office, 1952.

——. *Mutual Security Act of 1952.* Report of the Committee on Foreign Affairs. House of Representatives, House Report No. 1922.

82nd Congress, 2nd Session. Washington: Government Printing Office, 1952.

———. *Mutual Security Act of 1952*. Report of the Committee on Foreign Relations. U.S. Senate, Senate Report No. 1490. 82nd Congress, 2nd Session. Washington: Government Printing Office, 1952.

———. *Mutual Security Act of 1953*. Report of the Committee on Foreign Affairs. House of Representatives, House Report No. 569. 83rd Congress, 1st Session. Washington: Government Printing Office, 1953.

———. *The Mutual Security Act of 1953*. Report of the Committee on Foreign Relations. U.S. Senate, Senate Report No. 403, 83rd Congress, 1st Session. Washington: Government Printing Office, 1953.

———. *The United States and the Korean Problem*. Senate Document No. 74, 83rd Congress, 1st Session (Collection of Documents, 1943–53). Washington: Government Printing Office, 1953.

———. *Mutual Defense Treaty with Korea*. Report of the Committee on Foreign Relations. U.S. Senate, Senate Executive Report No. 1. 83rd Congress, 2nd Session. Washington: Government Printing Office, 1954.

———. *Relief and Rehabilitation in Korea*. Twenty-Third Intermediate Report of the Committee on Government Operations. House of Representatives, House Report No. 2574. 83rd Congress, 2nd Session. Washington: Government Printing Office, 1954.

———. *Budgetary and Financial Problems of the United Nations*. Staff Study No. 6. Subcommittee on the United Nations Charter, Committee on Foreign Relations, U.S. Senate, Senate Document No. 164. 83rd Congress, 2nd Session. Washington: Government Printing Office, 1955.

COMMISSION ON ORGANIZATION OF THE EXECUTIVE BRANCH OF THE GOVERNMENT. *Task Force Report on Overseas Economic Operations*. Washington: Government Printing Office, 1954.

DEPARTMENT OF STATE. *The Conferences at Malta and Yalta, 1945*. Foreign Relations of the United States. Diplomatic Papers. Washington: Government Printing Office, 1955.

———. *Korea: 1945 to 1948*. Publication 3305. Washington: Government Printing Office, 1948.

———. *The Economy of South Korea: Basic Survey*. Prepared in conjunction with the Korea Division, Economic Cooperation Administration. Washington, May, 1949.

DEPARTMENT OF STATE, and Economic Cooperation Administration. *Economic Aid to the Republic of Korea.* ECA Recovery Program for Fiscal Year 1950. June, 1949.

————. *United States Policy in the Korean Crisis.* Publication 3922, Far Eastern Series 35. Washington: Government Printing Office, 1950.

————. *The Korean Problem at the Geneva Conference, April 26– June 15, 1954.* Publication 5609, International Organization and Conference Series II (Far Eastern), 4. Washington: Government Printing Office, 1954.

————, *Bulletin,* Vol. XXIII, No. 576. July 17, 1950. The United Nations and Korea, Philip C. Jessup, p. 84.

————, *Bulletin,* Vol. XXIII, No. 578. July 31, 1950. The President's Message to the Congress on the Korean Situation, p. 163.

————, *Bulletin,* Vol. XXIII, No. 582. August 28, 1950. ECA Authorization for Aid to Korea in July and August, p. 334.

————, *Bulletin,* Vol. XXIII, No. 584. September 11, 1950. Aims and Objectives in Resisting Aggression in Korea, Address by the President, p. 407.

————, *Bulletin,* Vol. XXIII, No. 586. September 25, 1950. Korean Relief Assistance Fund Established, p. 492.

————, *Bulletin,* Vol. XXIII, No. 590. October 23, 1950. The President and General MacArthur Confer on Korean and Far Eastern Policies, p. 643.

————, *Bulletin,* Vol. XXIII, No. 595. November 27, 1950. Relief and Rehabilitation of Korea, p. 859.

————, *Bulletin,* Vol. XXIV, No. 604. January 29, 1951. UN Action on Korean Relief and Rehabilitation, p. 179.

————, *Bulletin,* Vol. XXIV, No. 605. February 5, 1951. Point Four Program after Korea, p. 225.

————, *Bulletin,* Vol. XXIV, No. 607. February 19, 1951. The Strategy of Freedom in Asia, Dean Rusk, p. 295.

————, *Bulletin,* Vol. XXIV, No. 611. March 19, 1951. Contributions to Aid Programs for Korea and Palestine, p. 469.

————, *Bulletin,* Vol. XXIV, No. 615. April 16, 1951. Preventing a New World War, Address by the President, p. 603.

————, *Bulletin,* Vol. XXIV, No. 623. June 11, 1951. Current Status of Contributions for Korea and Palestine Relief Programs, p. 950.

————, *Bulletin,* Vol. XXV, No. 628. July 9, 1951. Documents relating to Preliminary Truce Talk in Korea, p. 43.

————, *Bulletin,* Vol. XXV, No. 628. July 9, 1951. Unified Command Requests additional Forces in Korea, p. 53.

————, *Bulletin,* Vol. XXV, No. 630. July 23, 1951. Documents on Armistice Negotiations in Korea, p. 151.

————, *Bulletin,* Vol. XXV, No. 630. July 23, 1951. An Estimate of the Present World Situation, Remarks by Secretary Acheson, p. 123.

————, *Bulletin,* Vol. XXV, No. 632. August 6, 1951. U.S. Concludes Agreement with UNKRA, p. 232.

————, *Bulletin,* Vol. XXV, No. 633. August 13, 1951. Documents on Armistice Negotiations in Korea, p. 268.

————, *Bulletin,* Vol. XXV, No. 634. August 20, 1951. UN Commander praises work of Civilian Specialists, p. 305; also Documents on Armistice Negotiations in Korea, p. 306.

————, *Bulletin,* Vol. XXV, No. 635. August 27, 1951. Documents on Armistice Negotiations in Korea, p. 357.

————, *Bulletin,* Vol. XXV, No. 636. September 3, 1951. Documents on Armistice Negotiations in Korea, p. 392.

————, *Bulletin,* Vol. XXV, No. 637. September 10, 1951. Documents on Armistice Negotiations in Korea, p. 439.

————, *Bulletin,* Vol. XXV, No. 641. October 8, 1951. UN Ground Commander Reports on Summer Campaign, p. 589.

————, *Bulletin,* Vol. XXV, No. 643. October 22, 1951. U.S. makes Interim Financial War Settlement with Korea, p. 666.

————, *Bulletin,* Vol. XXV, No. 650. December 10, 1951. Political Problems and Economic Developments in Korea, Arthur B. Emmons, 3rd, p. 927.

————, *Bulletin,* Vol. XXVI, No. 668. April 14, 1952. Presidential Mission to Korea, p. 602.

————, *Bulletin,* Vol. XXVI, No. 673. May 19, 1952. UN Command Proposals for Settlement of Korean Armistice Issues, p. 786.

————, *Bulletin,* Vol. XXVI, No. 677. June 16, 1952. Korea: The Explosion of a Communist Delusion, John J. Muccio, p. 939.

————, *Bulletin,* Vol. XXVII, No. 692. September 29, 1952. Agreement on Economic Coordination between the Republic of Korea and the Unified Command, text, p. 499.

DEPARTMENT OF STATE, *Bulletin,* Vol. XXVIII, No. 711. February 8, 1953. Excerpts from the President's First Message to Congress on the State of the Union, p. 207.

————, *Bulletin,* Vol. XXVIII, No. 715. March 9, 1953. U.S. to make full settlement for Korean Currency Advances, p. 381.

————, *Bulletin,* Vol. XXVIII, No. 716. March 16, 1953. The Question of War or Peace in Korea, General Omar N. Bradley, p. 412.

————, *Bulletin,* Vol. XXVIII, No. 719. April 6, 1953. Proposals for Exchange of Sick and Wounded Prisoners of War, p. 494.

————, *Bulletin,* Vol. XXVIII, No. 720. April 13, 1953. Proposal for Settlement of Korean Prisoner-of-War Question, p. 526.

————, *Bulletin,* Vol. XXVIII, No. 721. April 20, 1953. Talks on Repatriation of Sick and Wounded Prisoners, p. 570; also Special Representative for Korean Economic Affairs, p. 576.

————, *Bulletin,* Vol. XXVIII, No. 723. May 4, 1953. Press Conference Remarks by Secretary Dulles on Questions Relating to Korean Settlement, p. 655.

————, *Bulletin,* Vol. XXVIII, No. 724. May 11, 1953. Documents on Korean Armistice Negotiations, p. 686.

————, *Bulletin,* Vol. XXVIII, No. 725. May 18, 1953. Documents on Korean Armistice Negotiations, p. 726.

————, *Bulletin,* Vol. XXVIII, No. 726. May 25, 1953. Repatriation of Korean Prisoners of War, p. 755.

————, *Bulletin,* Vol. XXVIII, No. 729. June 15, 1953. President's Letter to Syngman Rhee on Proposed Korean Armistice, p. 835.

————, *Bulletin,* Vol. XXVIII, No. 730. June 22, 1953. Text of Agreement on Prisoners of War, p. 866.

————, *Bulletin,* Vol. XXVIII, No. 731. June 29, 1953. Release of Anti-Communist Prisoners from U.S. Camps in South Korea, p. 905.

————, *Bulletin,* Vol. XXIX, No. 732. July 6, 1953. Syngman Rhee's Reply to President's Letter on Korean Armistice, p. 13.

————, *Bulletin,* Vol. XXIX, No. 735. July 27, 1953. Report on World Political Situation, Secretary Dulles and Assistant Secretary Robertson, p. 99.

————, *Bulletin,* Vol. XXIX, No. 736. August 3, 1953. Armistice in Korea, p. 131; also, Press Conference Remarks by Secretary Dulles on Korean Armistice Problems, p. 140.

———, *Bulletin,* Vol. XXIX, No. 737. August 10, 1953. Korea, p. 175 and p. 193.

———, *Bulletin,* Vol. XXIX, No. 738. August 17, 1953. Results of Secretary Dulles' Consultations with Syngman Rhee, p. 203.

———, *Bulletin,* Vol. XXIX, No. 741. September 7, 1953. Recommendations for the Relief and Rehabilitation of Korea, p. 313.

———, *Bulletin,* Vol. XXX, No. 758. January 4, 1954. Reduction of U.S. Forces in Korea, p. 14.

———, *Bulletin,* Vol. XXX, No. 759. January 11, 1954. Withdrawal of Two U.S. Divisions from Korea, p. 42; also, Agreement Reached on Program for Strengthening Korean Economy, p. 65.

———, *Bulletin,* Vol. XXX, No. 761. January 25, 1954. The Evolution of Foreign Policy, Address by Secretary Dulles, p. 107.

*United Nations Command Publications*

UNITED NATIONS COMMAND. *Civilian Relief and Economic Aid—Korea.* 7 July 1950–30 September 1951. Tokyo, 1952.

———. *Civil Assistance and Economic Affairs—Korea.* 1 October 1951–30 June 1952. Tokyo, 1952.

———. *Civil Assistance and Economic Affairs—Korea.* 1 July 1952–30 June 1953. Tokyo, 1953.

———. *Civil Assistance and Economic Affairs—Korea.* 1 July 1953–30 June 1954. Tokyo, 1954.

———. *Civil Assistance and Economic Affairs—Korea.* 1 July 1954–30 June 1955. Tokyo, 1955.

UNITED NATIONS CIVIL ASSISTANCE COMMAND IN KOREA (later, Korea Civil Assistance Command). *Monthly Civil Affairs Summary for Korea.* 1952–55. Seoul, Korea.

KOREA CIVIL ASSISTANCE COMMAND. *Reference Handbook: Government of the Republic of Korea.* Korea, September, 1953.

———. *United States Agreements with the Republic of Korea.* Korea, December, 1954.

*Other Publications and Articles*

BEAL, JOHN B. *John Foster Dulles.* New York: Harper & Bros., 1957.

BERGER, CARL. *Korea Knot.* Philadelphia: University of Pennsylvania Press, 1957.

BLOOMFIELD, ARTHUR. *Report and Recommendation on Banking in South Korea.* Pusan, Korea: March 31, 1952. Report prepared for the United Nations Civil Assistance Command in Korea. (Mimeographed.)

————, and JENSEN, JOHN P. *Banking Reform in South Korea.* New York: Federal Reserve Bank of New York, 1951.

CLARK, MARK. *From the Danube to the Yalu.* New York: Harper & Bros., 1954.

CHUNG, KYUNG CHO. *Korea Tomorrow.* New York: Macmillan Co., 1956.

DONOVAN, ROBERT J. *Eisenhower: the Inside Story.* New York: Harper & Bros., 1956.

FOOD AND AGRICULTURE ORGANIZATION. *Rehabilitation and Development of Agriculture, Forestry and Fisheries in South Korea.* New York: Columbia University Press, 1954.

GOLDMAN, ERIC L. *The Crucial Decade.* New York: Alfred A. Knopf, 1955.

GOODRICH, LELAND M. *Korea: A Study of U.S. Policy in the United Nations.* New York: Council on Foreign Relations, 1956.

————. "Korea, Collective Measures against Agression," *International Conciliation,* No. 494 (October, 1954).

————. "American National Interests and the Responsibilities of United Nations Membership," *International Organization,* VI, No. 3 (August, 1952), 369.

————. "The United Nations and Korea," *Journal of International Affairs,* VI, No. 2 (Spring, 1952), 115.

GORDENKER, LEON. *The United Nations and the Peaceful Unification of Korea.* The Hague: Martinus Nijhoff, 1959.

GOSORN, COLONEL LOUIS. "The Army and Foreign Civilian Supply," *Military Review,* XXXII, No. 2 (May, 1952), 27.

GRADJANSKY, ANDREW. *Modern Korea.* New York: Institute of Pacific Relations, 1944.

GRAEBNER, NORMAN. *The New Isolationism.* New York: Ronald Press, 1956.

HEER, CLARENCE. *Report on Relationship of Proposed UNKRA Program to Counter-inflationary Objectives of the Agreement on Economic Coordination.* Prepared for Under-Secretary of Defense Karl Bendetson. Chapel Hill, N.C.: August, 1952.

HOOPES, LIEUTENANT COLONEL E. L. "Civil Affairs Control Organization," *Military Review,* XXIV, No. 6 (September, 1944), 49.

HUSTON, JAMES A. "Korea and Logistics," *Military Review,* XXXVI, No. 11 (February, 1957), 18.

KENNEDY, EDGAR. *Mission to Korea.* London: Verschoyle, 1952.

KISSINGER, HENRY A. "Military Policy and Defense of the 'Grey Areas,' " *Foreign Affairs,* XXXIII, No. 3 (April, 1955), 416.

————. *Nuclear Weapons and Foreign Policy.* New York: Harper & Bros., 1957.

*Korean Report, 1948–1952.* A review of Governmental Procedures during Two Years of Peace and Two of War. Washington: Korean Pacific Press, August 15, 1952.

LIE, TRYGVE. *In the Cause of Peace.* New York: Macmillan & Co., 1954.

LEWIS, JOHN P. *Reconstruction and Development in South Korea.* Planning Pamphlet No. 94. Washington: National Planning Association, December, 1955.

LIMB, BEN C. "The Pacific Pact: Looking Forward or Backward?", *Foreign Affairs,* XXIX, No. 4 (July, 1951), 539.

MAY, LIEUTENANT COLONEL ROBERT W. "The Supply of Civilians in Liberated and Occupied Areas," *Military Review,* XXVIII, No. 1 (April, 1948), 29.

MCCUNE, GEORGE. *Korea, Today.* Cambridge, Mass.: Harvard University Press, 1950.

————, and HARRISON, JOHN A. *Korean-American Relations.* Documents Pertaining to the Far East Diplomacy of the United States, Vol. I, The Initial Period, 1883–1886. Berkeley: University of California Press, 1951.

MCCUNE, SHANNON. *Korea's Heritage.* A Social and Economic Geography. Rutland, Vermont: Chas. Tuttle & Co., 1956.

MEADE, E. GRANT. *American Military Government in Korea.* New York: King's Crown Press, 1951.

MILLER, JOHN, JR., CARROL, OWEN J., and TACKLEY, MARGARET E. *Korea, 1951–1953.* Washington: Office of the Chief of Military History, Department of the Army, 1956.

MILLIS, WALTER (ed.). *The Forrestal Diaries.* New York: Viking Press, 1951.

MORGANTHAU, HANS J. *Politics Among Nations.* New York: Alfred A. Knopf, 3rd ed., 1960.

292    MILITARY POLICY AND ECONOMIC AID

MORGANTHAU, HANS J. *In Defense of the National Interest.* New York: Alfred A. Knopf, 1951.

MROZEK, COLONEL JAMES E. "Civil Assistance in Action," *Military Review,* XXXV, No. 7 (October, 1955), 30.

NAPIER, LIEUTENANT COLONEL JACK P., and NESTEL, ARNOLD. "Military-Civilian Relations in the Occupation of Japan and Korea," *Journal of International Affairs,* VIII, No. 2 (1954), 151.

NATHAN ASSOCIATES, ROBERT R. *An Economic Programme for Korean Reconstruction.* A Report prepared for the United Nations Korean Reconstruction Agency. New York: March, 1954.

————. *A Preliminary Report on the Economic Reconstruction of Korea.* A Report prepared for the United Nations Korean Reconstruction Agency. New York: 1952. (Mimeographed.)

OLIVER, ROBERT T. *Verdict in Korea.* State College, Pa.: Bald Eagle Press, 1952.

————. *Syngman Rhee: The Man behind the Myth.* New York: Dodd, Mead & Co., 1954.

OSGOOD, CORNELIUS. *The Koreans and their Culture.* New York: Ronald Press, 1951.

OSGOOD, ROBERT E. *Limited War: Challenge to American Strategy.* Chicago: University of Chicago Press, 1957.

PERKINS, DEXTER. "Foreign Policy in Presidential Campaigns," *Foreign Affairs,* Vol. XXXV, No. 2 (January, 1957).

POQUE, FORREST C. The United States Army in World War II; The European Theatre of Operations; *The Supreme Command.* Washington: Office of the Chief of Military History, Department of the Army, 1954.

PORTWAY, DONALD. *Korea—Land of the Morning Calm.* London: George C. Harrap & Co., 1953.

REISCHAUER, EDWIN O. *Wanted: An Asian Policy.* New York: Alfred A. Knopf, 1955.

RIDGWAY, MATTHEW B. *Soldier.* New York: Harper & Bros., 1956.

ROVERE, RICHARD. *The Eisenhower Years.* New York: Farrar, Straus and Cudahy, 1956.

RUCKER, SIR ARTHUR. "Korea—The Next Stage," *International Affairs,* XXX, No. 3 (July, 1954), 313.

SAWYER, CAPTAIN ROBERT K. *United States Military Advisory Group to the Republic of Korea: A Monograph.* 2 vols. Washington: Office of the Chief of Military History, Department of the Army, 1955. (Mimeographed.)

Soward, F. H. "The Korean Crisis and the Commonwealth," *Pacific Affairs,* XXIV, No. 2 (June, 1951), 115.

Spanier, John. *The Truman-MacArthur Controversy.* Cambridge, Mass.: Harvard University Press, 1959.

Sterns, Brigadier General C. P. "The Army's Civilian Responsibilities in the European Campaign," *Military Review,* XXV, No. 9 (December, 1945), 67.

Stimson, Henry L., and Bundy, McGeorge. *On Active Service in Peace and War.* New York: Harper & Bros., 1947.

Taft, Robert A. *A Foreign Policy for Americans.* Garden City, New York: Doubleday & Co., Inc., 1952.

Truman, Harry S. *Memoirs,* Vol. II. Garden City, New York: Doubleday & Co., 1956.

United Nations Educational, Scientific and Cultural Organization. *Rebuilding Education in the Republic of Korea.* Report of the UNESCO-UNKRA Educational Planning Mission to Korea. UNESCO, 1954.

Vagts, Alfred. *Defense and Diplomacy.* New York: King's Crown Press, 1956.

Vernon, Colonel E. H. "Civil Affairs and Military Government," *Military Review,* XXVI, No. 3 (June, 1946), 25.

White, William S. *The Taft Story.* New York: Harper & Bros., 1954.

World Health Organization. *Report of the WHO/UNKRA Health Planning Mission in Korea.* World Health Organization, 1954. (Mimeographed.)

Zanzi, A. W. *Economic Reconstruction Problems in South Korea.* New York: Institute of Pacific Studies, 1954.

# INDEX